NATUREGUIDE

GEMS

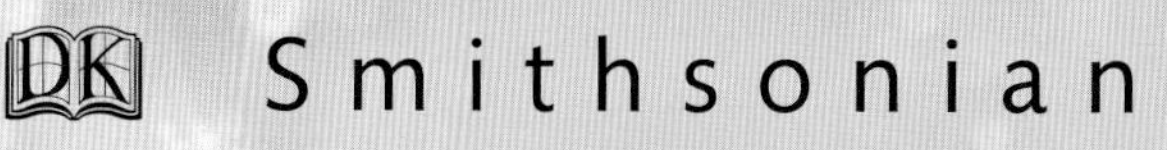

Smithsonian

NATUREGUIDE

GEMS

Ronald Louis Bonewitz

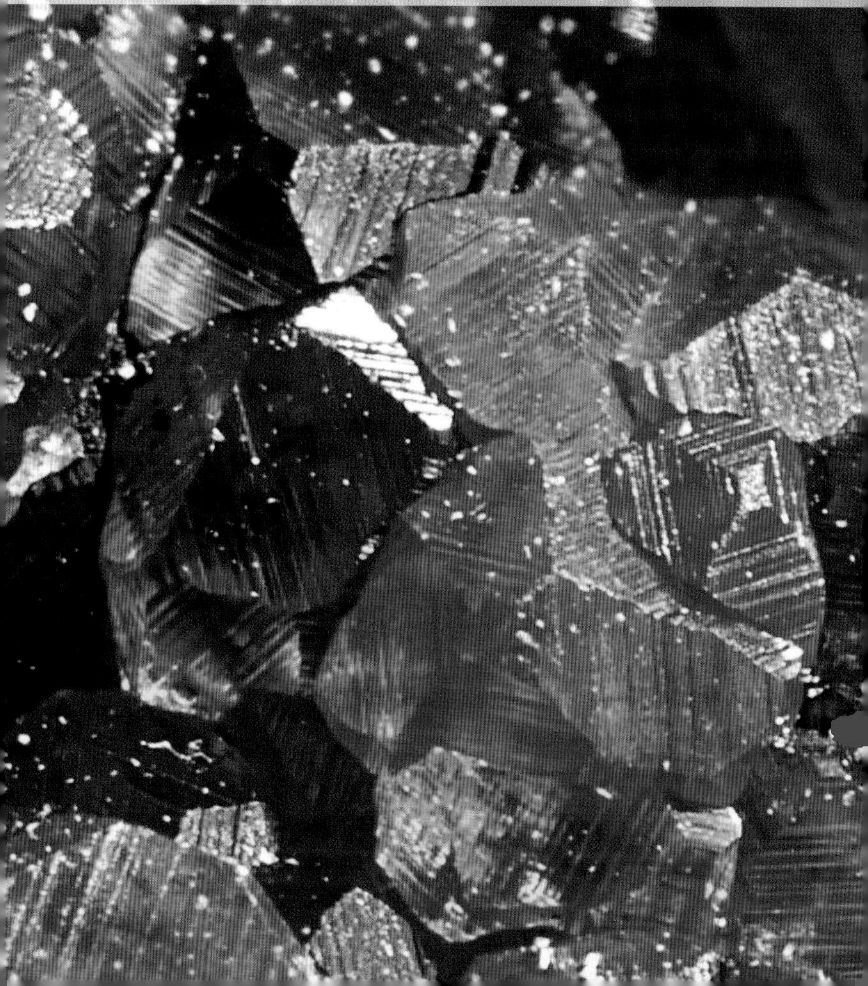

LONDON, NEW YORK, MELBOURNE,
MUNICH, AND DELHI

DORLING KINDERSLEY

Senior Editor Peter Frances

Editor Miezan van Zyl

US Senior Editor Rebecca Warren

US Editor Jill Hamilton

Jacket Editor Manisha Majithia

Managing Editor Angeles Gavira Guerrero

Pre-production Producer Lucy Sims

Associate Publishing Director Liz Wheeler

Publishing Director Jonathan Metcalf

Senior Art Editors Spencer Holbrook, Ina Stradins

Jacket Designer Laura Brim

Jacket Design Development Manager Sophia Tampakopoulos

Picture Researcher Jo Walton

Managing Art Editor Michelle Baxter

Senior Producer Alice Sykes

Publisher Sarah Larter

Art Director Philip Ormerod

DK INDIA

Senior Editor Soma B. Chowdhury

Editors Dharini Ganesh, Priyaneet Singh

Managing Editor Rohan Sinha

DTP Designers Arvind Kumar, Shanker Prasad, Tanveer Zaidi

Production Manager Pankaj Sharma

Senior Art Editor Devika Dwarkadas

Art Editor Parul Gambhir

Deputy Managing Art Editor Sudakshina Basu

Design Consultant Shefali Upadhyay

DTP Manager Balwant Singh

Picture Researcher Aditya Katyal

CONSULTANT

Dr. Jeffrey E. Post, Geologist, Curator-in-Charge, National Gem and Mineral Collection, National Museum of Natural History, Smithsonian Institution

First American edition, 2013

Published by DK Publishing
345 Hudson Street, New York, New York, 10014

14 15 10 9 8 7 6 5 4
005 – 188036 – March/2013

Published in Great Britain by Dorling Kindersley Limited

A catalog record for this book is available from the Library of Congress

ISBN 978-1-4654-0218-9

DK books are available at special discounts when purchased in bulk for sales promotions, premiums, fund-raising, or educational use. For details, contact: DK Publishing Special Markets, 345 Hudson Street, New York, NY 10014 or SpecialSales@dk.com

Printed and bound in China by Leo Paper Products

Discover more at **www.dk.com**

CONTENTS

INTRODUCTION

GEMSTONES

HOW THE GEM PROFILES WORK

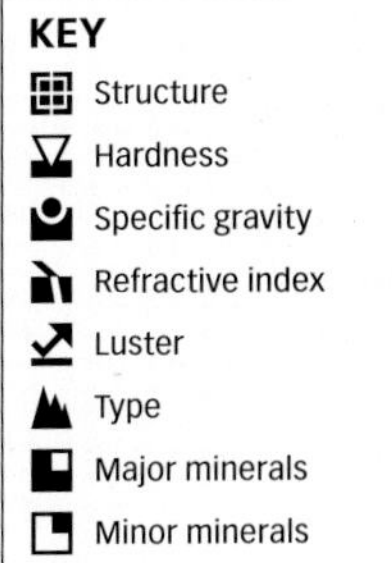

INTRODUCTION

WHAT IS A GEM?

Gems are generally defined as precious or semiprecious minerals that are polished for personal adornment. A wider definition includes a few rocks, such as obsidian, and a few organic substances, such as amber. By far the majority of gems are cut from minerals.

MINERALS, CRYSTALS, AND GEMS

A mineral is a naturally occurring inorganic substance that has a specific chemical composition and a specific internal atomic structure. When the atoms arrange themselves precisely in the mineral, the result is the formation of a crystal. Transparent gems, such as diamonds, rubies, and sapphires, are almost always cut from crystals or pieces of crystals. Translucent or opaque gems, such as jade and malachite, are cut from aggregates of small or microscopic crystals. A few gems, such as obsidian and some organic gems, have no crystal structure.

BEAUTY

The first quality that is noted in a gem is its beauty. The beauty of a gemstone rough is brought out by cutting it. Every piece of rough has unique possibilities—whether it is the sparkle of diamond, the rainbow colors of opal, or the subtle pastels of jade. These qualities are released by the skill of the craftsperson who cuts and polishes gemstones, so that in the finished stone, the shape, setting, and the interplay of colour and light are combined to the best effect. Endless combinations of color, shape, and fire are possible. Even within a single gem lie myriad possibilities: with changing light and movement, each new environment creates new colors and reflections in the same gemstone.

Bejewelled peacock
The creative use of gems, as seen in this opal, sapphire, and diamond brooch, increases their value.

Purple beauty
Tanzanite is valued because it is a newly discovered gem and has an intense and desirable blue color.

Colorful sapphires
Although it is normally thought of as blue, the variety of corundum known as sapphire actually comes in a wide range of colors.

RARITY

While beauty makes a gem more desirable, rarity takes it a step further. Rarity can imply the scarcity of the gem material itself, such as in the case of emerald. It can also refer to the occurrence of an unusual color or clarity in an otherwise common material. For example, quartz, which occurs in several colors, is a very common mineral. However, the rich, deep reddish purple color of the finest amethyst—a semiprecious quartz variety—is relatively rare.

ALMANDINE GARNET

RUBY

Rarity of occurrence
Garnet and ruby are two red gemstones. Ruby is considerably more expensive, partly because of its rarity. Its greater hardness and more intense red coloration also account for the difference in price.

DURABILITY

The phrase "diamonds are forever" underscores a prime quality sought in gemstones: durability. The durability of a gem is determined by its resistance to abrasion (hardness), its vulnerability to chip and break (brittleness), and its ease of splitting (cleavability). It must also be impervious to the many chemicals we encounter on a daily basis. Gemstones that do not meet these criteria are not commonly worn but cut only for collectors.

DIAMOND RING

BLUE JOHN RING

Hardness, brittleness, and cleavability
Diamond is the hardest substance and cannot be scratched easily, making it ideal for jewelry. Blue John is soft and vulnerable to scratching and breaking.

DIAMOND

BLUE SAPPHIRE

Valuable gems
The "four Cs" include the purity and intensity of color. Colorless diamonds are valued for their lack of color and blue sapphires for the depth of their coloration.

WHAT MAKES GEMS VALUABLE

Gemstones are graded by the "four Cs": color, clarity, cut, and carats. Color may indicate the intensity and purity of the color; clarity refers to a lack of flaws and inclusions; the technical perfection of the cut is graded; and carats is a weight measurement used for gemstones. Once these are determined, there are two other factors that influence a gemstone's value: overall beauty and rarity. Larger stones are rarer than smaller ones; therefore, an increase in weight can lead to a disproportionately large increase in price. When a gemstone doubles in weight, its price may go up by as much as four or five times.

HOW GEMS FORM

Apart from organic gems, all gemstones form by the geological processes that create, shape, and reshape Earth. Organic gems are created by biological processes, which often result in matter that is chemically and structurally identical to that created by geology.

ROCKS

Gemstones are created as rocks form in Earth. These can be the rock itself, crystals that are part of the rock structure, or that form from residual fluids as rocks are formed, or as a result of the alterations that change one rock into another. There are three types of rock—igneous, metamorphic, and sedimentary—and each creates gems.

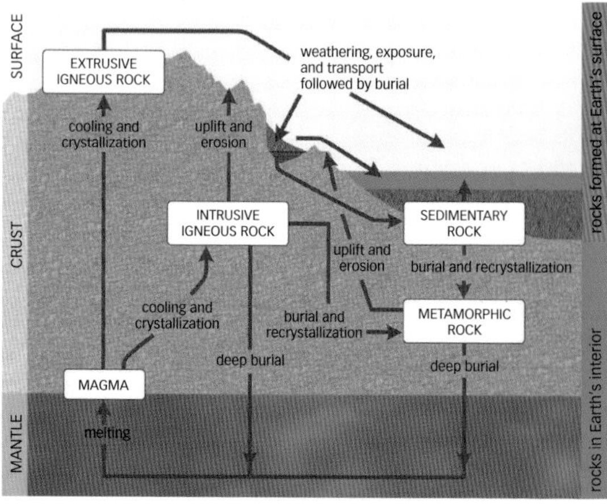

The rock cycle
This diagram illustrates the processes by which rocks (and gems) are continuously formed, broken down, and reformed. It is an endless and ongoing process.

Igneous rocks form from molten rock called magma. Gems such as peridot and diamond crystallize directly from the magma as part of the rock. Others, such as topaz, crystallize from residual fluids given off by magmas, and form in veins called hydrothermal veins.

Metamorphic rocks are rocks altered by temperature and pressure without remelting. The original rocks can be igneous, sedimentary, or other metamorphic rocks. Ruby and sapphire are created by metamorphic processes.

Sedimentary rocks form from the fragmentary remains of any or all of the three rock types, the remains of plants and animals, or chemicals dissolved in freshwater or seawater. Alabaster, celestine, and calcite are some of the gems that form from these processes.

TOPAZ IN IGNEOUS ROCK

STAUROLITE IN METAMORPHIC ROCK

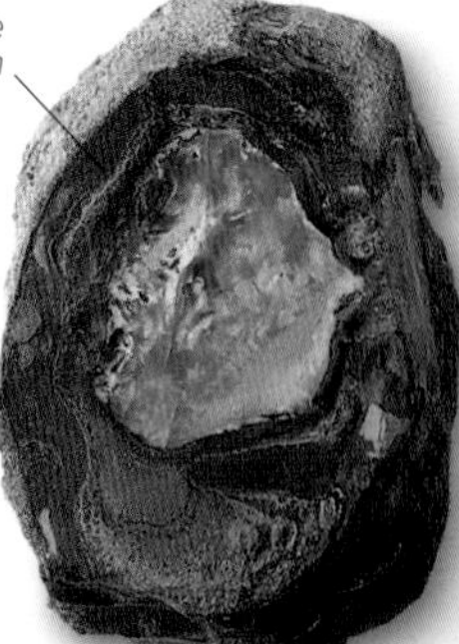

PRECIOUS OPAL IN SEDIMENTARY ROCK

Gems in different rocks
Igenous gems form from molten rocks or the fluids from them; metamorphic gems are created when minerals reform under heat and pressure without remelting; and sedimentary gems form from chemicals dissolved in water.

ALTERATION OF ROCKS

As Earth formed, all rocks originated as igneous rocks—that is, rocks formed from molten rock. Over time, these rocks have been broken down, altered, melted, remelted, and ground down as part of an endless reprocessing of Earth's mineral matter. These processes are referred to as the rock cycle (see opposite). At each stage of the cycle, different gems form as reprocessed minerals stabilize in a new set of geological conditions. Some gemstones are recovered from gravels, called placer deposits, before those gravels are reconstituted into new rocks.

Garnet in schist
This almandine garnet crystal has formed through alteration by the metamorphism of a preexisting rock. It has recrystallized from preexisting minerals without remelting.

Amethyst geode
These amethyst crystals were formed inside a hollow ball of stone referred to as a geode. They form when silica-rich waters flow into a cavity in a solidified lava flow.

ORGANIC GEMS

Organic gems fall into two general categories: those that contain crystalline matter and those that do not. Pearl, mother-of-pearl, shell, and coral are all partly made up of crystalline minerals that are created by biological, rather than geological, processes. The minerals in pearl, mother-of-pearl, and shell are calcium carbonate, which occurs either in the form of aragonite or calcite secreted by cells in the mantles of many molluscs. In hard corals, the mineral is secreted by coral polyps. In noncrystalline organic gems, the material is organic and includes tree sap (amber and copal), wood (jet), dentin (ivory), and conchiolin (black coral).

Amber nugget on seashore
Washed up on the north coast of Europe, this amber nugget is fossil resin from trees that were submerged when land was flooded at the end of the last ice age.

CRYSTALS

Almost all gems are cut from crystalline minerals—solids in which the component atoms are arranged in a particular, repeating, three-dimensional pattern. When these internal patterns produce a series of external flat faces arranged in geometric forms, a crystal is formed.

CRYSTAL SYMMETRY

Crystals are placed in systems according to their geometry or symmetry. In the following systems, crystals are grouped by their axes of rotational symmetry—axes around which a shape can be rotated and still appear the same once or more in a complete rotation. For example, a crystal has a fourfold axis of symmetry if it appears identical four times as it is turned 360 degrees around that axis.

CUBIC

The cubic system is sometimes known as the isometric system. Crystals forming in this system have three fourfold axes of symmetry at right angles to each other. The main geometric forms within this system are: cube, octahedron, and dodecahedron. Gemstone minerals and precious metals that crystallize in the cubic system include gold, silver, platinum, diamond, and spinel.

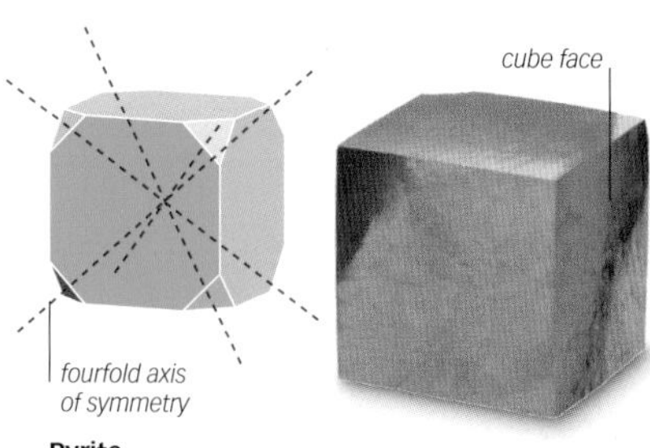

Pyrite
This crystal of pyrite is a prime example of crystals within the cubic system. Of all the systems, cubic crystals have the most axes of symmetry.

TETRAGONAL

Crystals forming in the tetragonal system have one fourfold axis of rotation. They have the look of elongated square prisms, appearing square in cross section and elongated in the third direction. Relatively few gemstone minerals crystallize in this system; some of them are vesuvianite, rutile, scapolite, and zircon.

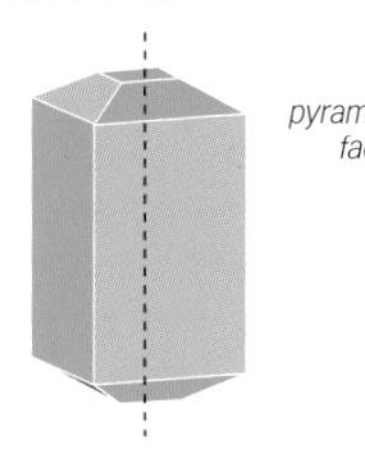

Zircon
Zircon has classic tetragonal crystals that have a square prism body with pyramidal terminations, often at both ends of the prism.

HEXAGONAL AND TRIGONAL

Some crystallographers separate the hexagonal and trigonal crystal systems, as hexagonal crystals have sixfold symmetry and trigonal crystals have threefold symmetry. However, other crystallographers regard them as comprising a single system because they share some geometrical properties. Gemstone minerals in the hexagonal system include emerald, aquamarine, and apatite. Calcite, quartz, and tourmaline are trigonal minerals.

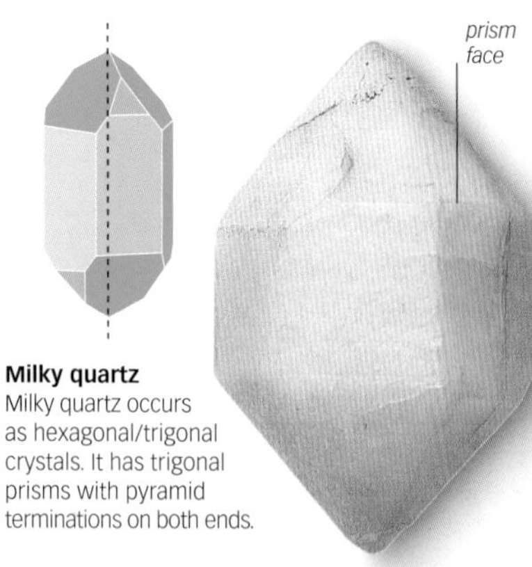

Milky quartz
Milky quartz occurs as hexagonal/trigonal crystals. It has trigonal prisms with pyramid terminations on both ends.

MONOCLINIC

The term monoclinic means "having one incline." Crystals forming in this system have one twofold axis of rotation. The largest numbers of minerals crystallize in the monoclinic system, including many gemstone minerals. Some examples are gypsum (alabaster and satin spar), orthoclase (moonstone), jade (both jadeite and nephrite), azurite, malachite, spodumene (hiddenite and kunzite), serpentine, diopside, meerschaum, and sphene.

ORTHOCLASE

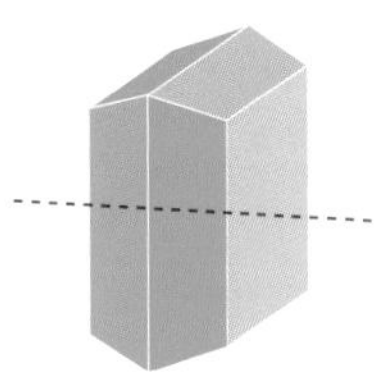

Monoclinic system
Selenite gypsum crystals perfectly illustrate the typical shape of monoclinic crystals: one elongated direction with a short direction at a right angle and another at an oblique angle.

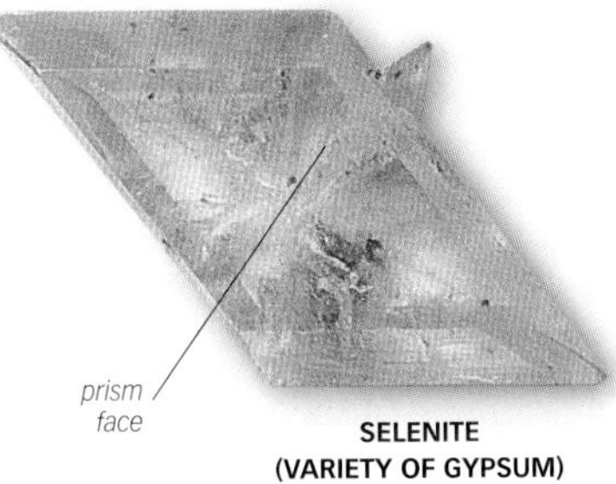

SELENITE (VARIETY OF GYPSUM)

ORTHORHOMBIC

The name orthorhombic means "shaped like a perpendicular parallelogram." Crystals in the orthorhombic system have three twofold axes of rotation, and have a shape like that of a cereal box. Gemstone minerals that crystallize in this system include olivine (peridot), chrysoberyl (alexandrite), aragonite, iolite, staurolite, zoisite (tanzanite), topaz, and barite.

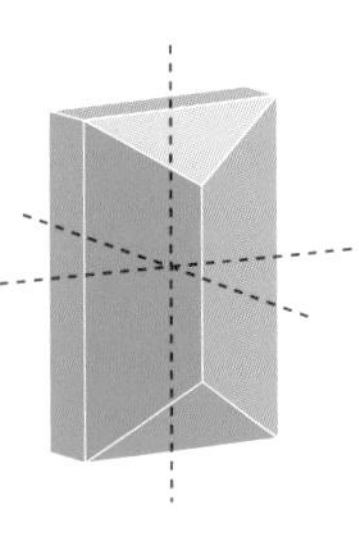

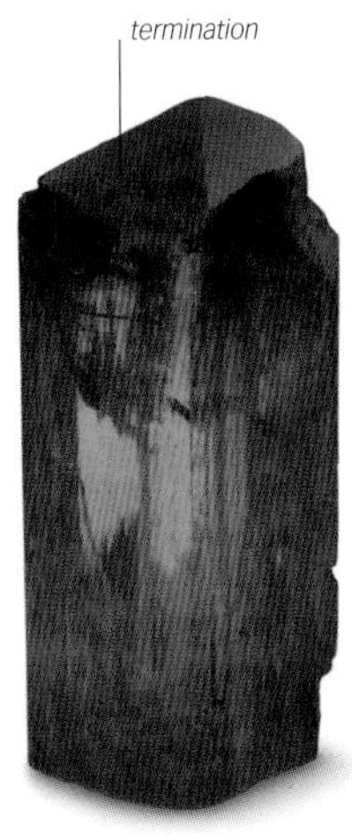

Topaz
This topaz crystal shows the general shape of orthorhombic crystals: one elongated direction and two unequal directions perpendicular to the elongated one.

TRICLINIC

Gemstone crystals forming in the triclinic system have the least symmetrical shape of all crystals. They have no rotational axes of symmetry and no symmetry in any of the crystal's three dimensions. The orientation of a triclinic crystal is thus arbitrary. Gemstone minerals that crystallize in this system include oligoclase (sunstone), microcline (amazonite), albite (some moonstones), and turquoise.

Amazonite
Crystals of amazonite—the green variety of the feldspar microcline—have no symmetry in any of their three dimensions.

» CRYSTAL GROWTH

A crystal is made of individual, identical structural units of atoms or molecules. These are repeated over and over in three dimensions. The symmetry of the structural units determines the position and shape of the crystal's faces. The geological conditions at the time of the crystal's formation determine the faces that are emphasized. The final form a crystal takes is known as its habit.

TWINNING

When two or more crystals of the same species form a symmetrical intergrowth, they are referred to as twinned crystals. Such crystals are described as contact or interpenetration twins. Penetration twinning may occur with the individual crystals at an angle to one another, as in a staurolite cross, or with them parallel to one another, as in the Carlsbad twin of orthoclase. If a twin involves three or more individual crystals, it is referred to as a multiple or repeated twin. It is multiple twinning that produces the sheen in some moonstone.

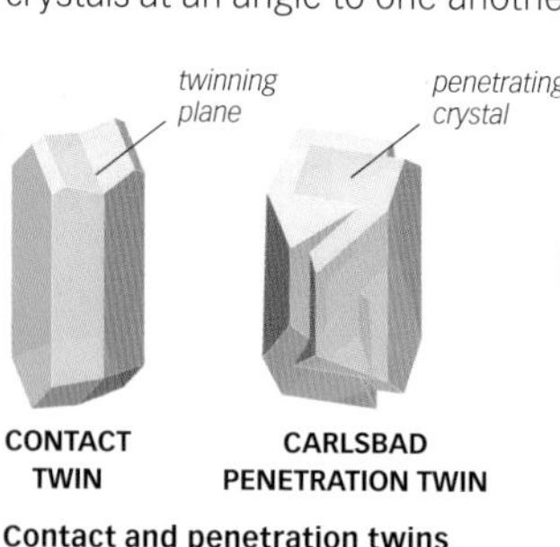

Contact and penetration twins
In contact twins, two or more crystals grow with faces in contact. In penetration twins, individual crystals penetrate each other.

Cyclic twin
A group of crystals that radiates outward from a common center, as in this specimen of chrysoberyl, is called a cyclic twin.

STRIATION

Striations are a series of parallel grooves that appear on a crystal. A close examination of striations shows that they are actually crystal faces. They form by the oscillation between two systems attempting to crystallize, or as an indication of multiple twinning, as seen in plagioclase.

Striated growth
This specimen of rutile has striations parallel to its prism faces, created by the oscillation between crystal faces during the crystallization process.

Starlike effect
The star effect in sapphires is produced by inclusions of oriented microscopic needles of rutile.

Mosslike effect
Inclusions of dendritic oxides of manganese, iron, and other minerals can produce a branching effect in moss agates.

INCLUSIONS

Minerals, liquids, and gas bubbles trapped inside another mineral are known as inclusions. In faceted stones, inclusions are sometimes considered flaws. In other gemstones, they produce an effect that makes the gemstone valuable. These include the stars in star sapphire, ruby, and other star stones; the spangles in sunstone; and the "eyes" in cat's eye chrysoberyl and cat's eye quartz.

CRYSTALLINE AND NONCRYSTALLINE HABITS

A crystal's habit is a description of its external shape and visible characteristics. It incorporates the names of the crystal's faces, such as prismatic or pyramidal, and the name of its form, such as cubic or octahedral. It also includes more general descriptive terms, such as grapelike or dendritic. Several terms are also used to describe the habits of crystal agglomerations that have no apparent structure.

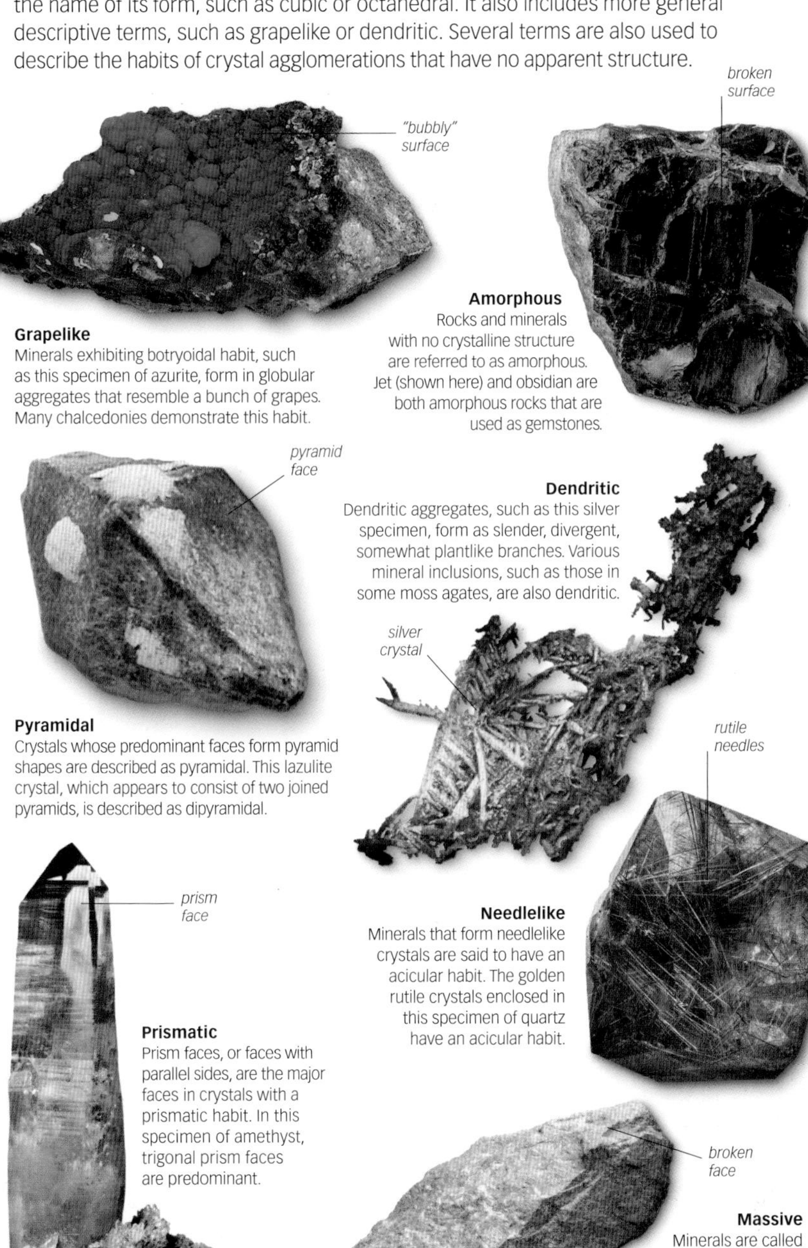

Grapelike
Minerals exhibiting botryoidal habit, such as this specimen of azurite, form in globular aggregates that resemble a bunch of grapes. Many chalcedonies demonstrate this habit.

Amorphous
Rocks and minerals with no crystalline structure are referred to as amorphous. Jet (shown here) and obsidian are both amorphous rocks that are used as gemstones.

Pyramidal
Crystals whose predominant faces form pyramid shapes are described as pyramidal. This lazulite crystal, which appears to consist of two joined pyramids, is described as dipyramidal.

Dendritic
Dendritic aggregates, such as this silver specimen, form as slender, divergent, somewhat plantlike branches. Various mineral inclusions, such as those in some moss agates, are also dendritic.

Needlelike
Minerals that form needlelike crystals are said to have an acicular habit. The golden rutile crystals enclosed in this specimen of quartz have an acicular habit.

Prismatic
Prism faces, or faces with parallel sides, are the major faces in crystals with a prismatic habit. In this specimen of amethyst, trigonal prism faces are predominant.

Massive
Minerals are called massive when they consist of a mass of crystals that cannot be seen individually. This thulite specimen is massive.

CLASSIFYING GEMS

Many gemstone names date back to antiquity, long before the science of mineralogy had given a scientific basis for classification. Modern texts identify gemstones first by their mineralogical classification and then by name of the variety of the mineral.

CLASSIFYING MINERALS

Mineralogical classification is based on chemical composition and internal atomic structure. Marcasite and pyrite have the same chemical formula but a different internal structure. Gems are grouped by their mineralogical classification. A radical is a group of atoms that act as a single unit.

SPHALERITE

Sulfides
A sulfide mineral is formed when a metal or semimetal combines with sulfur. In sphalerite, zinc is the metal.

DIAMOND

Native elements
Minerals formed from a single chemical element are called native elements. They include metals such as gold and nonmetals such as diamond, which is made up of carbon.

BLUE SAPPHIRE

Oxides
When oxygen alone combines with a metal or semimetal, an oxide mineral is formed. Corundum is aluminum oxide; when blue, it is called sapphire.

Hydroxides
These minerals contain a hydroxyl (hydrogen and oxygen) radical combined with a metal. In diaspore, aluminum is the metal.

DIASPORE

Halides
A halide is a halogen element (chlorine, bromine, fluorine, or iodine) combined with a metal or semimetal. Fluorite is fluorine and calcium combined.

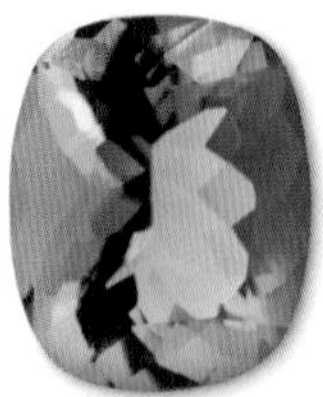

FLUORITE

Carbonates
The carbonate radical, carbon and oxygen, combines with a metal or semimetal to form a carbonate. In the case of azurite, copper is the metal.

AZURITE

LAZULITE

Phosphates
In the phosphates, a radical of oxygen and phosphorous combines with a metal or semimetal. Magnesium and aluminum are the combined metals in lazulite.

Borates
These minerals contain boron and oxygen. In howlite, boron, oxygen, and silicon combine with calcium and water.

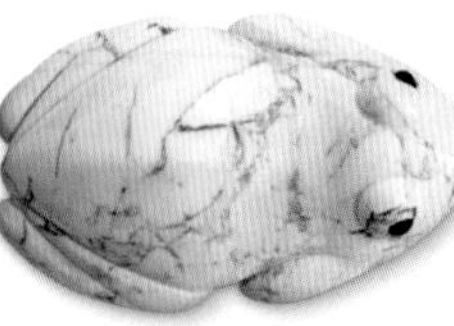

HOWLITE

Sulfates
Sulfur forms a radical with oxygen that combines with a metal or semimetal to form minerals of the sulfate group. Barite is barium sulfate.

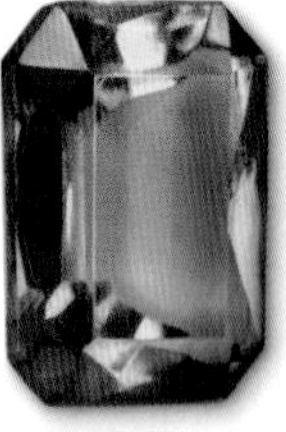

BARITE

AMETHYST

Silicates
In this group, a silica (silicon and oxygen) radical combines with various metals or semimetals. Silica also occurs uncombined as quartz, whose purple variety is amethyst.

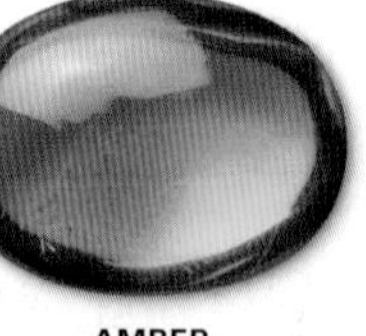

AMBER

Organics
Pearl, shell, and coral are organic compounds with well-defined crystal structures and are classified as minerals. Amber, copal, and jet are amorphous, and are not considered minerals.

CHEMICAL FORMULAS

The chemical makeup of a mineral is expressed in its chemical formula. The formula indicates the relative proportions of each chemical element that makes up a single structural unit of the mineral. Some minerals grade into each other chemically, and this is also noted in the formula. Minor amounts of other elements, called trace elements, may also be present in a mineral and influence its color. However, these are not included in the formula.

HOW GEMS ARE NAMED

Until relatively recent times, there was no real basis for classification of gems except color. However, color names referred to a number of different stones. The term "ruby" was used for many red stones that were not the red variety of the mineral corundum—the current definition of ruby. One such example is the Black Prince's "Ruby" in the British crown jewels, which is actually a spinel. Today, gemstones are named after the mineral from which they are cut, such as topaz. Some older names still persist. These include rubellite and indicolite for colored varieties of tourmaline. Many old names are dropping away as modern science is being applied to gemology. However, a number of gem names that are in use today are trade names, with no scientific or mineralogical connection.

ALEXANDRITE

CZAR ALEXANDER II

Date of discovery
Some gems have names related to the time they were discovered. Alexandrite was supposedly discovered on the birthday of Russia's Czar Alexander II and so is named after him.

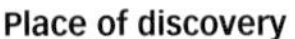

VESUVIANITE

Place of discovery
Gems are frequently named after a locality associated with them. Vesuvianite is named after its discovery on Mount Vesuvius, Italy.

MOUNT VESUVIUS

PHYSICAL PROPERTIES

Durability is an essential quality of gemstones. The physical properties of the mineral from which the gem is cut determine its susceptibility to wear, breakage, and deterioration. Diamonds may be "forever," but other gems may not be, depending on their properties.

HARDNESS

The hardness of a gem—the relative ease or difficulty with which it can be scratched—is a factor in its durability. Hardness should not be confused with toughness or strength. Very hard minerals, such as diamond, can be quite brittle. Gemstones below 5 on the Mohs scale (below) are too soft for general wear, and stones that are 6 or 7 in hardness will scratch and abrade. Very soft stones are only cut for collectors.

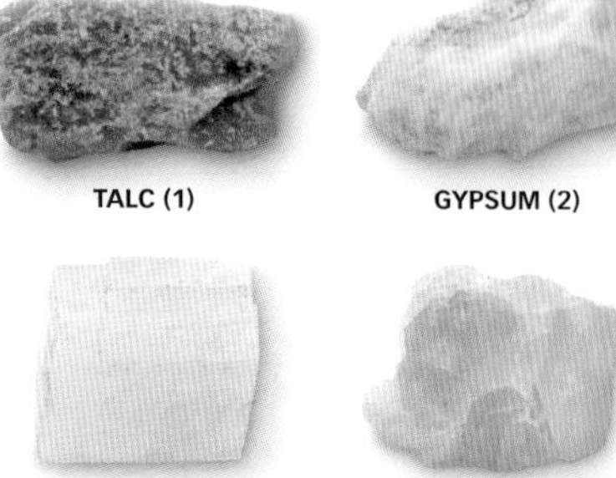

TALC (1)

GYPSUM (2)

CALCITE (3)

FLUORITE (4)

APATITE (5)

FELDSPAR (6–6½)

QUARTZ (7)

BERYL (7½–8)

CORUNDUM (9)

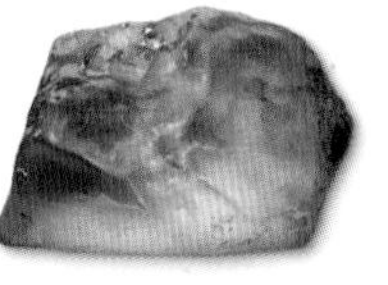

DIAMOND (10)

Mohs scale of hardness
The Mohs scale measures hardness relative to 10 minerals of increasing hardness, from 1 (as soft as talc) to 10 (as hard as diamond).

SPECIFIC GRAVITY

Specific gravity is a measure of the density of a substance. It is the ratio of the weight of the substance to the weight of an equal volume of water. For example, a mineral with a specific gravity of 2 is twice as heavy as water of the same volume. Specific gravity has two important functions in the realm of gems. First, it is a characteristic that is easy to determine when attempting to identify a cut gem. Second, a number of gems have a higher-than-average specific gravity, which allows them to concentrate in placer deposits.

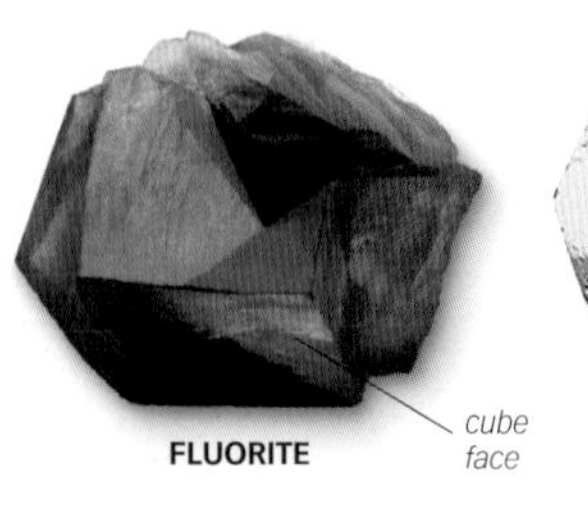

FLUORITE

PYRITE

Relative specific gravity
The "feel" of the weight of a gem or its rough is referred to as relative specific gravity. In two stones of the same size, as shown here, the one with the higher specific gravity (pyrite) will feel "heavy."

CLEAVAGE

Cleavage is the property of a mineral that causes it to break along flat, planar surfaces along the atomic layers, where the forces bonding the atoms are the weakest. Many gems have relatively strong bonds in all directions, but some gems have cleavages in several directions. Some cleavage is very easy to trigger, and this affects the durability of the finished gem. Cut and polished gems with easily triggered cleavages can break if knocked sharply. A mineral's breakage across its atomic planes is called its fracture.

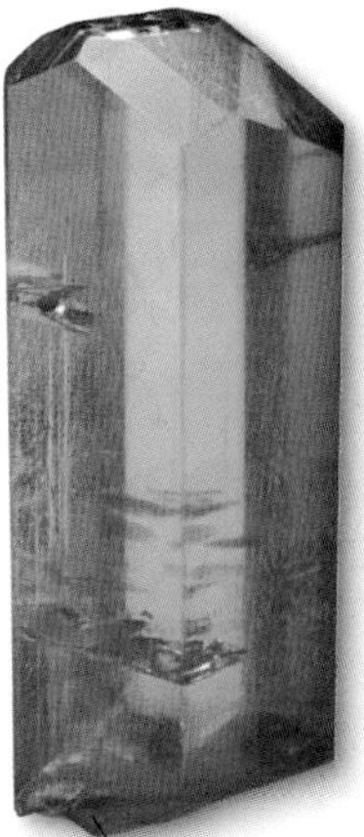

Indistinct cleavage
This cleavage is produced when a mineral breaks along relatively well-bonded atomic planes, producing irregular breakage surfaces, as seen at the base of this aquamarine specimen.

cleavage plane

Perfect cleavage
If a mineral has perfect cleavage, the breakage occurs as a flat surface along an atomic plane where the bonds are weakest. Topaz exhibits perfect cleavage.

crystal face

broken base

Distinct cleavage
As seen in cerussite, distinct cleavage occurs when a mineral breaks along weakly bonded atomic planes but not in perfectly flat surfaces.

TENACITY

The term tenacity refers to a set of physical properties that depend on the cohesive force between atoms in the mineral structures. In gemstones, tenacity affects durability. Brittleness is a type of tenacity that is particularly important, as it relates to a gem's tendency to chip. Most gemstones, including diamond, are brittle to a certain degree. Whether a stone will chip in the cutting process or when worn depends on the strength and direction of its atomic bonds. Gemstones made up of matted aggregates of small crystals, such as jade, are very tenacious. When gems are set, their mountings need to reflect their tenacity.

Conchoidal fracture
Many gemstones have conchoidal fracture, where the breakage has a shell-like appearance. The chip in this haüyne gemstone shows conchoidal fracture.

Uneven fracture
In minerals with uneven fracture, the broken surface is rough and irregular, with no evident pattern. Nephrite breaks with an uneven fracture.

OPTICAL PROPERTIES

Interaction with light is the essence of a gemstone. Light is the source of all color, sparkle, and beauty of the gem. Understanding the interaction between light and gemstone varieties is useful for gem identification.

CAUSES OF COLOR IN GEMS

Along with durability, beauty is one of the prime qualities necessary for a gemstone. Color is an important part of a gemstone's beauty. In gems, color is caused by the absorption or refraction of light. White light is composed of many colors; when one or more of these are removed, the remaining light that emerges from the gem appears colored. The color may either be intrinsic to the gem itself or caused by the presence of trace elements that result in certain wavelengths being absorbed.

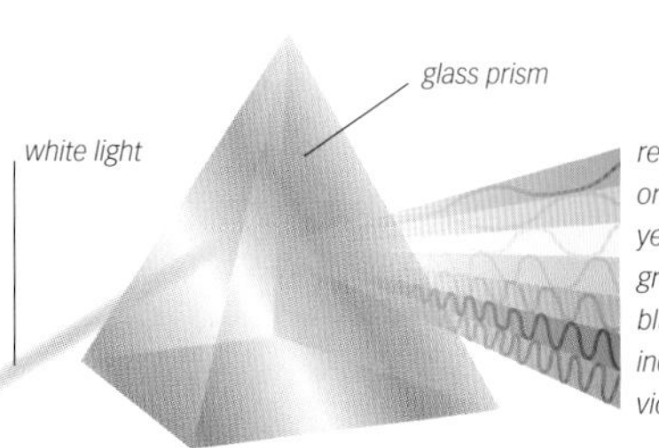

Splitting light
When light passes through a prism, it separates into its constituent colors. Each color has its own wavelength and is consequently diffracted at a different angle.

IDIOCHROMATIC AND ALLOCHROMATIC GEMS

The term idiochromatic (self-colored) is used for gems whose colors are intrinsic to the stone itself; for example, the bright blue of azurite and the green of malachite. These colors result from chemical elements that are essential constituents of the gem. In other gems, color is caused by the presence of trace elements—elements that are not part of the chemical composition of the mineral. Gems that are colored in this way are known as allochromatic gems. For example, traces of chromium result in the color of ruby and emerald. However, chromium causes a different absorption in each of the two gems, leading to different colors.

ROCK CRYSTAL (QUARTZ)

CITRINE

AMETHYST

Allochromatic gems
Amethyst and citrine are examples of allochromatic gems. Both are quartz varieties colored by trace elements. Amethyst is colored by traces of iron, and citrine by iron and natural irradiation.

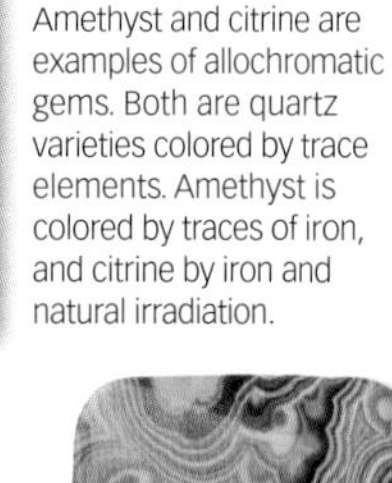

Idiochromatic gems
A manganese carbonate, rhodochrosite is naturally pink to red due to the presence of manganese. Malachite—a copper carbonate—is naturally green due to the presence of copper.

RHODOCHROSITE

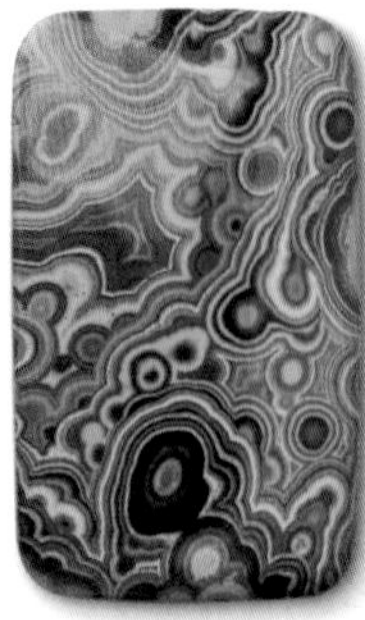

MALACHITE

PARTI-COLORING

Gems that exhibit different colors within the same stone are called parti-colored. The divisions between the colors can be abrupt or gradual. Gems with two colors are called bicolored and those with three, tricolored. Parti-coloring is a result of changes in the chemical medium in which a crystal grows or preferential absorption of different impurities by different growing crystal faces.

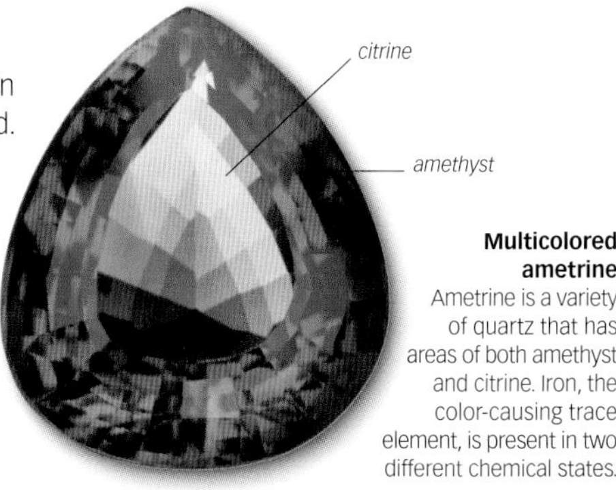

Multicolored ametrine
Ametrine is a variety of quartz that has areas of both amethyst and citrine. Iron, the color-causing trace element, is present in two different chemical states.

PLEOCHROIC GEMS

As white light passes through many gemstones, its colors are absorbed differently in different directions because of the way light interacts with the internal structure. As a consequence, a gemstone can appear different colors or shades when viewed from different directions. This effect is called pleochroism. Gem cutters orient pleochroic stones keeping in mind their most desirable color. Pleochroism is also an important aid for the identification of cut stones.

IOLITE (BLUE ASPECT)

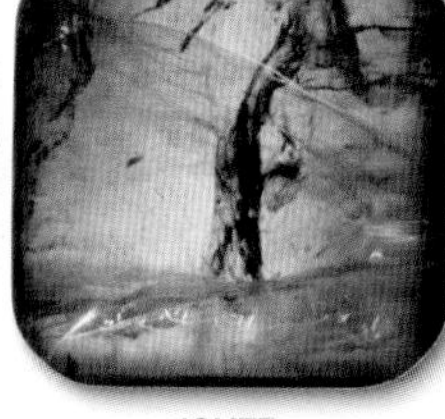

IOLITE (COLORLESS ASPECT)

Pleochroism in iolite
Iolite, a gem variety of the mineral cordierite, is strongly pleochroic. This rounded cube of iolite appears blue in one direction, but when rotated 90 degrees, it appears colorless.

REFRACTIVE INDEX

When light passes from air into a transparent or translucent gem, it changes velocity and direction, resulting in a phenomenon known as refraction. The extent of refraction is called the refractive index, measured as a ratio of the angle at which light strikes a stone and the angle at which the light bends as it passes through it. Gemstone minerals in the cubic system bend light equally in all directions; other crystal systems bend light in two directions—a phenomenon known as double refraction.

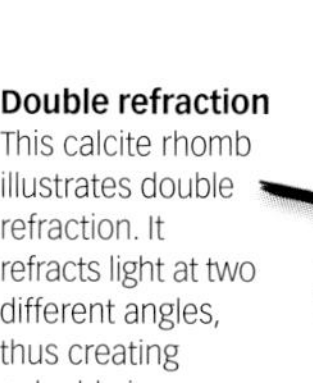

Double refraction
This calcite rhomb illustrates double refraction. It refracts light at two different angles, thus creating a double image.

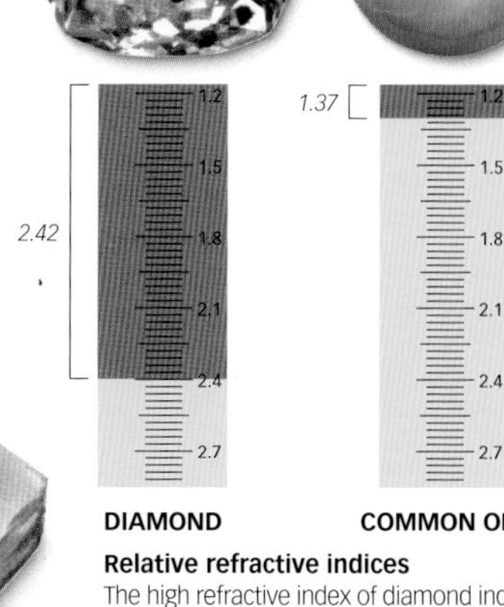

DIAMOND

COMMON OPAL

Relative refractive indices
The high refractive index of diamond indicates high bending and splitting of light, resulting in its "fire." The lower refractive index of opal indicates a stone that lacks "fire" even when faceted.

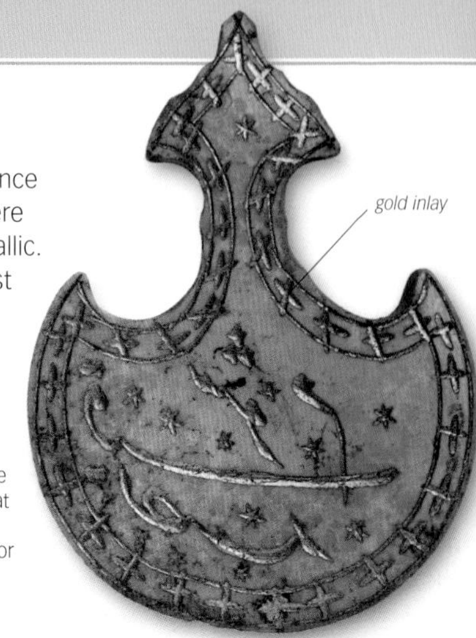

» LUSTER

The luster of a gem or mineral is the appearance of its surface in reflected light. In general, there are two types of luster: metallic and nonmetallic. Precious metals have metallic luster and most gemstones, nonmetallic. Pyrite, for example, is a mineral with a metallic luster. There are several kinds of nonmetallic lusters.

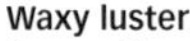

Waxy luster
Gems with a waxy luster have a surface appearance like that of a block of wax. Turquoise, shown to the right, is noted for this type of luster.

Pearly luster
A gem with pearly luster has a surface like that of pearl or mother-of-pearl. Apart from these organic gems, smithsonite (shown above) also has pearly luster.

Resinous luster
Gems with a resinous luster have the appearance of a piece of resin. Amber has a classic resinous luster.

Silky luster
As seen in this specimen of satin spar gypsum, silky luster is a sheen like that on the surface of a bolt of silk or satin.

Earthy luster
The nonlustrous appearance of raw earth or freshly broken, dry soil, as seen in this specimen of meerschaum, is known as earthy luster.

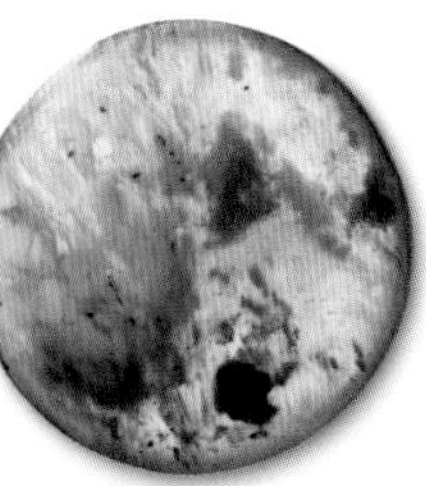

Greasy luster
Stones that exhibit this uncommon kind of luster appear to be coated with a thin film of oil. Jade has a greasy luster.

Adamantine luster
A relatively uncommon type of luster, adamantine refers to the brilliant luster of diamond. Apart from diamond, it can be seen in some zircons and in a few other gems.

Vitreous luster
Many gems exhibit vitreous luster, which resembles the surface of glass. This piece of obsidian perfectly illustrates vitreous luster on its broken surfaces.

Metallic luster
Metallic luster occurs when light is reflected on an untarnished metal surface. It is the luster of precious metals and of some gems and minerals, such as the pyrite specimen seen here.

FIRE

The term fire is used for the flashes of light that can be seen when a gemstone is moved. As with a prism, when white light enters a gem, its component colors are separated, or dispersed. The greater the dispersion of white light, the greater the fire. The refractive index (see p.21) is a measure of dispersion.

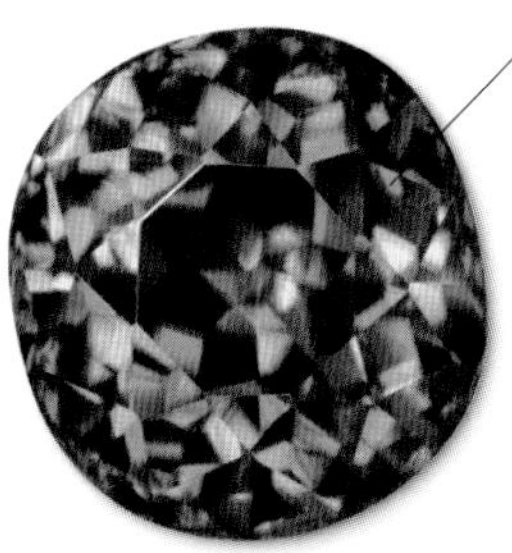

good color dispersion

Faceted zircon
Zircon has a high refractive index and thus shows good fire. It is also doubly refractive, with the pavilion facets, as seen in this specimen, showing doubling.

INTERFERENCE

The internal structures of a gemstone can cause interference between the light rays passing through it. For example, labradorite is composed of thin layers of plagioclase feldspar. When light passes through these layers, it is reflected from both their upper and lower surfaces. As the rays travel different distances, some waves are enhanced when the wave crests correspond, producing color. The colors depend on which wavelengths are enhanced. In other instances, the waves cancel each other.

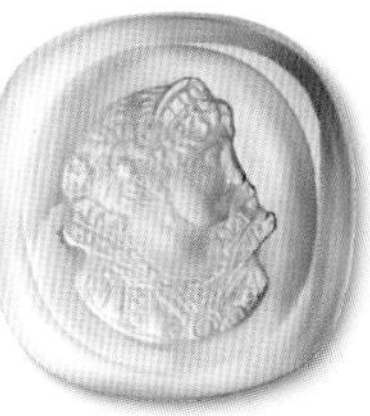

Adularescence
Moonstone contains thin layers of different feldspars. When each of these layers reflect light, a shimmering effect called adularesence is produced just below the surface.

PRECIOUS OPAL

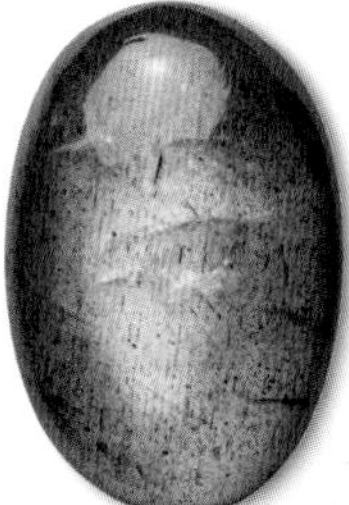

LABRADORITE

Iridescence
Precious opal is composed of regular-sized spheres of silica. Light is scattered by the spaces between the spheres, and colors are created where wave crests coincide. Different sphere sizes create different colors.

THE CAT'S EYE AND STAR EFFECTS

Both stars and cat's eyes result from chatoyancy—the reflection of light from microscopic inclusions of other minerals within the gemstone. A common cause of chatoyancy is the presence of microscopic needles of the mineral rutile. Star stones are cut *en cabochon* with the dome of the cabochon coinciding with the point of intersection of the rutile crystals.

SAPPHIRE

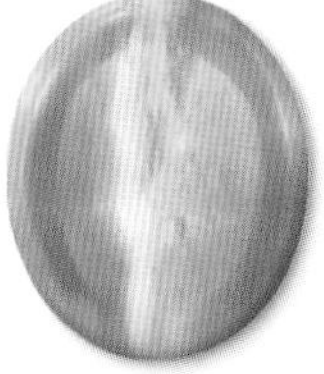

CAT'S EYE CHRYSOBERYL

Chatoyancy
Whether a gemstone produces a star or a cat's eye depends on the orientation of the inclusions of other minerals within the gemstone.

SPECTROSCOPY

A spectroscope is used to examine light passing through a gemstone. Spectroscopes have a small slit to admit light. The gem is placed between a light source and the slit, and a spectrum is produced as light enters the stone. Dark bands appear in the spectrum where various wavelengths are absorbed by the stone. These bands are characteristic of various chemical elements and help determine the gem's chemical makeup.

WHERE GEMSTONES ARE FOUND

There is scarcely a country where gems are not found. Some localities are tiny, producing mere handfuls; others produce tons of specimens on an industrial scale. New deposits are discovered regularly, keeping the gem market supplied with new material.

WHERE GEMSTONES ARE FOUND

Nearly 100 rocks and minerals and at least half a dozen organic materials are used as gemstones. While some countries have only a few small-scale gem sites, others have numerous large deposits of gemstones. The map shown here indicates some of the key deposits of many major gemstones. Given the scale of the map, the deposits have not been shown in their exact localities. In many instances, several varieties of gemstones or precious metals are sourced from the same locality. As a result of this, the symbols for the gemstones have been placed in the general area where the gemstones are found.

Gem localities

This map shows only the key deposits of major gemstones. Although no deposits are shown for some countries, it does not necessarily mean that there are no gems to be found there.

KEY

DIAMOND	SAPPHIRE	AMBER	AQUAMARINE
RUBY	EMERALD	TURQUOISE	TOURMALINE
TOPAZ	GOLD	ZIRCON	SPINEL
AMETHYST	JADE	PERIDOT	GARNET

Amber mine at Russia

The world's largest amber mine is in Kaliningrad Oblast—part of the Russian federation. The area is informally called Yantarny Kray, or "the Amber Region."

Mining emeralds at Colombia
Miners can be seen searching for emeralds in a mine in Muzo, Colombia. Although emerald deposits have recently been discovered elsewhere, Colombia remains the world's major supplier of the gem.

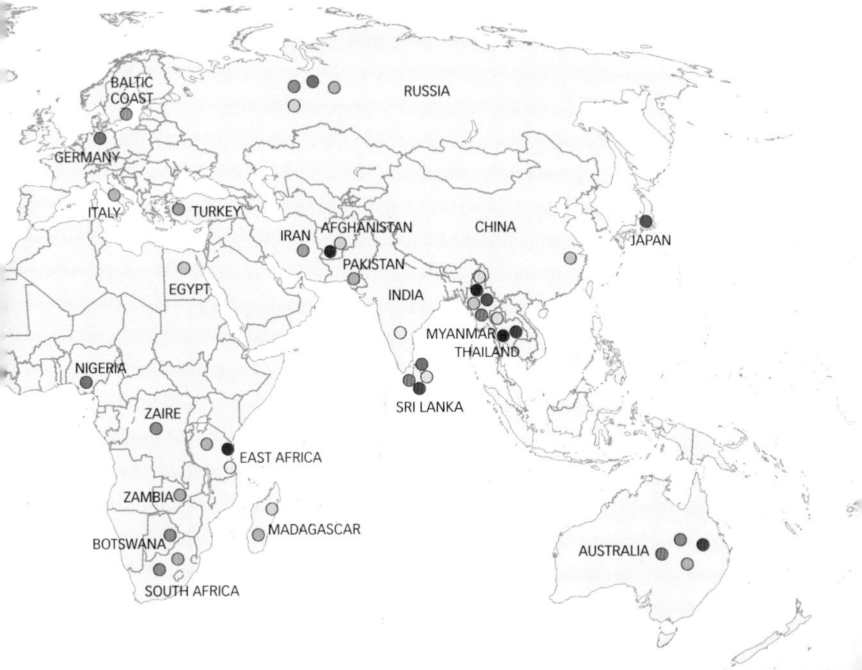

BALTIC COAST
RUSSIA
GERMANY
ITALY
TURKEY
IRAN
AFGHANISTAN
CHINA
JAPAN
PAKISTAN
EGYPT
INDIA
MYANMAR
THAILAND
NIGERIA
SRI LANKA
ZAIRE
EAST AFRICA
ZAMBIA
MADAGASCAR
BOTSWANA
AUSTRALIA
SOUTH AFRICA

MINING GEMSTONES

Gems are recovered in two ways: from the rocks in which they formed or from weathered rock debris. The first method is called hard-rock mining, while the second is called placer mining, in which gems are recovered from a concentration in a stream or beach deposit.

ANCIENT GEM MINING

Precious stones have been mined since antiquity. Lapis lazuli was mined in Afghanistan about 7,000 years ago, turquoise mining started on the Sinai Peninsula 5,000 years ago, and emeralds were mined in Egypt at the same time. Ancient mining techniques were quite efficient. Panning and sieving of stream gravels continues to be used today. Digging of decomposed gem veins has changed only in terms of the tools used.

Egyptian goldsmiths at work
In this wall painting from the tomb of the sculptors Ipuky and Nebamun (*c.*1390–60 BCE), goldsmiths are weighing and smelting gold and presenting gold jewelry.

HARD-ROCK MINING

Unless the gems are highly valuable, their concentration in the rocks in which they formed rarely justifies the extensive and expensive methods required to extract them. Although a large percentage of diamond is recovered from placers, it is also mined from "pipes" of kimberlite rock in which it formed. Solid kimberlite is mined by the usual hard-rock methods of drilling and blasting. The rock is crushed and the diamonds are extracted. Other examples of gems recovered through hard-rock mining are tourmaline, topaz, emerald, sapphire, ruby, aquamarine, opal, turquoise, and lapis lazuli. Most of these are mined on a small scale using basic tools.

Drilling for gold
The process of recovering precious metals from hard rock is the same as recovering gems. Holes are drilled in the rock and explosive charges are placed.

Open-cast mine
Large deposits of diamonds have been discovered in Australia. This mine at Argyle is a huge open-cast operation within a diamond pipe.

PLACER MINING

Because many gemstones are hard and dense, once released by weathering they can be transported by water to concentrate in river beds, beaches, and on the ocean floor. These concentrations are called placer deposits. Placer mining uses methods that mimic the original creation of the placer. Panning and sieving are the simplest methods. In panning, the lighter material is washed out of the pan, and in sieving, the denser minerals end up in the center of the sieve and are sorted from the concentrate by hand. In another method of placer mining, gem-bearing gravel is shoveled into a trough of flowing water with baffles at the bottom. Lighter material is washed away while the denser gemstones are retained by the baffles.

Sapphire sieving
In Sri Lanka and Laos, rubies and sapphires are mined by passing gravel through sieves and hand-washing and concentrating them to separate out the gems.

Sapphire gravels
These fancy sapphires were recovered from stream gravels at Rock Creek in Montana, USA, by hand-sieving gravels concentrated in the placer.

SORTING AND GRADING

A significant portion of gemstones recovered from mines and placers are not of gem quality. They lack the color, shape, or clarity to be cut. In the case of some gems, the rejection rate can be as high as 90 percent. To avoid discarding usable stones or retaining inferior ones, careful sorting and grading is necessary. Preliminary grading and sorting is done at the mine, and then at each stage before the rough reaches the cutter.

Sorting diamonds
This highly skilled diamond sorter is at work in Gaborone, Botswana. He is sorting rough diamonds for color and clarity before they are sent to the cutters.

CUTTING GEMS

The reshaping of natural materials to use them for personal adornment has occurred for millennia. Organic materials were probably the first to be shaped, because they are more easily worked, followed by softer stones, and finally hard stones.

WHY CUT GEMS?

There are several reasons for cutting or reshaping stones. Gems are cut to enhance their beauty, increase their value, and from ancient times to the present day, to increase their magical potency. Some of the earliest written records point to the belief that certain stones have potent supernatural powers. Although such beliefs still exist, gems are today cut principally to enhance their economic value. The value of a finished gem can be many times the value of its rough, and cut stones are far more salable than roughs.

CUTTING A GEM

The term "cutting" in the context of gemstones is a misnomer. Gemstone roughs may be sawn to remove poor areas, separate a gemmy area from within a larger stone, or create a preliminary shape. The actual "cutting" of the gem, however, is done through various stages of grinding and polishing. These stages are explained on the right. Some gemstones are not faceted and may be polished or used for engraving (pp.30–31).

Inspecting the cut
The general rule is to "cut a little and look a lot." The best brilliance is achieved when facets are cut at proper angles and are in their proper position.

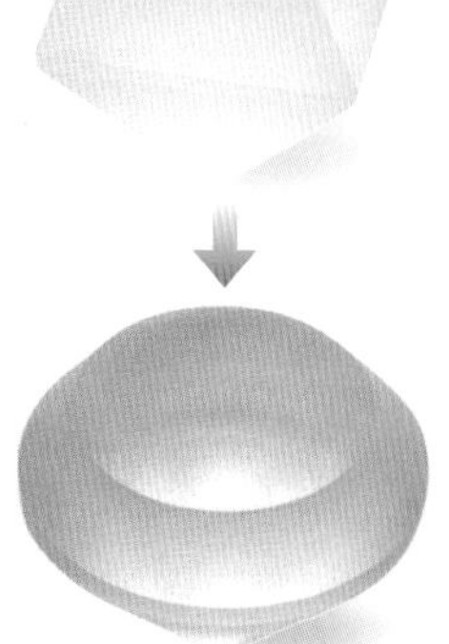

Rough choice
The rough is chosen for its clarity, shape, and absence of flaws and inclusions. If flaws and inclusions are present, the rough is carefully oriented to conceal them.

Sawn into two
The rough is sawn either into the general shape of the stone or to form the table facet in the top half of the stone, which is known as the crown.

Faceting begins
Large facets, called the main facets, are the first to be placed. In a brilliant cut, there are eight facets at the top and eight at the bottom.

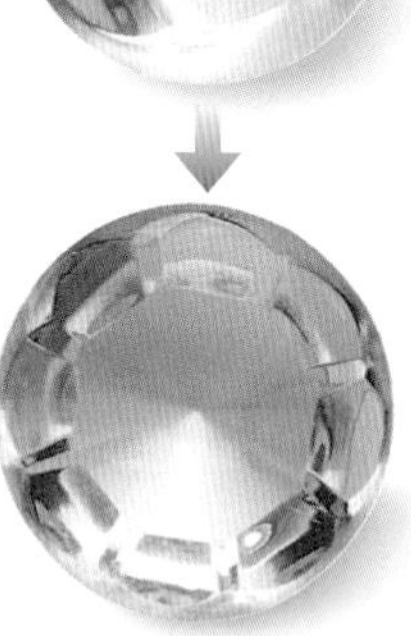

Further facets
Smaller facets are added around the main facets, both at the top (the crown) and the bottom (the pavilion). There are 40 such facets in a brilliant-cut stone.

Finished off
After the final facets are ground in, they are polished. This stage can be carried out either during cutting, which is preferred by most cutters, or afterward.

GEM CUTS

The cut used on any particular piece of gem rough is determined by a number of factors in combination. Keeping in mind the shape of the rough, gemcutters choose a cut that minimizes wastage. The position of flaws, fractures, and inclusions also determine the cut, as does a stone's cleavage. If the stone is pleochroic, it is orientated in a way that shows its best color. Stones that exhibit stars are cut so that the star is centred in the finished stone.

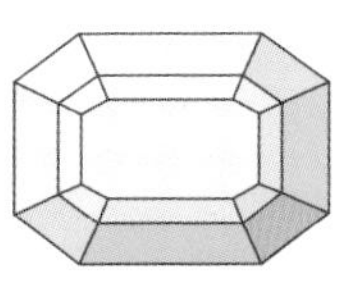
EMERALD

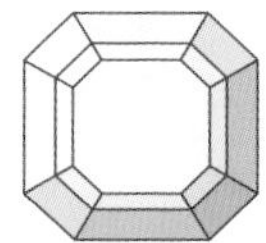
STEP

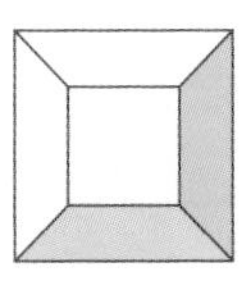
TABLE

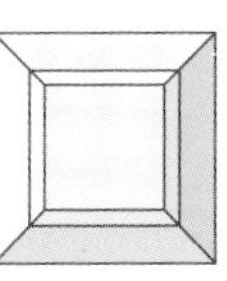
SQUARE

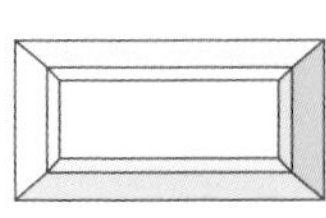
BAGUETTE

DIOPSIDE

TANZANITE

Step cuts
Step cuts are used to display the color of the stone. They are generally less brilliant, but in these specimens color is more important than brilliance. They have roughly rectangular facets.

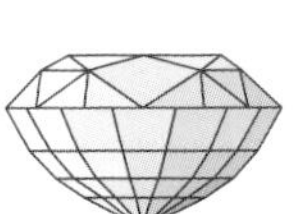
MIXED

CUSHION

Mixed cuts
Mixed cuts have a mixture of brilliant- and step-cut facets. They are used to enhance the brilliance of a colored stone while also emphasizing its color.

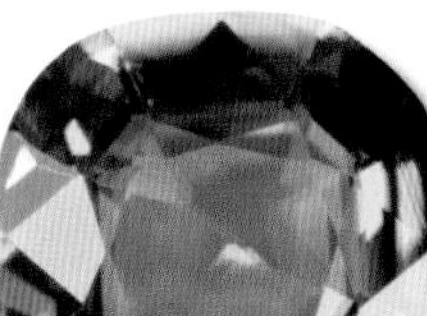
SPHENE

HESSONITE

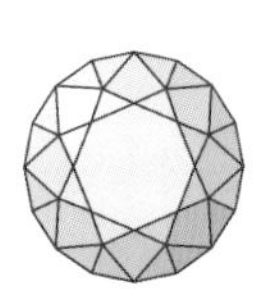
ROUND BRILLIANT

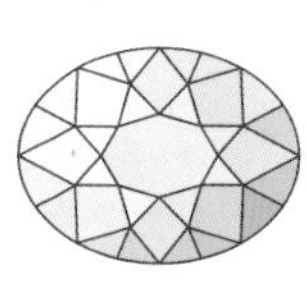
OVAL BRILLIANT

MARQUISE

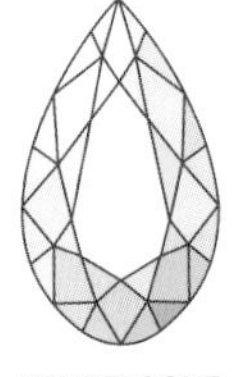
PENDELOQUE

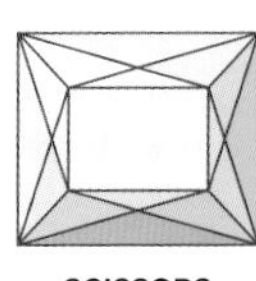
SCISSORS

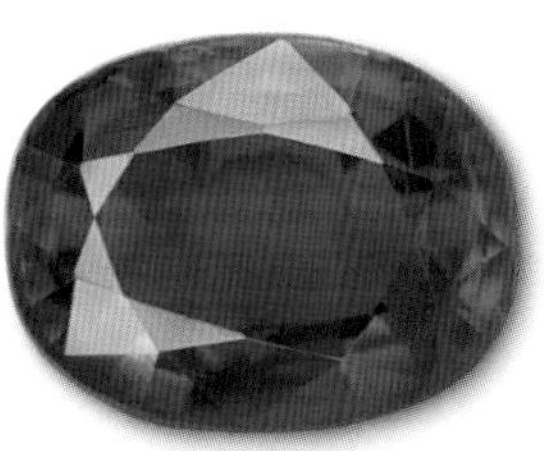

KYANITE

SUNSTONE

Brilliant cuts
Brilliant cuts maximize the brilliance of stones. They are also used on colored stones to deepen their color, conceal flaws, and even out patchy color. The facets are roughly triangular or kite-shaped.

POLISHING AND ENGRAVING GEMS

Transparent stones are generally faceted to maximize their fire and brilliance, and sometimes to enhance their color. Opaque or translucent semiprecious stones are tumble-polished, carved, engraved, or cut *en cabochon*.

POLISHING GEMS

The most common way of displaying colors and highlighting other optical effects in opaque or translucent stones is to cut them *en cabochon*—with a rounded upper surface and a flat underside. Cabochons are cut from slices of rock and polished on abrasive wheels. After sawing, the stone is ground to its outline shape, and then its top is ground and polished into a dome, using progressively finer abrasives. Some gemstones have oriented inclusions within them that produce a cat's-eye or star effect. These effects are revealed when the stones are cut *en cabochon*.

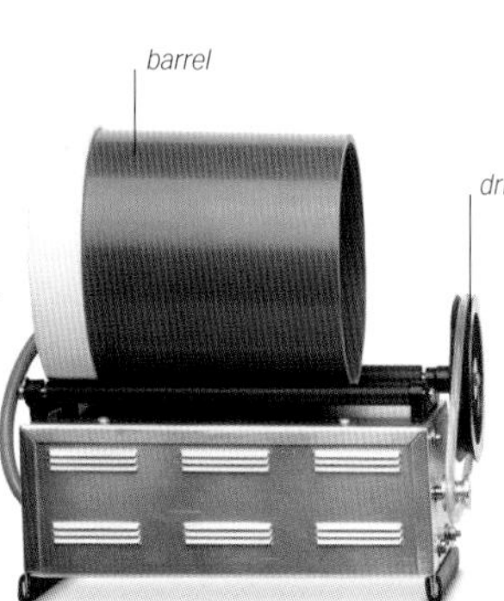

Tumbling drum
Rough stones are placed in a drum with water and progressively finer abrasives. When the drum is rotated, the stones wear themselves round in combination with the abrasives.

Many semiprecious stones are rounded and polished by tumble-polishing, which is essentially the same process that rounds beach pebbles. Nonspherical beads are rough-ground into shape and then tumbled. Spherical beads are produced in a bead mill. They are first rough-ground into shape and then placed between two counter-rotating iron plates with abrasives and rolled until spherical.

Tumble-polished gems
These semiprecious stones, most of which are varieties of quartz, have been rounded and polished in a tumbler similar to the one illustrated above.

THULITE

JADE

AVENTURINE

Slabs, beads, and cabochons
There are preferred ways of cutting and shaping some stones. As indicated by the symbols shown here, some stones are polished into flat surfaces, while others are rounded as beads and cabochons.

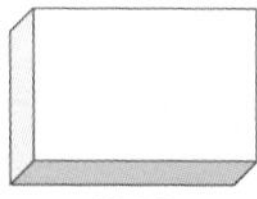

SLAB

BEAD

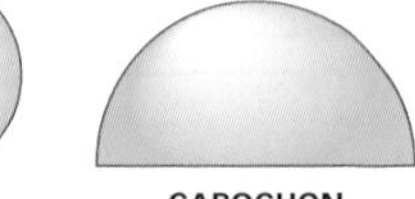

CABOCHON

ENGRAVING GEMS

Color-layered gemstones have been carved to create cameos and intaglios for around 2,000 years. In a cameo, the stone is cut around the design, so that it stands in relief against a differently colored background. In an intaglio, the subject is cut away to create a recessed image. The cutting process is exactly the same as in carving, except that cameos and intaglios are only cut into one surface of the stone.

AGATE

Cutting cameos
Cameos are cut from stones with layers of color. Different portions of the pattern are cut into different layers of color for emphasis.

CAMEO

Other engravings
Gemstone items such as the jet carving and the precious metal jewelry box shown here are also "carvings" and "engravings" in the broadest sense of the words.

SILVER

JET

CARVING GEMSTONES

Carving is the process of cutting gemstone material into a three-dimensional shape. It can be a simple "face" of the moon carved in moonstone, or an involved carving of human figures, plants, or animals. When carving, it is necessary to choose a stone that has a homogenous texture and uniform hardness. Stones lack tensile strength and are easily broken along directions or zones of weakness when carved. Although fine-grained stones can be carved with delicate detail, coarse-grained stones can only accept broad details. Semiprecious stones, often called hardstones, can be quite brittle and are more difficult to carve. In the past, they were carved with small rotating wheels using loose abrasives. Today, a selection of diamond-tipped tools are used.

Jade carving
This carver is working on an intricate jade carving with rotating, diamond-tipped tools. The tenacity and hardness of jade make it an ideal carving material.

GEM ENHANCEMENT

The enhancement of gemstones is any process other than the usual cutting and polishing that improves the appearance or durability of a natural stone. This practice is so widespread that buyers should presume gems are enhanced unless otherwise stated.

IRRADIATION

The color of gemstones may be altered by bombardment with neutrons, gamma rays, ultraviolet rays, or electrons. Virtually all blue topaz is irradiated and heat-treated colorless topaz. Most yellow-green quartz has been irradiated to attain its color. The two most common irradiation methods for color change in diamond are neutron and electron bombardment. Irradiated diamonds that are green and black are heat treated to produce orange, yellow, brown, or pink stones. Blue to blue-green stones are not usually heat treated, because they are considered desirable. Some irradiated diamonds, such as the Dresden Green Diamond, are completely natural. Although they undergo color change, irradiated gemstones themselves are not usually radioactive.

IRRADIATED UTAH TOPAZ

DARK BLUE IRRADIATED TOPAZ

Color change by irradiation
Most dark blue topaz in the market is produced by irradiating and heating colorless topaz. Some colorless topaz from Utah, such as the specimen on the left, turns rich golden-brown when irradiated.

HEAT TREATMENT

Heat treatment is probably the oldest form of gemstone enhancement. Today, heat treatment is used alone or in combination with other techniques. Sapphires and rubies are heat treated to dissolve microscopic rutile, which can make them appear cloudy. Some gemstones are heated in the presence of foreign elements that diffuse at a shallow depth in the stone's structure to change its color. Stones with fractures are heated with a flux that partially remelts the stone and heals the fractures.

Natural and heat-treated zircons
Zircons have been heat treated to change their color for at least a millennium. In the image below, the stones on the right are natural and those on the left, heat treated.

OILING, STAINING, AND BLEACHING

Many emeralds have small flaws or cracks that spoil their appearance. An age-old method to disguise these flaws is to simply soak the emerald in oil. This fills in the cracks and gives the appearance of a better-quality stone. Stones treated in this manner may have an oily feel.

Staining or dyeing is very widespread. Slices of agate are routinely dyed with vivid colors such as blue or red, and howlite is dyed to resemble turquoise. Turquoise itself is boiled in a hard wax that penetrates the surface and deepens the color. Other stones are often bleached to lighten or change their colors.

Oiling
This emerald has cracks and fissures that are typical of oiled specimens. The oil will eventually evaporate or be removed by cleaning, revealing the flaws.

Bleaching
Tiger's eye is one of the stones that are routinely bleached to change their color. Darker yellow-brown specimens are bleached to this lighter shade.

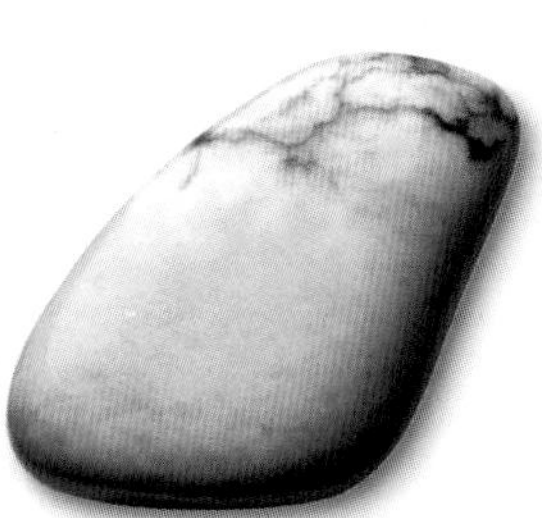

Staining
When howlite has dark inclusions that mimic those in turquoise, it can be stained blue to give it the appearance of turquoise.

FILLING, COATING, AND RECONSTRUCTION

Some gemstones with cracks are subjected to fillers other than oil (see above). Fillers such as glass, resins, plastic, or waxes can be colored to match the gemstone. Very thin coatings of gold, silver, or other metals can be applied to gems to alter their color or reflectivity, such as in "mystic" topaz. However, these coatings wear off very quickly. In reconstructed gems, heat pressure or solvents are used to fuse small pieces of a gems together into a larger whole.

Aqua aura quartz
This variety of quartz is a good example of a coated stone. Its crystals are coated with a surface film of gold to give the specimen a pale blue color.

LASER DRILLING

An expensive process, laser drilling is only used for diamonds. As diamonds are combustible, an infrared laser can be used to drill fine holes (less than 0.005 in or 0.2 mm in diameter) to reach flaws and inclusions by evaporating the diamond. Once a hole is drilled, many kinds of inclusions can be dissolved with acid. The hole left by the laser and the dissolved inclusion can then be filled with glass. The same technique is used to drill holes to cracks and other flaws, which can then be filled. The filled holes can usually be detected by a trained gemologist under the microscope.

SYNTHETIC GEMS

Gemstones have been simulated since ancient times. Modern chemistry allows virtually identical copies of natural gems to be produced in the laboratory along with simulations of gems that are hard to differentiate from genuine gems.

COMPOSITES

Some composites are meant to deceive, such as the grafting of a cheaper stone onto a more expensive one. Composites such as opal doublets and triplets exist to display and protect a slice of valuable and brittle thinner stone. When two stones are joined with the intent of deception, such as with a colored glass base and a mineral top, the joint can often be seen by immersing the gem in water.

Almandine garnet doublet
With a glass base, garnet-topped doublets can imitate gems of a number of colors. Looking sideways through the gem can often reveal the glued joint.

SYNTHETICS

Synthetic gemstones are made under laboratory conditions and are nearly exact copies of natural gems. Some are created by the flame-fusion process (see below); others by the flux-melt process. In the flux-melt process, gems are manufactured by melting or dissolving the appropriate mineral ingredients and coloring agents in a flux and allowing the solution or molten mass to crystallize at controlled pressures and temperatures. Synthetics, such as ruby, can be grown cheaply and quickly; others, such as emerald, take months.

Edmond Frémy ruby crystals
In 1877, the French chemist Edmond Frémy melted aluminum oxide and lead oxide together in a porcelain vat, artificially creating a number of small ruby crystals.

The flame-fusion process
In this process, mineral powder is sifted onto the end of the forming cylinder of the mineral. The end is bathed in hot flame, fusing the powder.

DISTINGUISHING BETWEEN NATURAL AND SYNTHETIC STONES

Because some synthetics are identical in both composition and crystal structure to the natural gem and possess similar optical and physical properties, they can only be identified by experts. Stones simulated by glass or plastic are much easier for an amateur to detect and can be identified by the unnatural look and "feel" of the stone. The reputation of the seller is usually the best guarantee of authenticity.

Different optical and physical properties
When synthetics are used to imitate natural stones, the optical and physical properties of the simulant help identify it.

SYNTHETIC OPAL

NATURAL OPAL

INCLUSIONS

One method of determining whether a gem is natural or synthetic is to look within the stone. Many methods of creating synthetics leave behind telltale growth structures and inclusions. For example, synthetics created by the flux-melt process (see below) leave curved growth zones, many synthetic emeralds have veils of fluid-filled tubes, and many synthetic opals show patterns that look like reptile scales.

Solid, liquid, or gas inclusions picked up by natural stones during the growth process also help to identify synthetics. Useful inclusions and patterns in natural stones are straight growth patterns, inclusions of other minerals, hollows filled with liquid or gas, and hollow or solid fibers. Although the absence of inclusions is considered desirable in natural stones, it can create problems with identification. This means that gemologists must resort to complex instruments and techniques to identify natural gems.

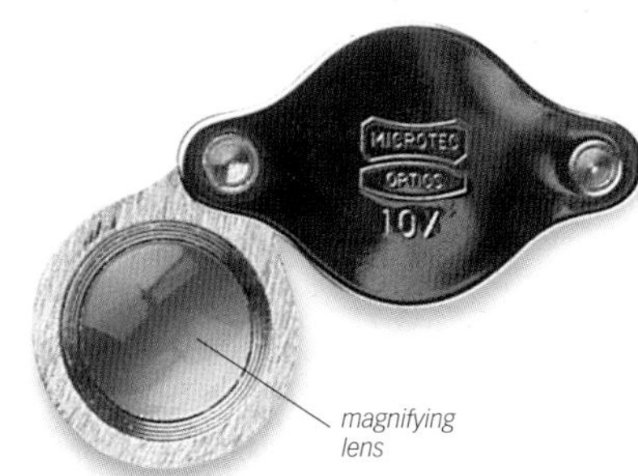

Hand loupe
Many inclusions and growth patterns of natural gem minerals can be seen with a loupe, which helps differentiate them from synthetics.

Gilson emerald
Pierre Gilson has been manufacturing synthetic emeralds since 1964. They are chemically and mineralogically identical to natural emeralds. Inclusions (far right) are a good way of differentiating synthetics.

GILSON FLUX-MELT EMERALD

FLUX-MELT EMERALD UNDER A MICROSCOPE

HISTORY AND FOLKLORE

The desire to wear adornments goes far back in human history. By the Upper Paleolithic Period (25,000–12,000 BCE), people were decorating themselves with shells, feathers, pieces of bone, teeth, and pebbles. The deliberate shaping of stones soon followed.

HISTORY OF GEMS

When the shaping of stones first began, opaque and soft specimens were used. By the 7th millennium BCE, the techniques of grinding, polishing, and drilling had improved and harder stones were being used. The belief that certain stones had mystical powers or properties was well established by the 3rd millennium BCE. Whether gemstones were worn for their mystical powers, for adornment, or both is unknown, but there was a lively lapidary industry throughout Egypt, India, and the Middle East by that time. Simultaneously, similar processes were underway in the Americas.

Aztec serpent
This 15th-century Aztec ceremonial pectoral is encrusted with turquoise mosaic. It has conch shell teeth and thorny oyster shell details around the nose and mouth.

Greek opal cameo
This cracked, painted opal cameo shows Cupid, the winged Greek god of love, embracing Psyche, the Greek goddess of the soul.

Egyptian earring
This gold earring from the tomb of Tutankhamun (*c.*1370–1352 BCE) has beads of lapis lazuli, carnelian, and emerald.

Necklace from Mohenjodaro
Crafted in the 19th century BCE in the Indus Valley Civilization, this necklace of agate, chalcedony, and jasper beads is probably from Mohenjodaro, Pakistan.

Chinese ivory snuff bottle
Dating back to the late Qing Dynasty (*c.*1800), this ivory snuff bottle features a dragon chasing the flaming pearl of wisdom.

SIGNIFICANCE OF GEMS IN TRADITION AND FOLKLORE

By 3000 BCE, "magical" amulets were being cut from agate, carnelian, turquoise, and lapis lazuli in Egypt and Mesopotamia. Babylonian and Assyrian cylinder seals were believed to have magical properties. The remnants of a Babylonian text states that a gem referred to as the "Ka-Gi-Ma" would help a man destroy his enemies, a seal made of rock crystal would help extend a man's possessions, a green serpentine seal would draw blessings, and a seal made of lapis lazuli contained a god. Using stones for medicinal purposes began in ancient Egypt, through the association of a gem's color with the colors produced in the body by the disease the gems were meant to treat. Many such beliefs persisted through the Middle Ages, and those to do with the healing powers of gems are still popular among New Age believers today.

Crystal gazing
This quartz crystal ball is set in an elaborate stand that is unusual for crystal gazing. Modern crystal gazers continue to value crystal balls as an aid to forseeing the future.

JANUARY (GARNET)

FEBRUARY (AMETHYST)

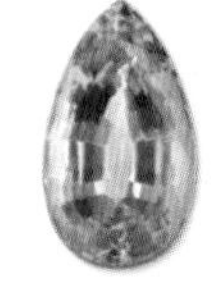
MARCH (AQUAMARINE)

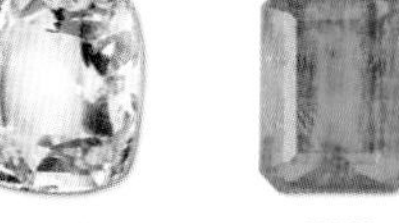
APRIL (DIAMOND)

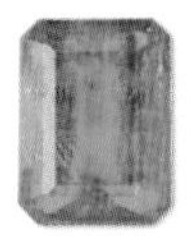
MAY (EMERALD)

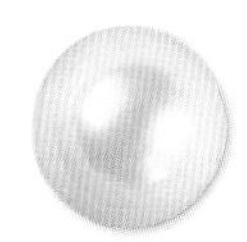
JUNE (PEARL)

JULY (RUBY)

AUGUST (PERIDOT)

SEPTEMBER (SAPPHIRE)

OCTOBER (OPAL)

NOVEMBER (TOPAZ)

DECEMBER (TURQUOISE)

Birthstones
Although principally a creation of the Victorian jewellery industry, the concept of birthstones is an echo of the ancient beliefs regarding the mystical power of gemstones.

HISTORY OF GEM CUTTING

Carnelian and rock crystal were fashioned into beads at Jarmo in Mesopotamia (now Iraq) in the 7th millennium BCE. By the 2nd millennium BCE, the craft of sophisticated engraving had developed and cameos were cut by the Romans. Faceted gems did not appear until the 16th century, and the brilliant cut was developed around 1700.

The Jewellers' Workshop
This Italian painting from 1672 shows the various activities undertaken in jewelers' workshops at the time, notably the shaping of metal and the cutting and setting of gemstones.

COLLECTING GEMS

Collecting gemstones need not be a hobby only for the wealthy. There are many beautiful and inexpensive gems available to the amateur. One can derive great satisfaction from building a collection of personally gathered and cut gems.

STARTING A COLLECTION

When starting a collection, many collectors accumulate stones as they become available. It is best to avoid expensive gems at first, since fluctuating market prices can significantly reduce the value of a purchase. Gems can be purchased wherever jewelry is sold; for example, at yard sales, auctions, or estate sales. Loose stones can be bought over the Internet or from specialist shops. Mineral clubs often have sections specifically for gems. Many collectors even take up digging for stones and cutting their own gemstones.

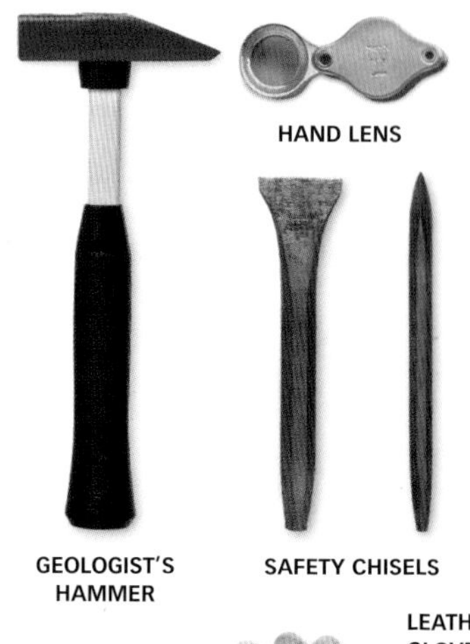

LEATHER GLOVES

SAFETY GOGGLES

HARD HAT

Panning for gems
The gold pan is an essential piece of gear for a collector. In addition to gold, many gemstones can be found by panning surface sediments.

Essential equipment
Digging for and extracting your own gemstones requires a minimum amount of equipment. The gear shown here is enough to get you started. As your experience increases, you can add more equipment as required.

Field experience
The likelihood of discovering some gems will increase as you gain experience in the field. Some collectors routinely find gem-quality material.

ORGANIZING A COLLECTION

Collections can be organized in a number of ways—on the basis of mineral species, color, inclusions, specific gemstone location, or just general interest. As a person becomes more involved in gem collecting, individual interests emerge. At all stages, it is important to keep records and retain as much information as possible about each gem, such as weight, location of discovery, and purchase price. If provided, gem dealers' labels should be retained. A collector may try various methods of organization at different times.

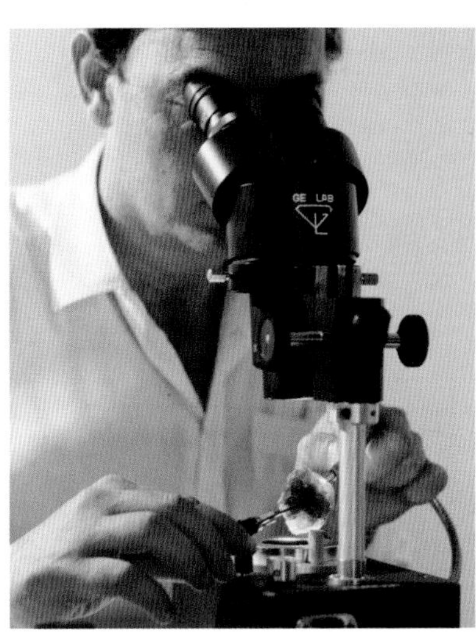

Examining a gem
Valuable gems should be examined under a microscope, and any diagnostic inclusions should be photographed to help with identification later.

STORING A COLLECTION

The difficulty of tracing and identifying loose gems makes them a desirable target for thieves. As a result, the safe storage of a potentially valuable collection is of major importance. Irrespective of how your collection is stored and displayed, discretion must be exercised in showing it and revealing the storage location. Photograph each stone individually, and keep a written record of its weight in carats along with the photograph. Other descriptive records should also be maintained for each gem. It is a good idea to have microscope photos taken of inclusions or inner markings in valuable stones. If the stone is stolen and recut, these photos can help identify it. A vault or safe is the safest, but gem collections can also be concealed in other difficult-to-discover places. Store all photos and written records separately.

Gem collection
Gemstones can be displayed in specialized cases such as the one shown here. If stones are exhibited in this manner, it is recommended that photos be taken of the display as a permanent record.

BUYING GEMS

With the development of new ways of enhancing gems, the purchase of genuine gems can be full of pitfalls. The best way to avoid these is to purchase gems from a reputable seller, with suitable guarantees. Buying altered stones is particularly risky since the long-term stability of some alterations is unproven.

Examining pearls
Pearls are valued under stringent grading criteria. When buying pearls, the reputation of the seller is the key to ensuring that they are correctly graded.

GEMSTONES

PRECIOUS METALS

A precious metal is defined as a naturally occurring metallic element of high economic value. However, this modern definition does not reflect the other values that metals such as gold and silver have held in the past.

MYSTICAL METALS

In ancient times, both gold and silver had mystical associations—gold with the Sun, and silver with the Moon. Like the Sun, gold was believed to be indestructible. In addition to its color, silver had another "lunar" quality: its color came and went like the waxing and waning of the Moon—in other words, it tarnished.

Both gold and silver occur in nature in a comparatively pure form and are easily worked. As a result, even while retaining their mystical associations, both metals soon became worked into objects of desire. Eventually, they were used as mediums of exchange and stores of wealth. Whatever ornamental purposes gold and silver have been put to, they have, for the most part, been associated with cut stones.

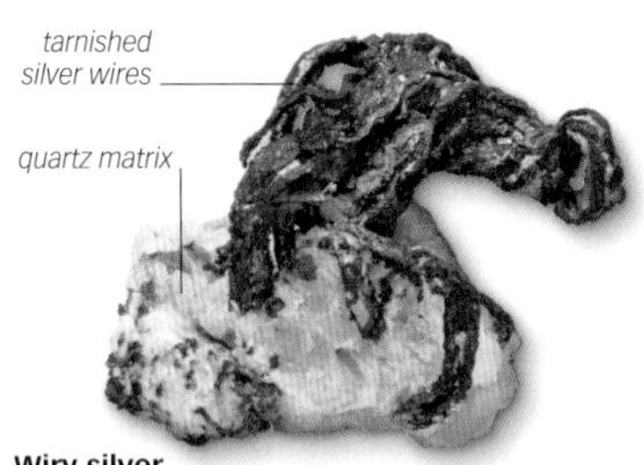

Wiry silver
In this specimen, crystalline wires of native silver run through and surmount a mass of quartz. The silver shows black tarnish.

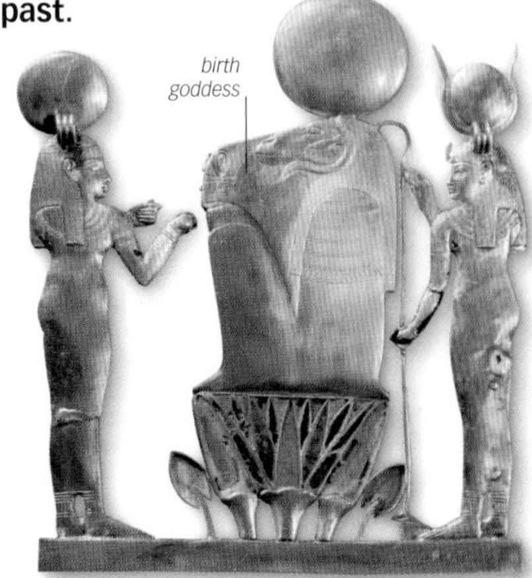

Egyptian pectoral
In this ancient Egyptian gold pectoral, the sky goddess Nut gives birth to the Sun, assisted by the cow goddess Hathor and the warrior goddess Sekhmet.

NEW METAL

Not recognized as a distinct metal until relatively recently, platinum has had a short career as a jewelry and coinage metal. As with gold and silver, platinum is as important an industrial metal today as it is a jewelry metal.

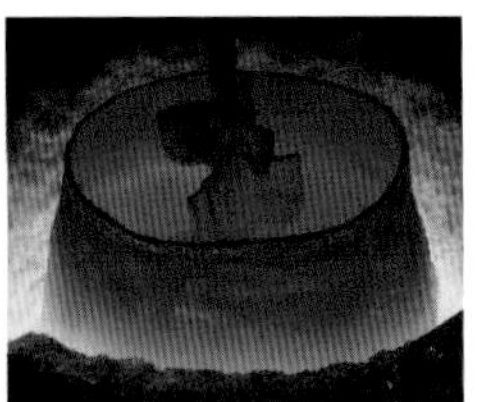

Industrial uses of platinum
Glass and other materials are often melted in platinum crucibles, because platinum has a high melting point and resists corrosion at high temperatures.

Fishpool hoard
These gold coins are part of a hoard that was buried in Fishpool, England, in 1463–64. It consisted of 1,237 gold coins and a number of pieces of jewelry.

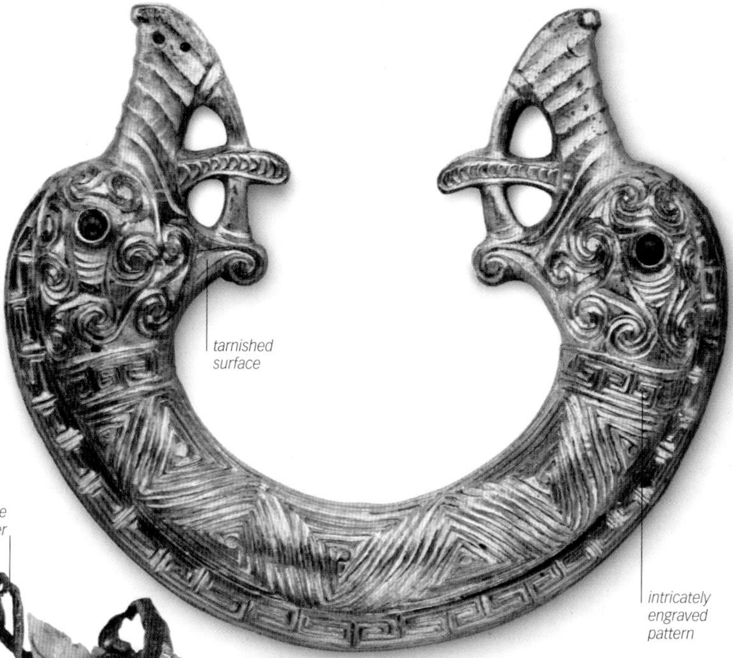

tarnished surface

wire silver

intricately engraved pattern

accessory quartz

NATURAL SILVER

Celtic bracelet
This antique Scottish silver bracelet—crafted in the Celtic style—shows intricate patterns.

PROFILE

- Cubic
- 2½–3
- 10.1–11.1
- Opaque
- Metallic

VARIANT

Modern chalice A silver chalice that has been wrought to bring out its natural luster

Ag

SILVER

The most malleable and ductile metal next to gold, silver is one of the earliest metals known to humans. It has been recovered in the form of ornaments and decorations from tombs that date as far back as 4000 BCE. Silver coinage is believed to have come into use around 550 BCE. Even today, silver is significant across cultures—as a symbol of purity for some and divine wisdom for others. Its chemical symbol, Ag, comes from the Latin word *argentum*, which is derived from a Sanskrit word meaning white and shining.

Silver is opaque, with a bright white luster and a pinkish tint, but readily tarnishes to either gray or black. Often found in its native form, silver primarily occurs in hydrothermal veins. It also forms by the alteration of other minerals. Much of the world's silver production is a by-product of refining lead, copper, and zinc. Major sources are Peru, Australia, Russia, Kazakhstan, Canada, and the USA. The world's largest producer of silver is Mexico, where silver has been mined since 1500.

PROFILE

- Cubic
- 2½–3
- 19.3
- Opaque
- Metallic

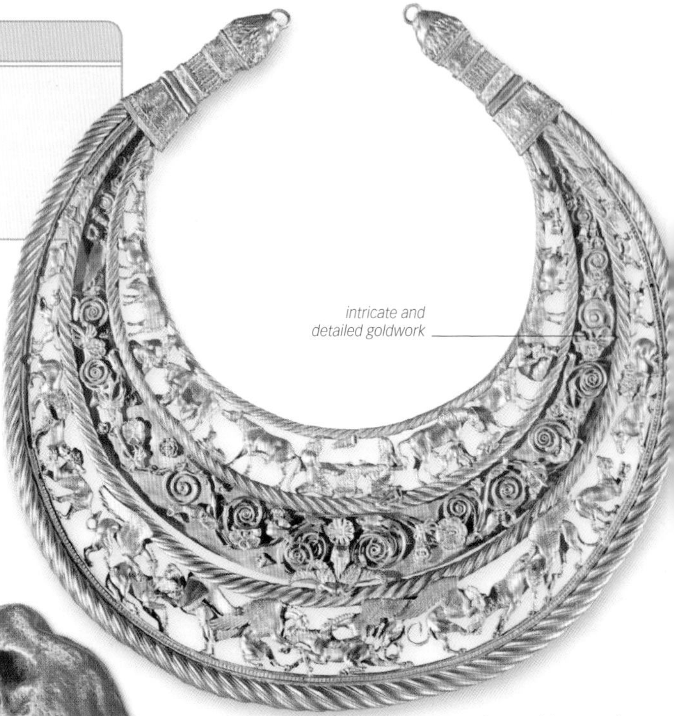

intricate and detailed goldwork

rounded surface from stream battering

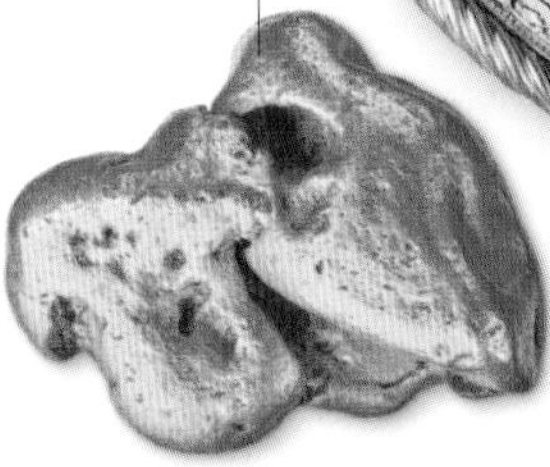

STREAM-ROUNDED NUGGET OF NEARLY PURE GOLD

Ancient gold pectoral
This gold Scythian pectoral, or neckpiece, is from a royal tomb in Ukraine. It dates back to the 4th century BCE.

GOLD

Gold has been used and treasured for at least 6,000 years, since the civilizations of ancient Egypt and Mesopotamia and Bronze-Age Britain. The metal's color, brightness, and malleability—and the fact that it is usually found in a relatively pure form—have made it exceptionally valuable. Gold is almost chemically inert and therefore resists tarnishing or corrosion.

In its native state, gold is opaque and a metallic golden yellow in color. When naturally alloyed with silver or other metals, it is paler. In its pure state, gold is too soft to be worn, so it is alloyed with other metals to increase its hardness. The purity of alloyed gold is expressed as its carat value, or the proportion of gold out of 24 parts. So, for example, 18 carat gold is three-quarters gold.

Gold is seldom found as well-formed crystals, although rare crystals measuring more than 1 in (2.5 cm) across have been found in California, USA. Crystals are typically octahedral and dodecahedral. Gold occurs more commonly as tree- or fernlike growths, and as grains and scaly masses. Nuggets weighing over 200 lb (90 kg) were found in Australia.

In ancient times, gold was almost exclusively recovered from river and stream gravels, where weathered particles were concentrated in placer deposits. Almost all igneous rocks contain low concentrations of mostly invisible, well-dispersed grains of gold. In some modern gold mines, the gold particles are too tiny to be seen with the naked eye.

INDUSTRIAL GOLD

Gold is an important industrial metal. Due to its high electrical conductivity, it is used in plating contacts, terminals, printed circuits, and semiconductor systems. Thin films of gold reflect up to 98 percent of infrared radiation. Gold coatings on windows reduce the need for air-conditioning, and gold compounds are used in medicines.

Gold in space
The mirror segments of the James Webb Space Telescope were plated with gold.

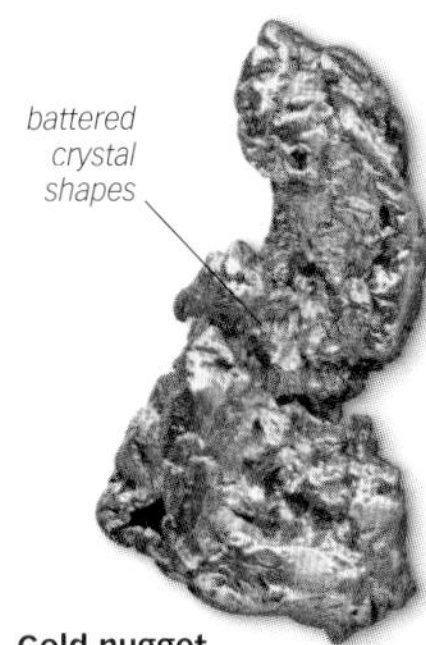

Gold nugget
Nuggets of gold, like the one above, are uncommon and are a welcome find for miners.

Gold crystals
Gold rarely occurs as well-formed crystals. The crystals in this cluster exhibit dodecahedral crystal form.

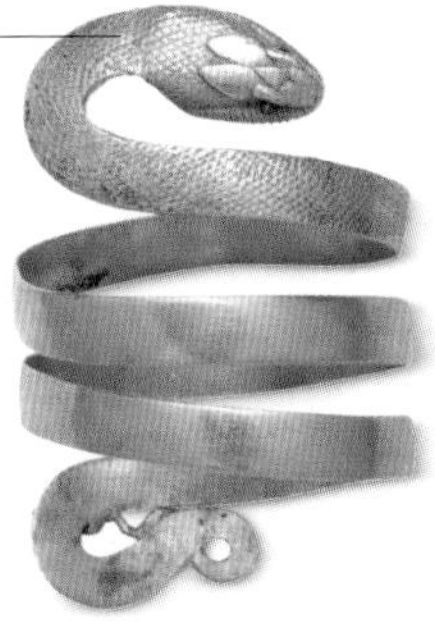

Roman armlet
This gold armlet in the form of a snake was recovered from Pompeii.

Flat gold plates
The gold in this specimen from Baita in Transylvania, Romania, has formed as thin plates set in a matrix of quartz.

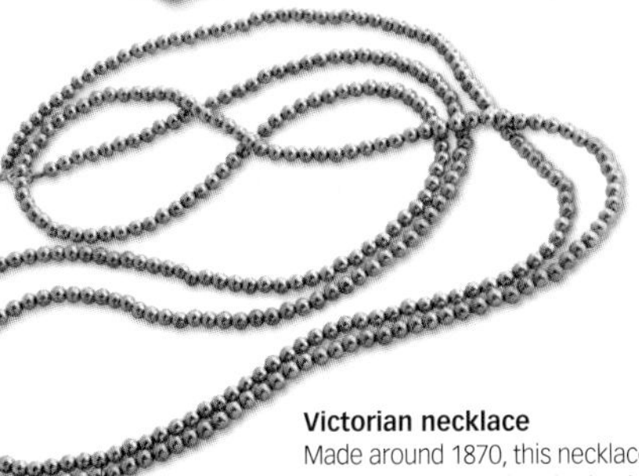

Victorian necklace
Made around 1870, this necklace is composed of uniformly sized gold beads that are 1/4 in (6 mm) in diameter.

Gold grains
Most of the gold that is recovered from placer deposits is found in the form of grains or scales.

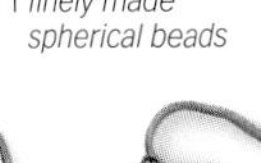

Roman earrings
This pair of gold earrings of diving dolphins with daisylike petals around the eyes shows fine granulation and filigree.

Inca statuette
This statuette of a llama was made of gold cast by the Inca of South America in the 16th century.

GOLD RUSHES

A gold rush occurs when fortune-seekers flock to the location of a newly discovered gold deposit. Large-scale gold rushes began in the 19th century, with the settlement of new lands by Europeans and the availability of mass transport.

THE FORTY-NINERS

The discovery of gold in California in 1848 triggered the most famous gold rush of all time. By 1849, about 80,000 "forty-niners" (the name given to that years' fortune-seekers) had dashed to the Californian gold fields; by 1853, the number had risen to 250,000. The first deposits, easy to mine by hand, were soon depleted, so mining moved to machinery-intensive methods. The gold rush gave impetus to a push for statehood, which California attained in 1851.

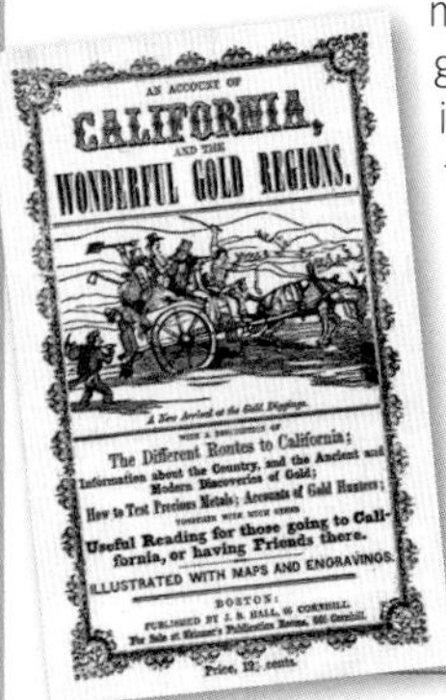

AN ACCOUNT OF
CALIFORNIA,
AND THE
WONDERFUL GOLD REGIONS.

A New Arrival at the Gold Diggings.

The Different Routes to California;
Information about the Country, and the Ancient and Modern Discoveries of Gold;
How to Test Precious Metals; Accounts of Gold Hunters;
Useful Reading for those going to California, or having Friends there.
ILLUSTRATED WITH MAPS AND ENGRAVINGS.

BOSTON:
PUBLISHED BY J. B. HALL, 66 CORNHILL.

Price, 12½ cents.

Routes to California
An Account of California and the Wonderful Gold Regions (left) was published in 1849. Booklets like these fueled the gold rush.

Sacramento
Gold seekers rush to the newly discovered gold deposits at Sacramento, California, in 1850. The city later became California's state capitol.

PIKE'S PEAK OR BUST

Gold was discovered in Colorado, USA, in the 1850s, in the area of Cripple Creek, on the western side of Pike's Peak. Other discoveries soon followed in the area of Clear Creek, Colorado, and the city of Denver developed where the creek flowed into the Platte River. The area around Central City, another mining camp, titled itself "The Richest Square Mile on Earth." The slogan "Pike's Peak or Bust" was painted on many wagons as prospectors flooded westward across the prairies to the newly discovered gold fields. As with most gold rushes, some miners grew rich, while many wound up with nothing. Soon, a steady stream of wagons was headed back east, painted with the word "Busted."

Garden of the Gods
The snow-covered Pikes Peak serves as a majestic backdrop for the Garden of the Gods, a city park in Colorado Springs, Colorado, USA.

THE KLONDIKE RUSH

In 1898, gold was discovered along the Klondike and Upper Yukon Rivers in Canada. Within a year, a gold rush was on. However, despite its legendary status, it quickly came to an end. The town of Dawson was at its core, but with little to sustain it when the gold ran out, it steeply declined, reflecting the fate suffered by many gold-rush boom towns.

On the White Pass
Miners travel on the White Pass and Yukon Railroad during the Klondike Gold Rush. Providing supplies and transport generated more wealth than digging gold.

MARCH TO VICTORIA

The gold rush that began in 1851 in the state of Victoria, Australia, was centered in the towns of Ballarat and Bendigo. Most gold in North America was found in flakes or small nuggets, but in the Australian fields, nuggets weighing 100 lb (48 kg) or more were common. Large nuggets are still found there today.

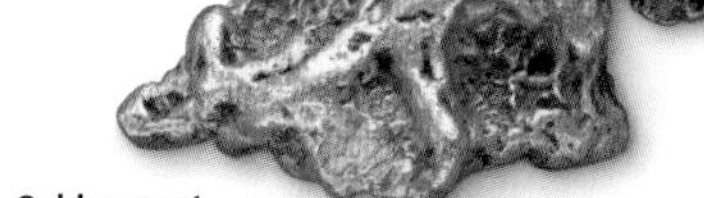

Gold nugget
This gold nugget is from the Australian National Mineral Collection. The largest nugget ever found, with a refined weight of 136 lb (62 kg), comes from Victoria.

THE AMAZONIAN RUSH

A large-scale gold rush has been under way in the Amazon Rain Forest since 1980. Although about 46.3 tons (42 tonnes) of gold have been recovered from a huge open-pit mine, most gold is recovered by thousands of independent miners working by hand. There is a great deal of concern about damage to the environment since a lot of mercury—used to extract gold—is being released into rivers and streams.

Panning for gold
Gold panning, in spite of being slow and inefficient, is still used by small-scale miners to separate gold from stream gravels.

Platinum necklace
This necklace designed by Leo DeVroomen, set with symmetrical rows of diamonds, shows the beauty and versatility of platinum to its fullest extent.

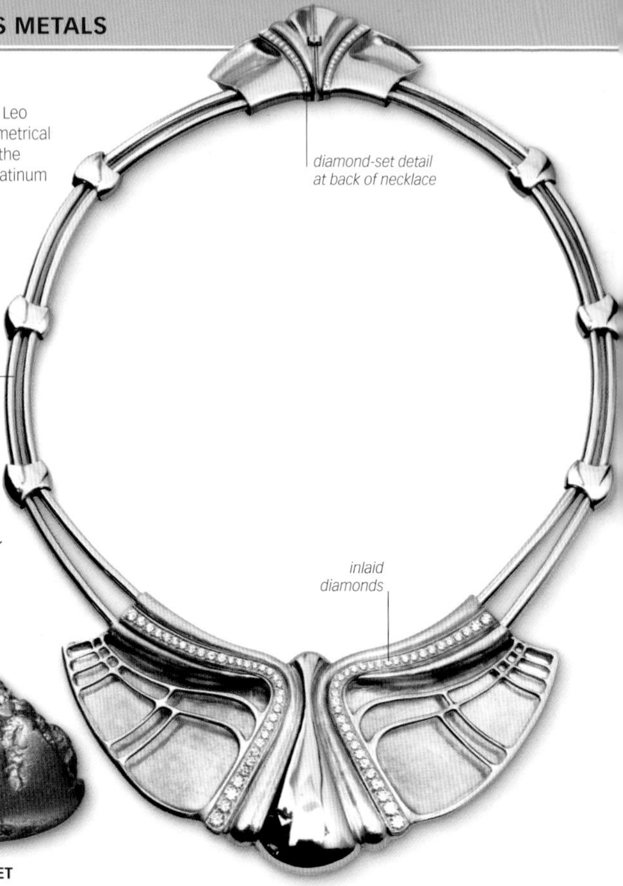

diamond-set detail at back of necklace

two hoops provide framewok for design

inlaid diamonds

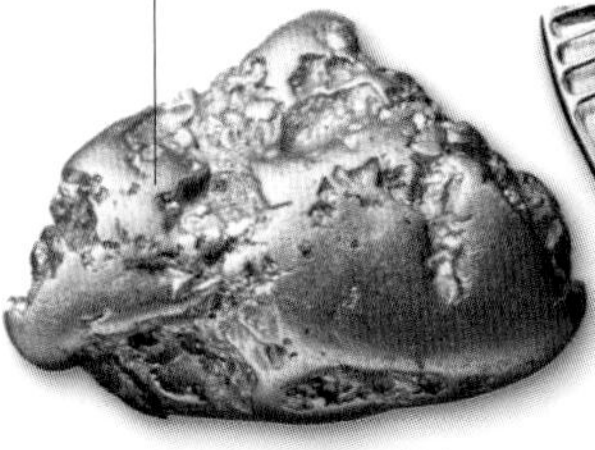

rounded surface

PLATINUM NUGGET

PROFILE

- Cubic
- 4–4½
- 14.0–19.0
- Opaque
- Metallic

 Pt

PLATINUM

Hard, durable, and noncorrosive when worn, platinum is an important metal for modern jewelry. Although it was used for thousands of years, the Spaniards are associated with the first documented discovery of the element in Río Pinto, Colombia, in the 1500s. They called it *platina del Pinto—platina* meaning "little silver"—thinking it to be an "unripe" ore of silver. It was recognized as a distinct metal only in 1735. Usually found as flakes or grains, and rarely as nuggets, this precious metal is opaque, silvery gray, and markedly dense.

Formerly recovered mainly from placer deposits, most commercial platinum today comes from primary deposits, and as a by-product of nickel mining. Important sources of platinum are in South Africa; Montana and Alaska, USA; Canada; and Russia.

Platinum and ruby ring
This Art Deco style ring, set with rubies, was designed by Van Cleef & Arpels.

CUT STONES

Cut stones can be defined as the end product of the artificial reshaping of any mineral, such as diamond, or rock, such as obsidian. The end product is used for the purpose of personal adornment or esthetic enjoyment.

WHAT IS A CUT STONE?

The term cut stone includes what were traditionally thought of as gemstones, as well as small carvings, cameos, tumble-polished stones, and stones from which utilitarian items, such as jewel boxes and vases, have been made. The term excludes bigger reshaped pieces, such as large sculptures and slabs of stone used to adorn buildings or as flooring—in other words, uses of a more public nature.

Jade carving
This finely carved, 13.7-carat piece of imperial jade from Myanmar shows the superb color and translucency for which the gem is known.

HEXAGONAL FACETED FIRE OPAL

FANCY ROUND-CUT ELBAITE

STEP-CUT AQUAMARINE

Gem cuts
Some of the many possible gem cuts are shown here. The cut is determined by the size, color, and shape of the gem rough.

OBJECTS OF BEAUTY

Cut stones come in an enormous range of shapes and sizes. With varying degrees of artificial reshaping, they can range from stones with little more than sliced and polished surfaces to the complex intricacies of faceted stones and some types of carvings. In each case, the objective is to either enhance the natural beauty of the material or transform an unattractive natural material into a thing of beauty and pleasure.

Inlaid gemstones
This marble specimen has been inlaid with stones such as cornelian (orange) and lapiz lazuli (blue). It is from the Uttar Pradesh Marble Crafts Palace in India.

PROFILE

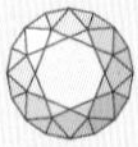

Round brilliant 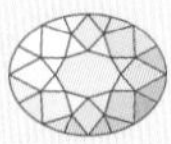 Oval brilliant

Pendaloque 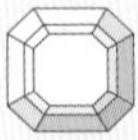 Step

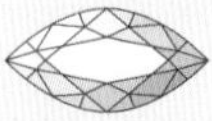

Marquise 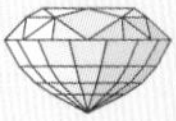 Mixed

Cubic

10

3.4–3.5

2.42

Adamantine

excellent color dispersion

adamantine luster

BORT DIAMOND

Brilliant-cut diamond
This stone has been cut with a 58-facet brilliant cut. The cut was developed specifically to bring out the brilliance of diamond.

C

DIAMOND

Recognized since ancient times as the hardest of all minerals, diamond is named after the Greek word *adamas*, which means "unconquerable." Gemstone crystals are usually found as octahedrons and cubes with rounded edges and slightly convex faces. Diamonds were known in India 2,300 years ago. For over three millennia, India was the only source of diamonds. However, diamonds were not cut for many centuries in the belief that they had magical properties that would be lost if cut. Sometime after 1300 CE, the polishing of the faces and the placement of simple table cuts began in Europe.

The exceptional luster and dispersion of diamond gives it the fiery brilliance for which it is prized. The color of diamonds has also been one of the prime factors in ascertaining their value. Colorless or pale blue gemstones are the most often used in jewelry, with red and green considered among the rarest colors. Pure orange and violet are much rarer still.

In the last few decades, the color of diamonds has been changed by exposure to intense radiation or by heat treatment. Many of the "fancy" colored stones—reds, greens, blues, and others—on the market today are the result of such treatments. When purchasing colored diamonds, buyers need to be aware that unless the stone is certified as natural, it may be artificially colored and therefore less valuable than a naturally colored stone.

SYNTHETIC DIAMONDS

Diamond press
This press exerts the tremendous pressure and high temperature required to create diamonds.

In the past few decades, laboratory-grown diamonds have reached sizes that are large enough to be used as gemstones. These diamonds are usually yellow or blue, and occasionally, colorless. Pink and green colors are achieved by irradiating the synthesized stones. These stones can be told apart from natural diamonds by gemologists.

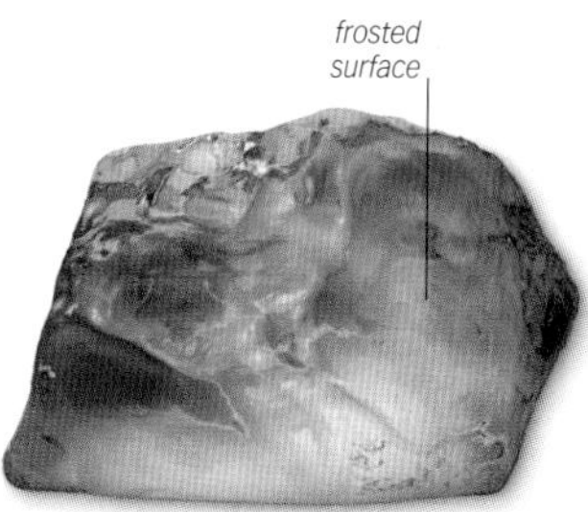

Cullinan diamond
The largest diamond ever found, the 3,106.75-carat Cullinan diamond was as big as a medium-sized potato.

Shepherd diamond
This 18.3-carat yellow diamond from South Africa is colored by the nitrogen in its structure.

Emerald-cut gem
This ice-blue diamond has been faceted with an emerald cut to emphasize its unusual color.

Red Diamond
Red is the rarest diamond color. The color-causing mechanism in red diamonds is not yet fully understood.

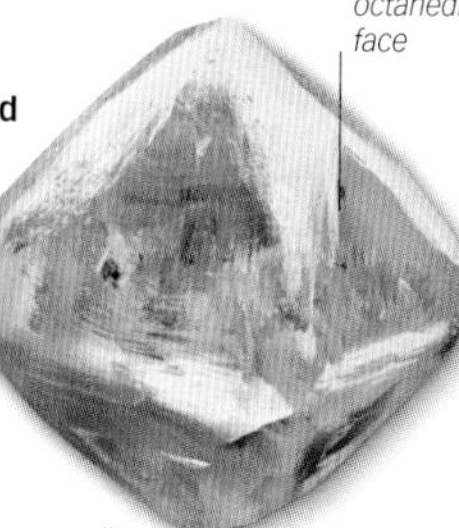

Oppenheimer diamond
Colored yellow by the presence of nitrogen, this 253.7-carat octahedral diamond crystal is the size of a walnut.

Art Deco ring
The emerald-cut diamond in this ring complements the symmetry of the mounting.

Green octahedron
This octahedral crystal of natural green diamond is perfectly formed and virtually flawless.

Pink diamond
This rare 2.86-carat pear-shaped pink diamond was found in the Williamson mine in Tanzania.

Flower spray brooch
This platinum brooch is set with 7.5 carats of baguette- and brilliant-cut diamonds.

CELEBRATED DIAMONDS

Since their discovery, diamonds have caught human imagination. Myths and legends have grown around them and magical properties have been attributed to them. A diamond does not have to be large to be celebrated. Its accumulated history is its own celebration.

On September 17, 2000, thieves broke into an exhibition of diamonds at London's Millennium Dome. One of the exhibits on display was the 234.04-carat flawless Millennium Star diamond. They were arrested by the police, literally inches away from their target. This incident is an example of how diamonds become legendary. Another diamond has a longer history: a 115-carat blue diamond was sold to King Louis XIV of France in 1669. It disappeared during the French Revolution, only to reappear in London in 1812. It was purchased first by King George IV and later by a banker, Henry Hope, whose name it bears. As it passed through various hands, it was recut into its current form.

Blue Heart Diamond
The Blue Heart diamond originated in South Africa. At 30.62 carats, it is somewhat smaller than the 45.52-carat Hope Diamond, but it has a unique character.

Dresden Green
The Dresden Green is a 41-carat, internally flawless, natural green diamond. Although found in India around 1720, it is named after the city of Dresden, Germany.

Marie Louise's necklace
Napoleon I gave this necklace to Empress Marie Louise in 1811 to celebrate the birth of their son. Its diamonds are old mine-cut (a type of brilliant cut) and weigh a total of about 263 carats.

Cullinan Blue Diamond
The world's largest diamond was found by Thomas Cullinan. Once it was cut, the largest pieces went to the British Crown Jewels. Cullinan gave his wife this necklace, which includes nine rare blue diamonds.

Koh-i-noor Diamond
The Koh-i-Noor diamond was found in India in 1304 and came to Britain in 1849. Weighing 109 carats, it is now set in the British Queen Mother's crown.

Marie Antoinette's earrings
Louis XVI of France gave these diamond earrings to Marie Antoinette, Queen of France. They were eventually sold to a Russian gem collector and then to Pierre Cartier, who sold them to Marjorie Merriweather Post.

Hope Diamond
The 45.52-carat Hope Diamond is currently held in the gemstone collection at the Smithsonian Institution, Washington, D.C. It was set in its current mounting in the early 20th century.

PROFILE

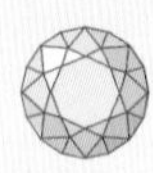

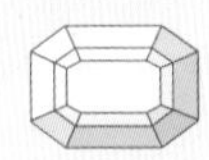

Round brilliant Emerald

Cubic

3–4

3.9–4.1

2.36–2.37

Resinous to adamantine, metallic

Yellowish brown sphalerite This emerald-cut gem shows the classic yellowish brown color of faceted sphalerite. Its crystals are very difficult to facet.

sphalerite crystal

accessory quartz

SPHALERITE CRYSTALS WITH QUARTZ

VARIANTS

Golden brown sphalerite A mixed-cut specimen of sphalerite

Scissors-cut sphalerite A golden-brown sphalerite with internal veiling

Yellow sphalerite A brilliant-cut sphalerite in an unusually light shade of yellow

ZnS

SPHALERITE

Usually cut only for collectors, sphalerite crystals are difficult to facet because of their softness and cleavability. When amateur gem and mineral clubs hold gem-cutting competitions, a faceted sphalerite is commonly awarded the maximum number of points for difficulty. Sphalerite ranges from pale greenish yellow to brown and black with increasing iron content. Pure, colorless sphalerite is rarely found. Red or reddish brown, transparent crystals are sometimes called ruby zinc or ruby blende. Gem-quality sphalerite is found in Spain and Mexico. Other important deposits that sometimes yield gem material are in the Mississippi River Valley, USA, and in Canada and Russia.

Sphalerite gets its name from the Greek *sphaleros*, which means "deceitful," since its lustrous dark crystals can be mistaken for other minerals. It occurs in contact metamorphic zones, hydrothermal vein deposits, and replacement deposits formed at high temperatures (1,065°F/575°C or above).

Pyrite necklace
The spherical beads of this necklace are made of finely crafted and highly polished pyrite.

uniformly sized beads

natural crystal shape

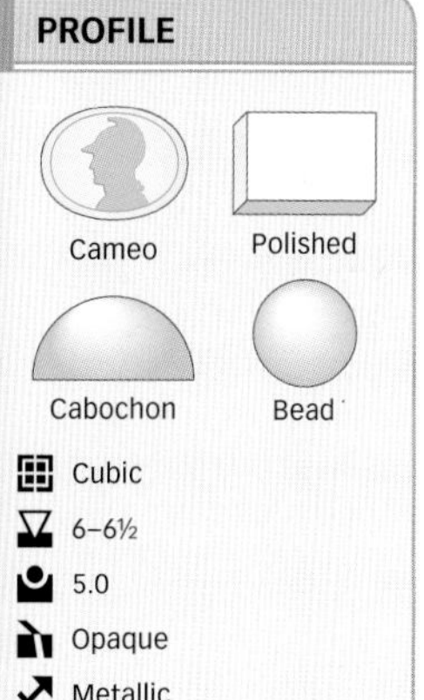

PYRITE CRYSTALS ON LIMESTONE MATRIX

PROFILE

Cameo
Polished
Cabochon
Bead

Cubic
6–6½
5.0
Opaque
Metallic

FeS_2

PYRITE

Known informally as "fool's gold," pyrite has been used since antiquity. Although it is lighter than gold, its brassy color often misled novice prospectors. Opaque and pale silvery yellow when fresh, pyrite turns darker and tarnishes with exposure. Pyrite's name is derived from the Greek word *pyr*, which means "fire," because it emits sparks when struck by iron.

As a gemstone, pyrite is usually polished as beads. Most "marcasite" in Victorian jewelry is in fact pyrite. Historically, however, bright crystals were themselves mounted as gemstones. Today, pyrite-replaced fossils are sometimes mounted and worn as pendants. Despite being a relatively hard and dense mineral, pyrite is also brittle, and it has traditionally been sliced and polished. In fact, polished crystal slices were often set edge to edge on wooden backing to make mirrors. It occurs in hydrothermal veins, in contact metamorphic rocks, and in sedimentary rocks.

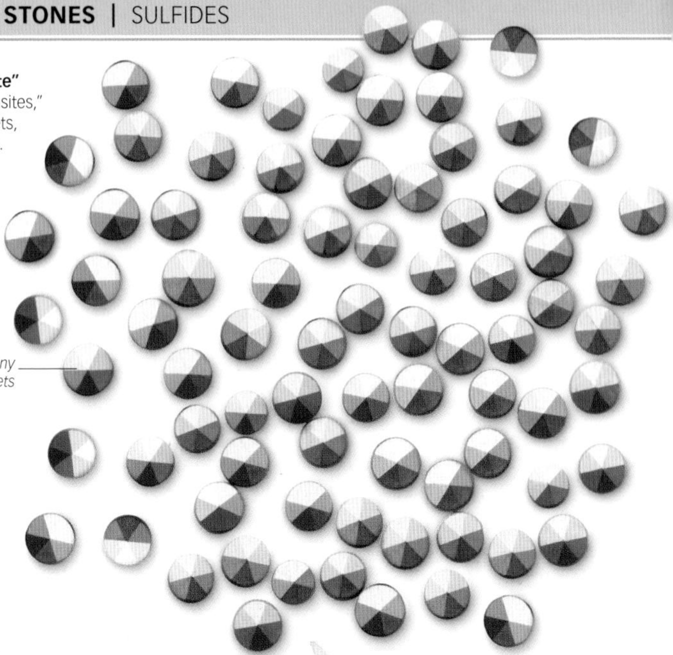

Pyrite "marcasite"
These tiny "marcasites," each with six facets, are actually pyrite.

tiny facets

bladed crystals

MARCASITE ROUGH

PYRITE ROUGH

Pyrite and marcasite
These two minerals have the same chemical composition, but only pyrite is used to make gemstones.

PROFILE

- Orthorhombic
- 6–6½
- 4.9
- Opaque
- Metallic

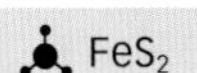

FeS_2

MARCASITE

Marcasite is an iron sulfide mineral. Its name is widely applied to an entire range of jewelry, although marcasite itself is never used as a gemstone. The word "marcasite" was applied to both pyrite (p.55) and marcasite from medieval times until the 19th century, when it was recognized as a separate mineral. Despite its name, "marcasite" jewelry is generally made from pyrite. Some "marcasite" jewelry, however, has been made from hematite (p.57) or even simulated from cut steel.

The mineral marcasite is chemically identical to pyrite but it has a different crystal form. It is opaque and pale silvery yellow when fresh. It darkens and tarnishes after exposure and eventually crumbles.

Victorian bracelet
This Victorian marcasite bracelet has pyrite "marcasites" set in a base metal frame.

PROFILE

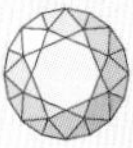

Round brilliant

Cameo

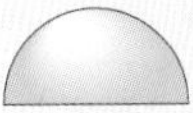

Cabochon

Hexagonal

5.6

5.3

2.94–3.22

Metalic to dull

faceted on top

Oval cabochon Hematite cabochons such as this black oval have been sold as "marcasites."

metallic luster

colorful tarnish on surface

SPECULAR HEMATITE

VARIANTS

Polished bead A specimen of hematite, popular for making polished beads

Oval marquise cabochon A specimen with a vulnerable faceted top due to hematite's brittleness

Fe_2O_3

HEMATITE

A dense and hard iron oxide, hematite comes in a number of different forms from soft, fine-grained, and earthy, to several crystal forms that are hard and dense. Powdered hematite is called red ocher and is used as a pigment. A form of ground hematite called rouge is used to polish plate glass and jewelry. Hard black hematite is used for beads, carvings, and as faceted and domed cabochons.

The name hematite is derived from the Greek *haimatitis*, meaning "blood-red," an allusion to the red color of its powder. This association with blood led to it being worn as an amulet to protect the wearer from bleeding and diseases of the blood. Polished hematite jewelry and amulets are known from ancient Roman and Egyptian times. The bones of Neolithic burials have been found smeared with powdered hematite.

Carved stone Larger pieces of hematite are a popular carving medium for lapidaries because they are easily shaped.

PROFILE

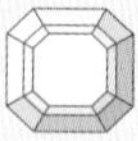

Step

Cubic

3½–4

6.1

2.85

Adamantine, submetallic

Large cuprite specimen Faceted cuprites tend to be small—this oval brilliant is unusually large.

table facet

CLUSTER OF CUPRITE CRYSTALS

VARIANT

Step-cut cuprite A small but very transparent rectangular step-cut cuprite

Cu_2O

CUPRITE

A copper oxide, cuprite is sometimes known as ruby copper due to its distinctive carmine-red color. Fresh cuprite is translucent bright red, but exposure to light and pollutants can turn its surfaces dull metallic gray. Massive or granular aggregates of cuprite with the appearance of sugar are common. Cuprite crystals are usually octahedral or cubic in shape and are commonly striated. Faceted stones are too soft to wear, but their exceptional brilliance and garnet-red color make them highly desirable as collectors' stones.

An important ore of copper, cuprite takes its name from the Latin word *cuprum*, which means "copper." It is a secondary mineral that forms in the oxidized zones of copper sulfide deposits. Almost every faceted stone over one carat, which is quite rare, has come from a single deposit in Namibia that is now exhausted. Other localities that produce lesser amounts of smaller gem material are Chile, Australia, and Bolivia.

Brilliant-cut sapphire
This blue sapphire of fine color and clarity is cut in a modified brilliant cushion, with the main facets divided horizontally.

horizontally split facet

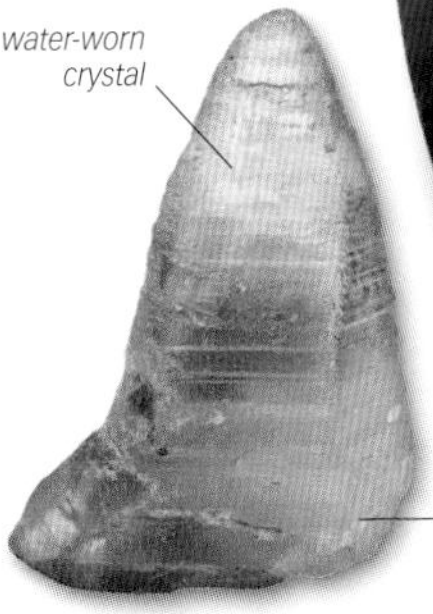

PROFILE

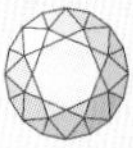

Round brilliant — Cameo

Cabochon

- Hexagonal or trigonal
- 9
- 4.0
- 1.76–1.77
- Vitreous

water-worn crystal

color zoning is common in uncut sapphires

CORUNDUM CRYSTAL

VARIANT

Blue sapphire cabochon
A star effect produced by light reflecting off the oriented rutile inclusions

Al_2O_3

BLUE SAPPHIRE

Although sapphire is found in various colors, it is popularly thought of as being blue, and the most valuable sapphires are blue ones. All sapphires are color varieties of corundum. The blue stones owe their color to traces of titanium and iron. They vary from light cornflower-blue to a dark blue that is almost black. A variety referred to as color-change or alexandrite sapphire appears blue in daylight and reddish or violet in artificial light.

Before the 19th century, the term "sapphire" was applied only to blue varieties of corundum, so most historical references to sapphire relate to this color. In the Middle Ages and ancient Greece, blue sapphire was believed to cure eye diseases and to set prisoners free. It was often used to make jewelry for medieval kings and was set in rings worn by those holding office in the Christian church. In the East, sapphire was traditionally believed to protect against the evil eye. Significant sources of blue sapphire include Myanmar, Sri Lanka, India, Thailand, Australia, Nigeria, Madagascar, and the USA.

PROFILE

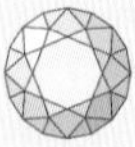

Round brilliant
Oval brilliant 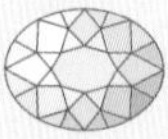
Emerald 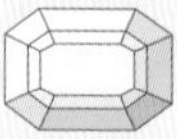
Cameo 
Cabochon 

Hexagonal or trigonal
9
4.0
1.76–1.77
Vitreous

star facet

Cushion mixed-cut ruby Many rubies contain flaws, but these can be hidden by cuts made up of many small facets.

rich purple-red color

prismatic ruby crystal

rock matrix

RUBY IN MATRIX

VARIANTS

Star cabochon A superb ruby with an unusually sharp star

Synthetic ruby A stone faceted into a step cut to display its brilliant red color

Brilliant cut A round brilliant ruby showing inner reflection

Al_2O_3

RUBY

Ruby is the name for the dark red, gem-quality variety of corundum. Its coloration is due to traces of chromium that replace some of the aluminum in the mineral's structure. As the amount of chromium increases, the color deepens. Although there is continuous gradation of color from pink sapphire to ruby, only the darker stones are recognized as rubies. Rubies of more than 10 carats are rare and valuable—good-quality rubies can fetch higher prices than diamonds of the same size. Ruby crystals tend to be prisms with tapering or flat ends.

Sources of high-quality stones include Myanmar, Thailand, and Sri Lanka, with smaller amounts found elsewhere. Synthetic rubies are also available. In the past, the term "ruby" has often been wrongly applied to other transparent red minerals.

Antique ruby ring The square-cut ruby in this ring is highlighted by being embedded at right angles to its square setting.

Mixed-cut gem
This mixed-cut padparadscha has been cut in the shape of a rounded keystone.

pavilion facet

cracks stained by iron oxide

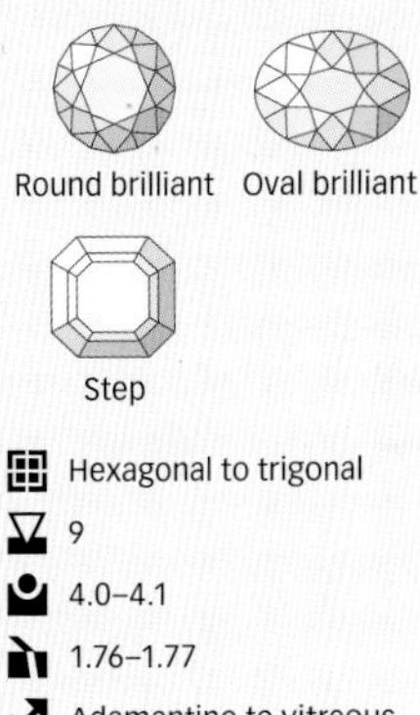

PADPARADSCHA ROUGH

PROFILE

Round brilliant
Oval brilliant
Step

- Hexagonal to trigonal
- 9
- 4.0–4.1
- 1.76–1.77
- Adamantine to vitreous

Al_2O_3

PADPARADSCHA

The only corundum to be given its own name apart from ruby is the pink-orange variety called padparadscha. All other colors, including blue, are identified by the term "sapphire" preceded by the color; for example, blue sapphire or yellow sapphire. Pink-orange is a very rare color, and padaparadscha gems of any size are even rarer. When cutting, gemstone rough in which the pink and orange are concentrated in separate areas are oriented so as to mix the two colors. Orange sapphires exist, but to be properly called padparadscha the orange must be noticeably tinged with pink.

The name "padparadscha" is derived from the Sanskrit or Sinhalese word *padma raga*, which means "lotus color." Corundum forms in syenites, certain pegmatites, and in high-grade metamorphic rocks. It is concentrated in placer deposits, from where most gem varieties, including padparadscha, are recovered. Padparadscha has been found in Sri Lanka, Vietnam, various localities in Africa, and in Montana, USA.

PROFILE

Cabochon Cameo

Emerald Mixed

Round brilliant

Hexagonal or trigonal

9

4.0–4.1

1.76–1.77

Adamantine to vitreous

main facet split for better brilliance

Yellow sapphire
This yellow sapphire is faceted in a mixed cut. Yellow is one of the more common colors of fancy sapphire.

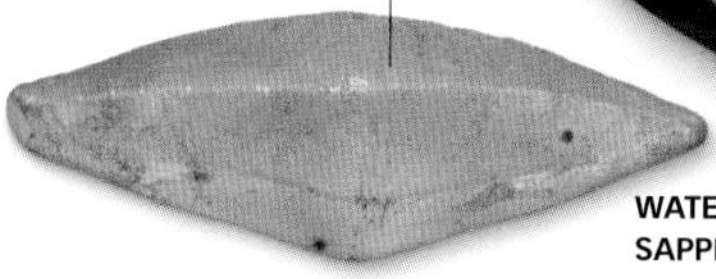

color zoning

WATERWORN, DIPYRAMIDAL SAPPHIRE CRYSTAL

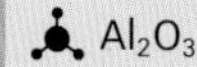

Al_2O_3

FANCY SAPPHIRES

Like ruby (p.60), sapphire is a gem variety of the mineral corundum, which, next to diamond (pp.50–51), is the hardest mineral on Earth. Although commonly thought of as being blue, sapphire can be colorless, green, yellow, orange, violet, pink, and a wide range of other hues. All sapphires other than the blue ones are collectively known as fancy sapphires. They are identified by the term "sapphire" preceded by their color; for example, "pink sapphire," "yellow sapphire," and the rare and colorless "white sapphire." Sapphire that appears blue in daylight and reddish or violet in artificial light is called color change sapphire. Apart from blue sapphire, which is just called "sapphire," the only color of sapphire to have its own specific name is orange-pink padparadscha (p.61). Sapphire crystals are hexagonal and tend to be either blocky or tapering and barrel-shaped. Many sapphires have inclusions of rutile (p.71), which produce a star when cut *en cabochon*. Other sapphires with rutile inclusions simply appear murky. Today, it is common practice to heat natural sapphires to enhance their color and clarity.

From medieval times until the end of the 19th century, green sapphire was called "oriental peridot" or "oriental emerald"; yellow sapphire was called "oriental topaz." One of the oldest gem sapphires is St. Edward's sapphire, believed to date back to the coronation of Edward the Confessor of England in 1042 CE.

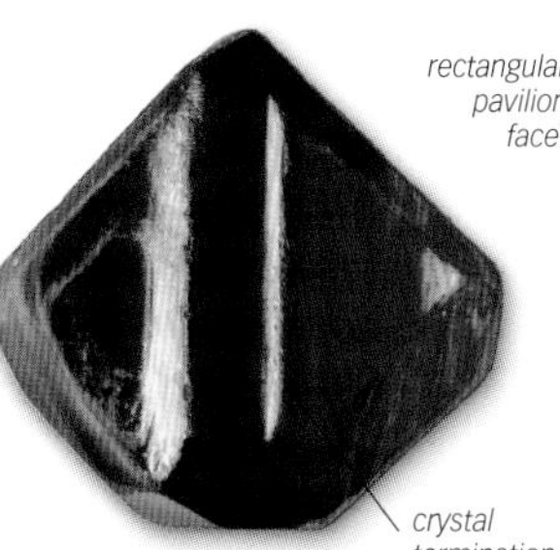

Pink sapphire rough
This dark and rich pink sapphire crystal will make a stunning gem.

Faceted pink sapphire
Pink is a desirable color for sapphires. As the color becomes redder, it grades into ruby.

Green sapphire
The color of this oval-cut green sapphire was once known as "oriental emerald."

Colorless sapphire
This specimen of relatively rare colorless sapphire is faceted into a mixed-cut cushion.

Multicolored sapphires
This flower-shaped brooch is composed of different colored sapphires: pink on the petals, yellow on the pistil, and colorless on the stem.

Sapphire brooch
The color range of sapphires from Montana, USA, is demonstrated in this butterfly brooch set with 331 brilliant-cut and two cabochon sapphires.

Yellow sapphire ring
The yellow sapphire in this 18-carat yellow gold ring weighs several carats, and is flanked by diamonds.

Lavender sapphire
These earrings are made of a matched pair of oval brilliant-cut lavender sapphires.

MONTANA SAPPHIRES

Montana, USA, has two deposits that produce literally every color of gem-quality fancy sapphire. One of them is located in the western mountains, near the border of Idaho. The other is on the Missouri River, near the state capitol. Between them, they have produced tens of thousands of carats of fancy sapphire.

Missouri River
This part of the Missouri River in Montana is alongside a sapphire deposit called El Dorado Bar.

FAMOUS RUBIES AND SAPPHIRES

Carat for carat, large rubies and sapphires are nearly as rare as large diamonds. The geological conditions under which they form tend to limit their size. Both gemstones owe their coloration to the presence of trace elements.

Rubies and sapphires are both colored varieties of the mineral corundum, which is aluminum oxide. Rubies are colored red by chromium traces in the crystal structure, and blue sapphires by traces of iron and titanium. Other sapphire colors are produced by a variety of trace elements—alone or in combination. On the whole, large rubies and sapphires have not acquired the history and legend of large diamonds. One reason for this is that, until the 19th century, other red or blue stones were also called ruby and sapphire. In Roman writings, the gem referred to as *sapphirus* is probably lapis lazuli; and the Black Prince's "Ruby" in the British Crown Jewels, known since the 14th century, was discovered to be a spinel.

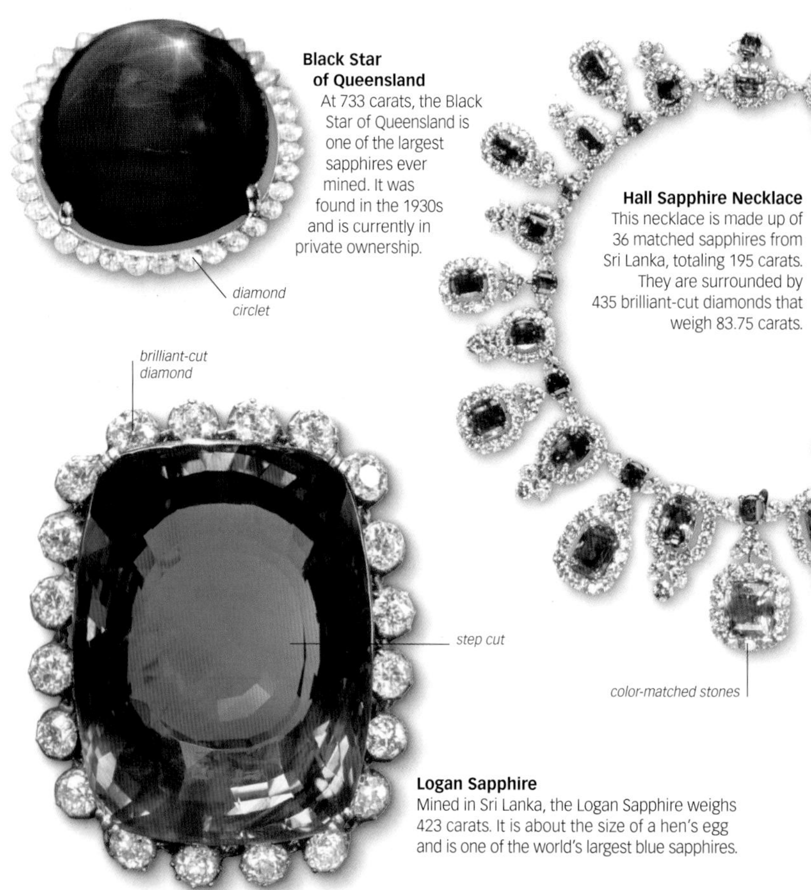

Black Star of Queensland
At 733 carats, the Black Star of Queensland is one of the largest sapphires ever mined. It was found in the 1930s and is currently in private ownership.

Hall Sapphire Necklace
This necklace is made up of 36 matched sapphires from Sri Lanka, totaling 195 carats. They are surrounded by 435 brilliant-cut diamonds that weigh 83.75 carats.

Logan Sapphire
Mined in Sri Lanka, the Logan Sapphire weighs 423 carats. It is about the size of a hen's egg and is one of the world's largest blue sapphires.

Bismarck Sapphire
Mounted in a pendant, this 98.6-carat, table-cut sapphire is surrounded by baguette-cut diamonds and four smaller sapphires. It is currently on display at the Smithsonian Institution, USA.

Star of Asia
A 330-carat star sapphire, the Star of Asia was discovered in the mines of Mogok, Myanmar. It probably once belonged to the Maharajah of Jodhpur in India.

Rosser Reeves Ruby
At 138.7 carats, the Rosser Reeves Ruby is one of the world's largest and finest star rubies, renowned for its color and well-defined star pattern.

Carmen Lúcia Ruby
This 23.1-carat Myanmar ruby was donated to the Smithsonian Institution by nuclear physicist Peter Buck in memory of his late wife Carmen Lúcia.

PROFILE

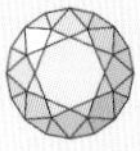

Round brilliant 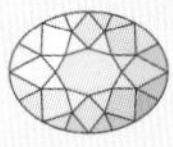 Oval brilliant

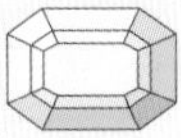

Emerald 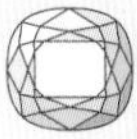 Cushion

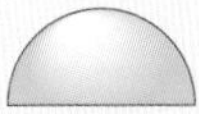

Cabochon

Cubic

7½–8

3.6

1.71–1.73

Vitreous

vitreous luster

sharply pointed octahedral crystal

quartz matrix

SPINEL CRYSTALS IN MATRIX

emerald cut

Ruby spinel The dark red variety of spinel is sometimes called ruby spinel, a reminder of the times when red spinel was mistaken for ruby.

VARIANTS

Star spinel A rare, cabochon-cut, six-rayed star spinel

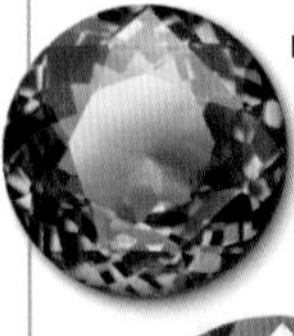

Medium blue spinel A modified brilliant-cut blue spinel

Purple spinel A cushion-cut spinel in unusual purple color

$MgAl_2O_4$

SPINEL

The earliest known gem-quality spinel dates back to 100 BCE. It was discovered in a Buddhist tomb near Kabul, Afghanistan. Gem-quality spinel is the magnesium aluminum oxide variety of the group of minerals called spinel. Although commonly seen as blue, purple, red, or pink gemstones, spinel can be of other colors. Some spinels contain parallel sets of rutile needles that give rise to a six- or four-rayed star effect in cabochon-cut gems.

The name spinel comes from the Latin word *spinella*, which means “little thorn”—a reference to the sharp points on spinel’s octahedral crystals. Spinel resists weathering, and most gem sources are placer deposits. Specimens have been found in Myanmar, Sri Lanka, and Madagascar. Gem-quality stones are also found in Pakistan, Australia, Tajikistan, and Afghanistan. Red spinel, called “ruby spinel,” has often been misidentified as ruby because of its blood-red color. Two such historic “rubies,” the Timur Ruby and the Black Prince’s Ruby, are part of the British Crown Jewels; they are, in fact, spinels.

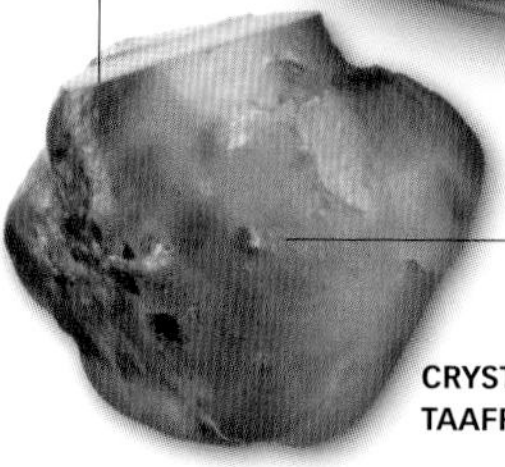

vitreous luster

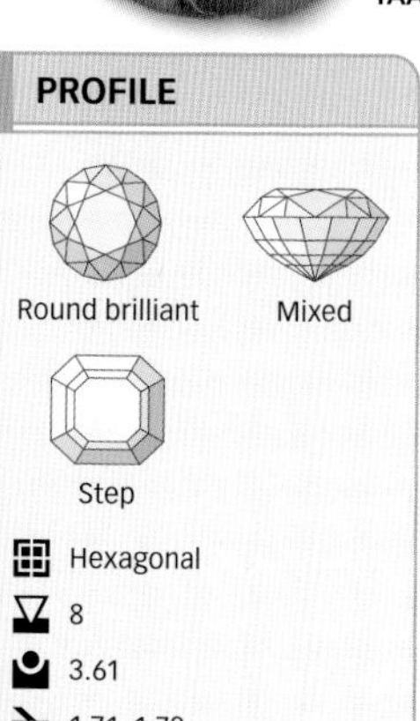

CRYSTAL OF TAAFFEITE ROUGH

pale grayish mauve color

Cushion-cut taaffeite
This cushion-cut taaffeite shows excellent clarity and brilliance.

PROFILE

Round brilliant

Mixed

Step

Hexagonal

8

3.61

1.71–1.72

Vitreous

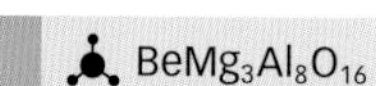

$BeMg_3Al_8O_{16}$

TAAFFEITE

One of the rarest gemstone minerals in the world, taaffeite was discovered as late as 1945. It was named after its discoverer, the Dublin gemologist Count Taaffe. This mineral was first discovered as a cut stone among some faceted gems recovered from old jewelry. It was originally mistaken for spinel (p.66), which is similar in appearance, hardness, and density. It was then noticed that the gem was doubly refractive, whereas spinel is singly refractive. On examination, the stone was discovered to be a beryllium, magnesium, and aluminum oxide. Other misidentified taaffeite gemstones were discovered later.

Taaffeite can occur as pale mauve, green, and sapphire-blue crystals. These have been found in the gem gravels of Sri Lanka and in Hunan, China, and South Australia. The geological origin of this mineral is uncertain but is thought to be magnesium- and aluminum-bearing schists. Because it is a rare mineral, the only economic use is as a gemstone.

PROFILE

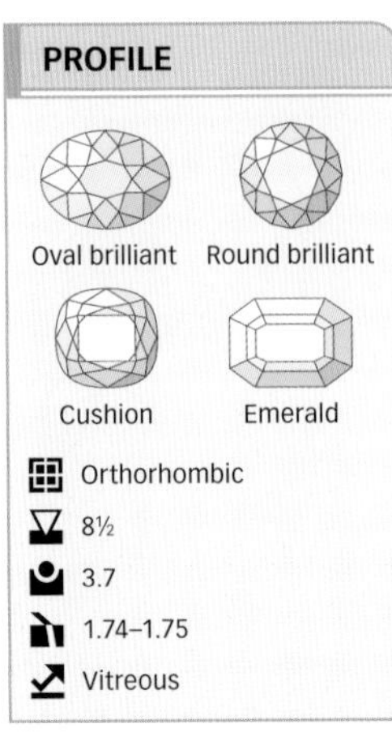

Orthorhombic

8½

3.7

1.74–1.75

Vitreous

ALEXANDRITE IN INCANDESCENT LIGHT

CLUSTER OF ALEXANDRITE CRYSTALS

ALEXANDRITE IN NATURAL LIGHT

Cushion-cut alexandrite This exceptionally large, 17.08-carat, mixed cushion-cut alexandrite shows the classic color change of the gem.

VARIANT

Greenish hue A cushion-cut specimen in natural light

$BeAl_2O_4$

ALEXANDRITE

A gemstone variety of chrysoberyl, alexandrite is one of the rarest and most expensive gems. However, crystals and faceted gems of ordinary chrysoberyl are more common. Like other chrysoberyls, alexandrite is durable and inferior in hardness only to corundum and diamond (pp.50–51). Alexandrite was discovered in the Ural Mountains in Russia in 1830 and was named after Czar Alexander II, on whose birthday it was believed to have been found. Alexandrite appears blue-green to green in daylight and red under incandescent light. It is usually recovered from mica schists, although chrysoberyl generally occurs in granites or granitic pegmatites. Faceted alexandrite rarely exceeds 10 carats in weight.

While the original deposit of alexandrite in the Urals is mostly exhausted, gem-quality material can still be recovered from Brazil, Sri Lanka, India, and Tanzania. Alexandrite can also be produced synthetically.

cloudy, opalescent surface

"eye" caused by minute inclusions

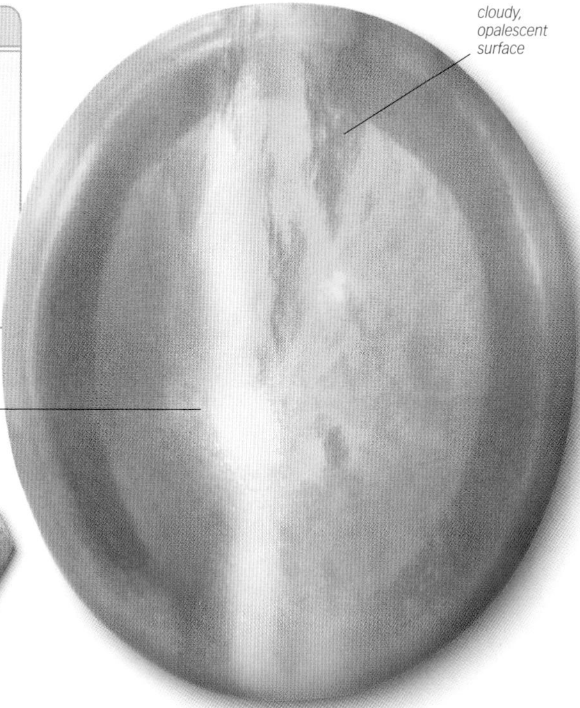

Honey-yellow cabochon This cat's eye gem has a fine "eye" and shows its highly prized honey-yellow color.

CAT'S EYE CHRYSOBERYL ROUGH

PROFILE

Cabochon

Orthorhombic

8½

3.7

1.74–1.75

Vitreous

$BeAl_2O_4$

CAT'S EYE CHRYSOBERYL

A cloudy, opalescent, and chatoyant variety of chrysoberyl, cat's eye chrysoberyl has numerous tiny, parallel, needlelike inclusions. It exhibits a cat's eye effect when cut *en cabochon*. This effect is achieved by orienting the crystal so that the inclusions focus the light into a bright band on the surface. Cut gems rarely exceed 100 carats, and the finest cost as much as fine sapphires.

Chrysoberyl is hard and durable, and can be yellow, green, or brown. It is strongly resistant to weathering, so crystals that weather out of the parent rock are concentrated in streams and gravel beds.

Cat's eye cross This pendant is made up of 11 cat's eye cabochons whose size and color match closely.

VARIANTS

Dark color A cat's eye cabochon with a dark honey color and a sharp eye

Yellow-green cabochon A specimen of chrysoberyl with a sharp cat's eye

PROFILE

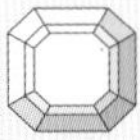

Step

Tetragonal

6–7

7.0

2.00–2.10

Adamantine to metallic

Oval cut This oval-cut cassiterite shows its classic reddish brown color. This rare gem is difficult to cut.

adamantine luster

double image of facet on far side

prismatic cassiterite crystals

muscovite matrix

CASSITERITE CRYSTALS ON MATRIX

VARIANT

Unusual color An atypical specimen of near-colorless, faceted cassiterite

SnO_2

CASSITERITE

Usually occurring as heavily striated prisms and pyramids, cassiterite crystals are colorless when pure but more commonly brown or black when containing iron impurities. Occasionally, reddish brown crystals are found, which are faceted for collectors. Most gem-quality cassiterite is recovered from placer deposits, where eroded crystal fragments concentrate due to their durability and density. However, crystals are also sometimes found on the rock matrix. Crystals are distinctly dichroic, exhibiting two different colors when viewed from different angles. This and the high specific gravity of cassiterite distinguish its reddish brown faceted crystals from brown diamond (pp.50–51) and sphene (p.197). Gem-quality crystals are found in Italy, Portugal, France, the Czech Republic, Brazil, and Myanmar.

A tin oxide, cassiterite takes its name from the Greek word for tin, *kassiteros*. The mineral forms in hydrothermal veins associated with granitic rocks at high temperatures (1,065°F/575°C).

Rutilated quartz
Golden crystals of rutile are enclosed within this transparent rock crystal cabochon.

bladed rutile crystals

vertical striations

DARK RED RUTILE CRYSTAL

PROFILE

Round brilliant

Oval brilliant

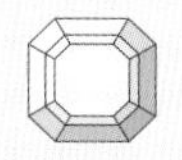
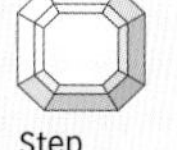
Step

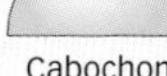
Cabochon

 Tetragonal

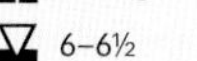 6–6½

 4.2

2.62–2.90

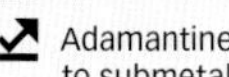 Adamantine to submetallic

TiO_2

RUTILE

Familiar to many people as the pale golden, needlelike crystals enclosed in crystals of quartz, rutile is a form of titanium dioxide. It is typically golden to yellowish brown, dark brown, black, or red in color. It takes its name from the Latin *rutilis*, which means "red" or "glowing." Rutile crystals are generally prismatic, but they can also be slender and needlelike. Prism faces typically have vertical striations.

Rutile is commonly found as a minor constituent of granites, pegmatites, gneisses, and schists, and also in hydrothermal veins. Its primary gemstone value is as an inclusion in other minerals. It commonly forms microscopic, oriented inclusions and produces the asterism shown by some sapphires (p.59, pp.62–63) and rubies (p.60). Rutilated quartz (p.108) has been used as an ornament since ancient times. Some reddish rutile crystals are darkly transparent, and have been faceted for collectors. Synthetic rutile is sold under a variety of names and comes in a number of colors.

PROFILE

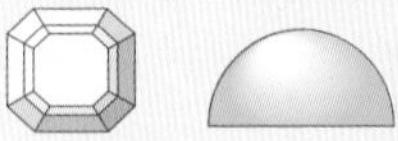

Step Cabochon

Orthorhombic

6½–7

3.4

1.68–1.75

Vitreous

complex faceting

Brilliant-cut diaspore
This square brilliant-cut diaspore has unusually fine clarity and brilliance.

fibrous structure

MASSIVE DIASPORE

VARIANT

Step-cut diaspore
A rectangular step-cut diaspore with a lavender cast

$\mathrm{AlO(OH)}$

DIASPORE

A relatively new gem to the market, diaspore is a hydrous aluminum oxide. It takes its name from the Greek word *diaspora*, which means "scattering"—a reference to the way diaspore crackles and depreciates under high heat. Specimens are strongly pleochroic, showing violet-blue in one direction, asparagus-green in another, and reddish plum in a third. The transparent variety of diaspore comes almost exclusively from one source in the Ibir Mountains in Anatolia, Turkey. Stones from this source exhibit multiple color changes in varying lights: greens in sunlight, raspberry-purplish pinks in candlelight, and champagne colors in indoor lighting. Translucent crystals cut *en cabochon* can display a strong cat's eye effect.

A gemstone trade name for diaspore is zultanite, although some gem dealers still market it as diaspore. Diaspore forms in metamorphic rocks, such as schists and marbles, and is also found in hydrothermally altered rocks. Gem-quality crystals are occasionally found in the Ural Mountains of Russia and in the USA.

Blue John vase
This finely crafted Blue John vase illustrates classic color banding.

intricate banding and interlayering

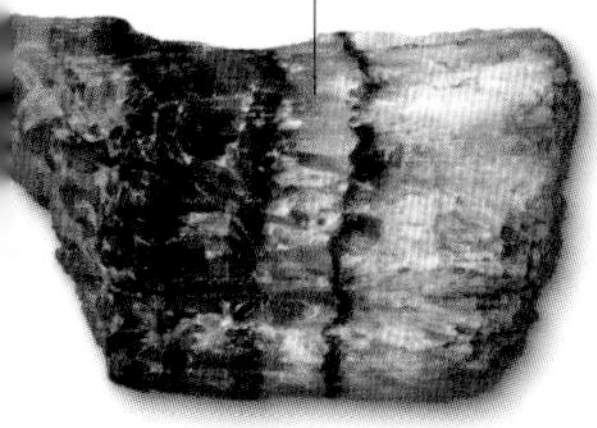

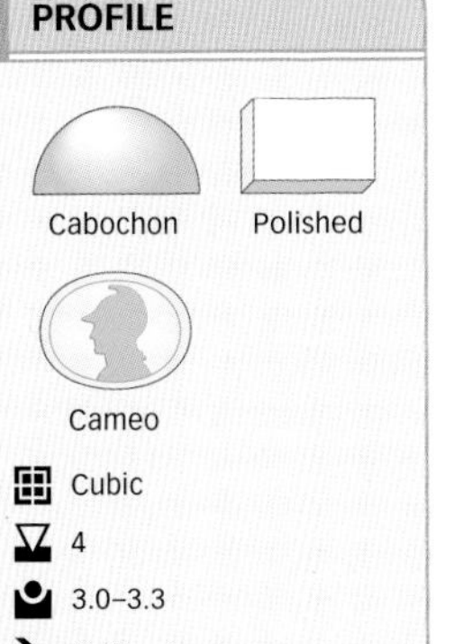

TYPICAL PIECE OF UNWORKED BLUE JOHN

PROFILE

Cabochon
Polished
Cameo

- Cubic
- 4
- 3.0–3.3
- 1.43
- Vitreous

CaF_2

BLUE JOHN

The distinctive purple and colorless or purple and pale yellow banded variety of fluorite (pp.74–75) is called Blue John. The name may be a corruption of the French words *bleu jaune*, which mean "blue yellow"—a reference to the interbanded colors. Blue John is brittle and is usually bonded with resins to increase resilience. It is used to make vases, urns, dishes, ornaments, and jewelry.

The major source of Blue John is Castleton in England, where it is found in a number of different veins, each producing a differently patterned variety. It was first mined there by the Romans, who prized Blue John vessels for the special flavor they imparted to the wine. This flavor actually came from resins used to manufacture these vessels. Although mining at Castleton peaked in the 18th and 19th centuries, it continues to the present day.

Blue John cabochon
This silver ring is set with a Blue John cabochon. It is a soft stone and needs to be worn carefully.

PROFILE

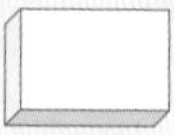

Polished

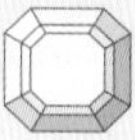

Step

Cameo

Cubic

4

3.0–3.3

1.43

Vitreous

complex faceting on pavilion

Yellow fluorite
This intense yellow 40.01-carat fluorite was recently found in Tanzania and is held in the USA's National Gem Collection.

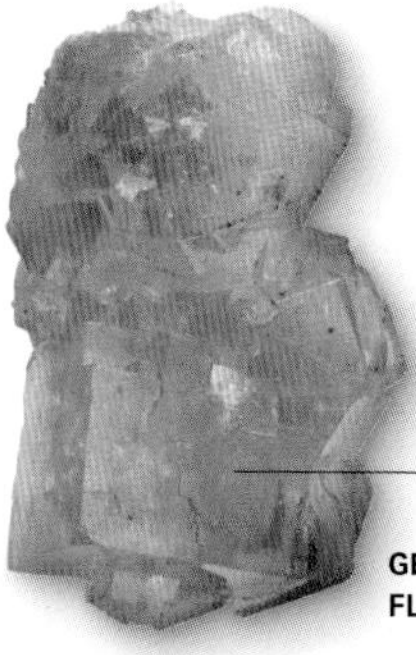

cube face

GEM-QUALITY YELLOW FLUORITE CRYSTALS

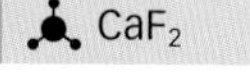

CaF_2

FLUORITE

Fluorite has one of the widest color ranges of any mineral. It usually occurs in vibrant colors, with violet, green, and yellow being the most common. Zones of different colors commonly occur within a single crystal, following the contour of the crystal faces. Extremely difficult to facet, fluorite is usually cut only for collectors.

Fluorite is calcium fluoride. As much as 20 percent of the calcium in fluorite can be replaced by yttrium or cerium, producing fluorescence—the emission of visible light on exposure to ultraviolet light. This phenomenon was first observed in fluorite.

Well-formed crystals are common in fluorite and are widely found in cubes and octahedra. Fluorite can also be massive, granular, or compact.

Massive English fluorite called Blue John (p.73) has been carved since Roman times. The ancient Egyptians carved massive fluorite into statues and scarabs, and the Chinese used it in carvings for more than 300 years. Some Chinese fluorite carvings have been passed off as jade (pp.154–55), but their softness can give them away. The name fluorite is derived from the Latin word *fluere*, which means "to flow"—a reference to the use of the mineral as a flux in the smelting and refining of metals since ancient times. Fluorspar, an old name for fluorite, is now an industrial term that refers to massive fluorite used as a flux in steel-making. Fluorite occurs mainly in hydrothermal deposits formed at low temperatures (up to 400°F/200°C).

Orange cubes
Orange fluorite, such as this specimen of interpenetrating cubic crystals, is unusual.

FACETING FLUORITE

Fluorite is a faceter's nightmare due to its several cleavages—the planes along which the mineral easily breaks. The stone is carefully oriented to avoid these planes, and it is cut and polished slowly to avoid heat or vibration. The final polish is done on a wax-impregnated wooden lapping wheel as a precaution against breakage.

Faceted fluorite
These faceted fluorites have been cut with extreme difficulty.

Lavender cluster
Several crystals in this cluster of lavender fluorite have areas of transparent material.

Purple fluorite rough
This group of purple fluorite crystals is facet-grade.

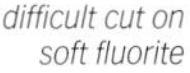

Cushion-cut fluorite
This nearly colorless specimen of fluorite has been faceted in a cushion fancy cut.

Green uncut fluorite
Several green fluorite cubes in this cluster have areas of facet-grade material.

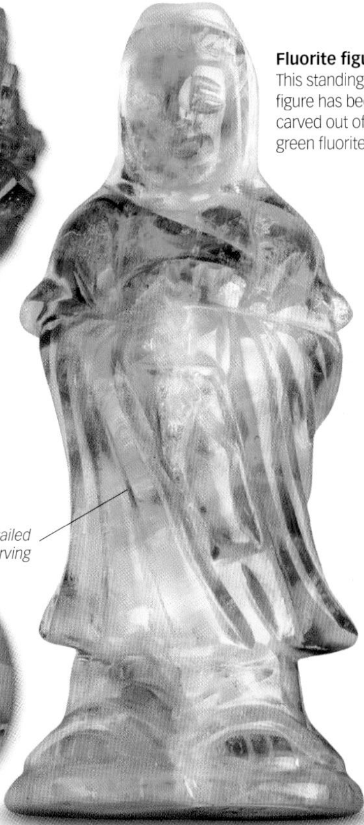

unusually rich green color

Cusion-cut fluorite
This intense green 9.24-carat fluorite is from England.

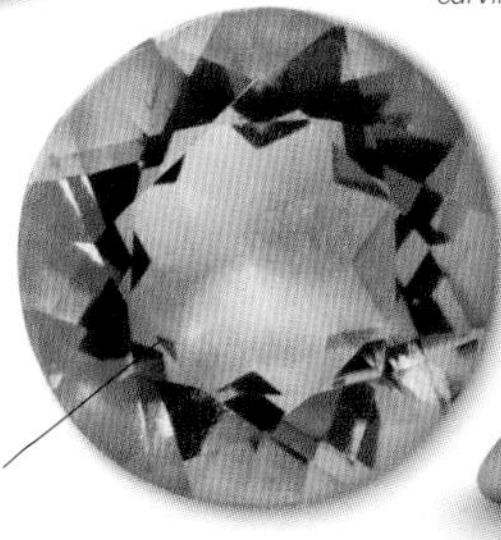

Fluorite figure
This standing figure has been carved out of green fluorite.

detailed carving

Brilliant-cut fluorite
This yellow-green fluorite has been faceted in a brilliant cut.

table facet

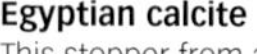

Egyptian calcite
This stopper from a canopic jar found in Tutankhamun's tomb is carved from calcite, often incorrectly identified as alabaster.

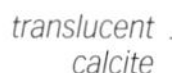

TRANSPARENT, SCALENOHEDRAL CALCITE CRYSTALS

PROFILE

Cameo

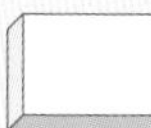

Polished

Cabochon

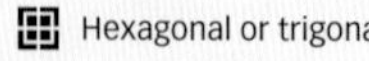

Hexagonal or trigonal

3

2.7

1.48–1.66

Vitreous

$CaCO_3$

CALCITE

The most common form of calcium carbonate, calcite is known for the great variety and beautiful development of its crystals. However, most calcite is massive, occurring either as limestone, marble, or travertine. The most common use of calcite in its massive forms is as an ornamental and carving stone. Optical-grade calcite is occasionally faceted for collectors—but with difficulty, since it is both soft and easily cleaved. In its pure form, calcite is colorless, pale, or white, but it is found in virtually all colors, including blue, green, and black.

Travertine is a dense, banded rock formed by the evaporation of river and spring waters, which deposit layers of calcite. Travertine takes a good polish, and it is often used for walls and interior decorations in public buildings. Deposits of ten feet or more are found along the Aniene River near Rome. Many ancient Egyptian carvings described as alabaster are actually calcite, although it is becoming common to refer to calcite as alabaster.

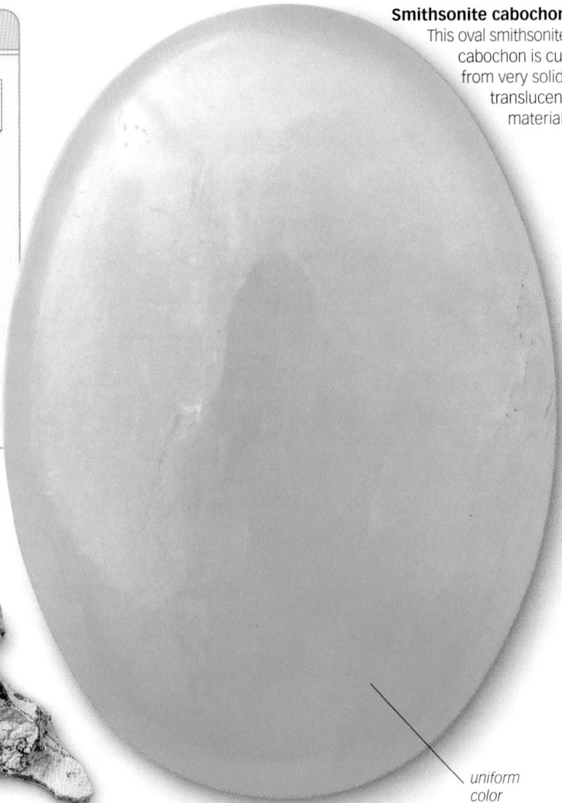

Smithsonite cabochon This oval smithsonite cabochon is cut from very solid, translucent material.

uniform color

PROFILE

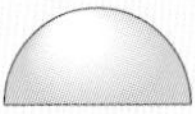

Cabochon
Polished 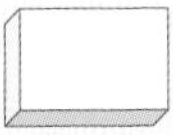
Step 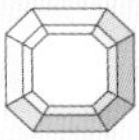

Hexagonal or trigonal
4–4½
4.4
1.62–1.85
Vitreous to pearly

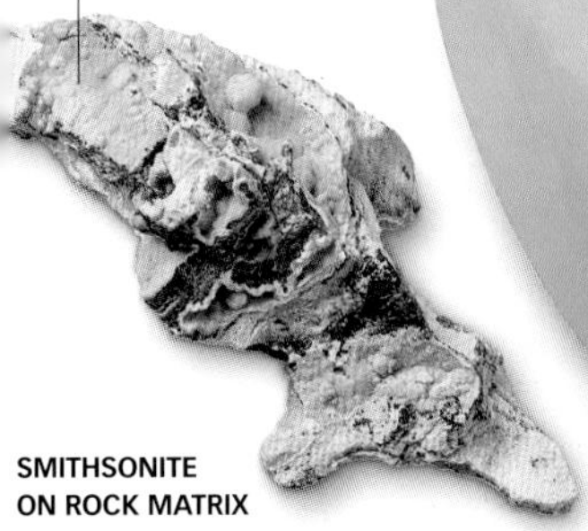

blue smithsonite

SMITHSONITE ON ROCK MATRIX

VARIANTS

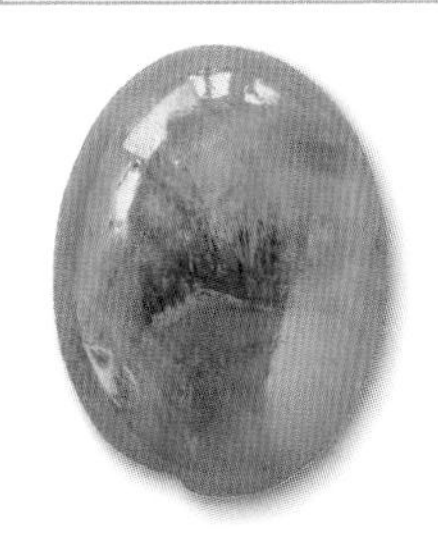

Blue smithsonite A cabochon of unusually blue smithsonite

Rectangular cabochon A rectangular cabochon of blue-green smithsonite

$ZnCO_3$

SMITHSONITE

A zinc carbonate, smithsonite is named after James Smithson, whose bequest supported the foundation of the Smithsonian Institution in the USA. Blue-green is the most prized color of smithsonite. Specimens can also be other colors, including yellow, orange, brown, pink, lilac, white, gray, green, or blue. These colors variously result from the presence of small amounts of cadmium, cobalt, copper, manganese, or lead. Smithsonite is typically found as spherular, grapelike, or stalactitic masses, or as honeycombed aggregates called "dry-bone" ore. Crystals are rare, with rhombohedral crystals generally having curved faces. Smithsonite is too soft for general wear, and is brittle and easily abraded or chipped. It is sometimes faceted for collectors. Most gemstone material is either cut *en cabochon* or carved into ornaments.

Smithsonite is found in the oxidation zones of zinc ore deposits, and in adjacent rocks rich in calcium carbonate. Significant deposits are in Germany, Mexico, Zambia, Italy, Australia, and the USA.

PROFILE

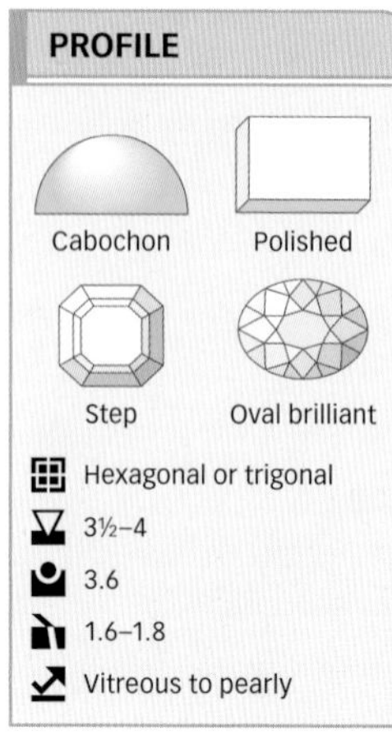

Hexagonal or trigonal

3½–4

3.6

1.6–1.8

Vitreous to pearly

GEM-GRADE RHODOCHROSITE IN CALCITE MATRIX

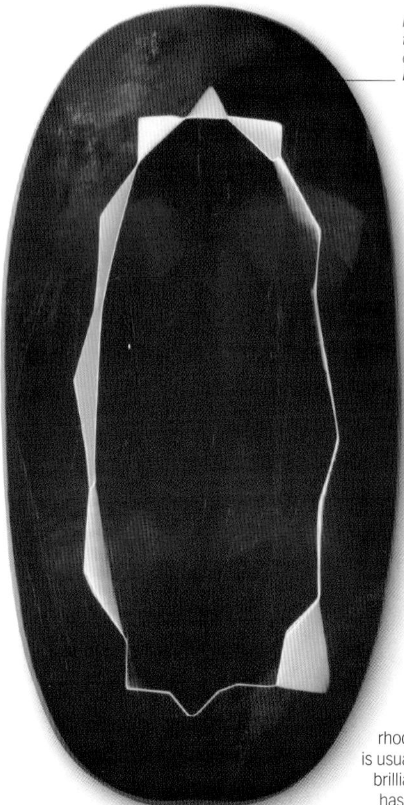

Rich color Unlike other rhodochrosite, which is usually pink, this oval brilliant-cut specimen has a deep red color.

VARIANT

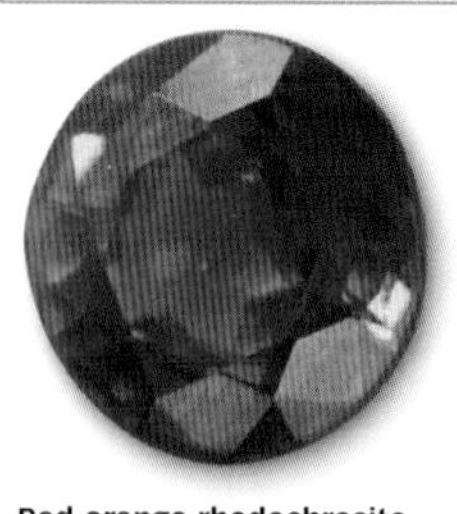

Red-orange rhodochrosite An unusual red-orange specimen faceted in a brilliant cut

$MnCO_3$

RHODOCHROSITE

A manganese carbonate, rhodochrosite derives its name from the Greek word *rhodokhros*, which means "of rosy color"—a reference to its classic rose-pink color. Specimens can also be brown or gray. Rhodochrosite forms dogtooth or rhombohedral crystals, but it can also be stalactitic, granular, nodular, grapelike, or massive. Because it is soft and fragile, faceted stones are rare and are usually collectors' pieces. The more common, fine-grained, banded stalactitic stones are used for decoration or polished and worn as pendants. They are also cut into beads and cabochons, and used as a carving medium.

Rhodochrosite is found in hydrothermal ore veins formed at moderate temperatures (400–1,065°F/200–575°C). Localities include South Africa and South America.

Carved ducks These charming ducks have been carved using rhodochrosite for the bodies and calcite for the heads.

PROFILE

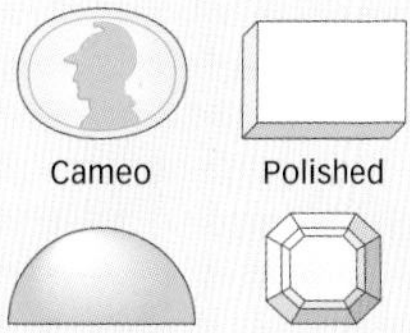

Cameo Polished

Cabochon Step

Orthorhombic

3½–4

2.9

1.53–1.68

Vitreous inclining to resinous

multicolored layering

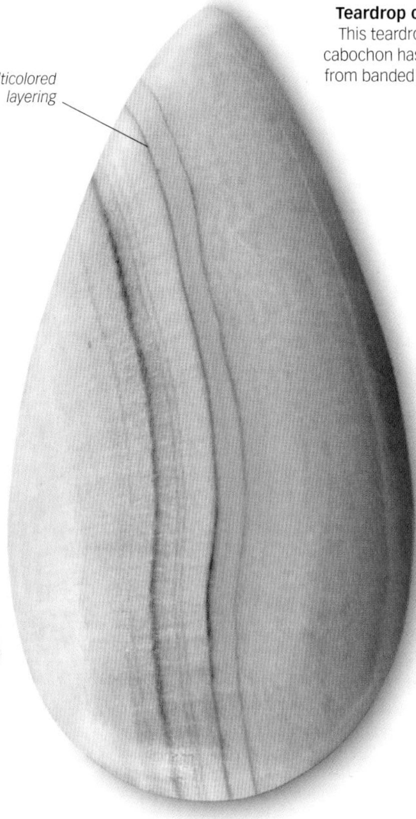

Teardrop cabochon This teardrop-shaped cabochon has been cut from banded aragonite.

individual crystal

ARAGONITE CRYSTALS

VARIANT

Banded aragonite A sawn specimen of good-quality banded aragonite

$CaCO_3$

ARAGONITE

A calcium carbonate, aragonite is chemically identical to the more common mineral calcite (p.76), but it crystallizes in a different crystal system and forms under more limited geological conditions than calcite. Aragonite is found as crystals or in columnar, stalactitic, radiating, or fibrous forms. It is also produced by biological processes and constitutes the shells of many marine mollusks and pearls. It can be colorless, white, gray, yellowish, green, blue, reddish, violet, or brown. Aragonite is very soft and brittle. As a result, facet-grade crystals that come from the Czech Republic are faceted only for collectors, and with great difficulty. Banded stalactitic material or layered material from around hot springs is sometimes polished as ornamental stones.

Aragonite is named after its place of discovery—Aragon, Spain. It forms at low temperatures (up to 400°F/200°C) near the surface of Earth. It is found in the oxidized zones of ore deposits, around hot springs, in mineral veins, and as stalactites in caves.

Brilliant-cut cerussite
This faceted crystal of cerussite shows a faint yellow color.

chipped facet edge

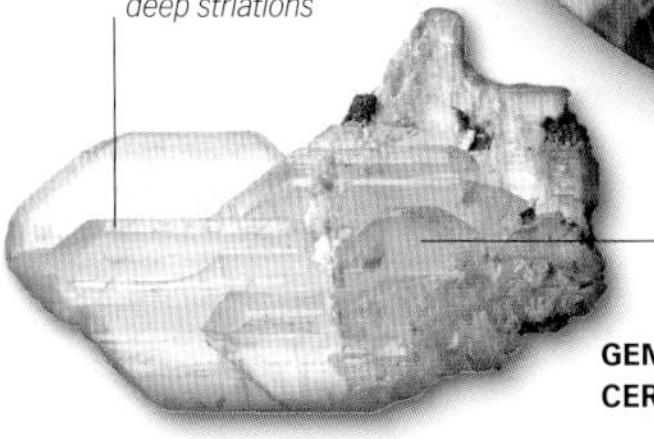

deep striations

colorless crystal

GEM-QUALITY CERUSSITE CRYSTAL

PROFILE

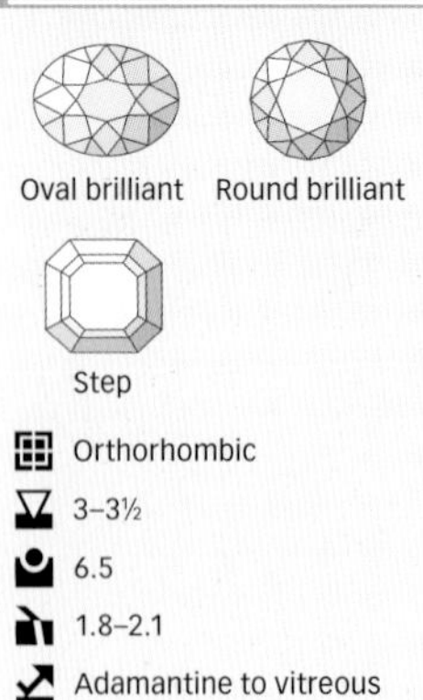

Orthorhombic

3–3½

6.5

1.8–2.1

Adamantine to vitreous

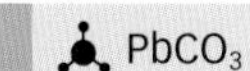

$PbCO_3$

CERUSSITE

The bright adamantine luster of cerussite crystals is similar to that of diamond (pp.50–51) and distinguishes the mineral. Specimens are generally colorless or white to gray but may be blue to green due to the presence of copper impurities. Cerussite crystals are difficult to facet and wear as gemstones because they are soft, brittle, and cleave easily. However, faceted specimens are especially brilliant owing to the high refractive index of the mineral. For this reason, gem-quality material is sometimes faceted for collectors. A widespread mineral, cerussite is found in locations such as Namibia, Australia, Bolivia, Spain, and Arizona and California in the USA, all of which yield gem-quality material.

A lead carbonate, cerussite has been known since antiquity and is named after the Latin word *cerussa*, which describes a white lead pigment. It occurs in the oxidation zones of lead veins, where it is formed by the action of carbonated water on other lead minerals.

PROFILE

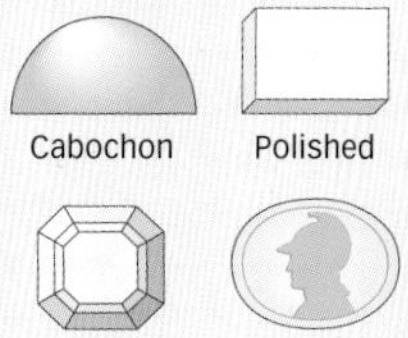

Cabochon
Polished
Step
Cameo

- Monoclinic
- 3½–4
- 3.8
- 1.73–1.84
- Vitreous to dull to earthy

vitreous luster
azurite crystal
goethite matrix

AZURITE CRYSTALS ON MATRIX

azurite
malachite layer
chessylite banding

Cabochon heart
This cabochon-cut azurite heart has layers of malachite within it. The two minerals are sometimes found together.

VARIANTS

Mixed cabochon A cabochon showing an intermixture of blue azurite and green malachite

Azurite ball A natural sphere of azurite that can be used in jewelry

Step-cut azurite A dark blue, translucent to near transparent azurite gem

$Cu_3(CO_3)_2(OH)_2$

AZURITE

Typically deep blue in color, azurite takes its name from the Persian word *lazhuward*, which means “blue.” Azurite was probably used in the production of blue glaze in ancient Egypt, where it was mined from the Sinai and the Eastern Desert. It was also used as a blue pigment in 15th- to 17th-century European art. Azurite usually occurs as complex crystals. It can also be massive, stalactitic, or in grapelike masses. Spherical concretions of radiating crystals are sometimes mounted and worn as jewelry—these can, for example, be sliced and mounted on silver frames as pendants. A massive variety of azurite that is interbanded with malachite (p.82) is called chessylite after Chessy, France—the place of its discovery. Used mostly for ornamentation, chessylite is typically cut *en cabochon* and, rarely, faceted for collectors.

Azurite is a secondary mineral that forms in the oxidized portion of copper deposits. Sources of azurite are France, Mexico, Australia, Chile, Russia, Morocco, Namibia, USA, and others.

PROFILE

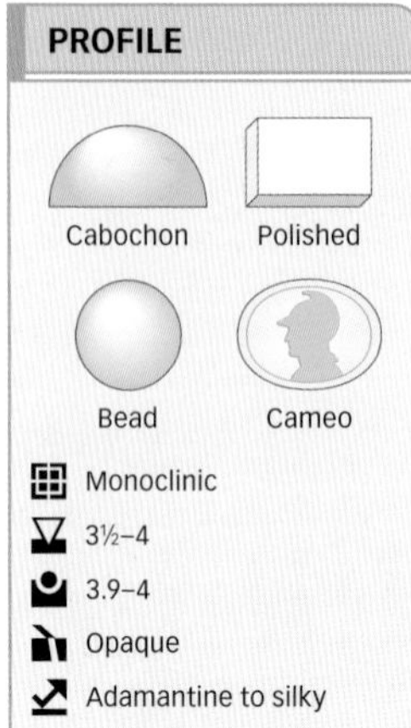

Monoclinic

3½–4

3.9–4

Opaque

Adamantine to silky

GRAPELIKE MALACHITE ON MATRIX

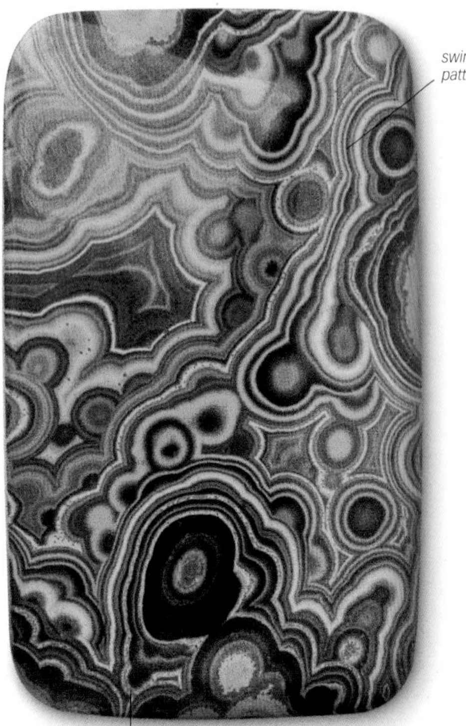

Patterned malachite
This polished slab exhibits the intricate patterns that can be seen in some malachite.

VARIANTS

Banded malachite
A polished fragment displaying concentric banding

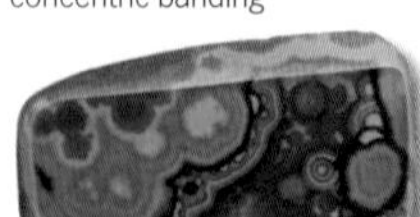

Azurite in malachite
A malachite gem with a small area of blue azurite

$Cu_2CO_3(OH)_2$

MALACHITE

A leaf-green copper carbonate, malachite was used as a cosmetic and a pigment by the Egyptians as far back as 3000 BCE. It was also used in amulets for children by the ancient Greeks and later in Italy as a talisman to ward off the "evil eye." Malachite's principal value today is as an ornamental material and gemstone, and it is used in cabochons, polished slabs, and carvings.

Malachite is often found as grapelike masses with a radiating, fibrous structure. Single masses of malachite weighing up to 56 tons (51 tonnes) were found in Russia in the 19th century. These were used to panel entire rooms, such as in the Malachite Room at the Winter Palace in St. Petersburg, Russia, and to create huge pillars, such as those at St. Isaac's Church in the same city.

Jewelry box
This jewelry box was veneered from a single piece of Russian malachite in the workshops of the jeweler Carl Fabergé.

Green cabochon
This variscite cabochon shows the darker green color of the best material.

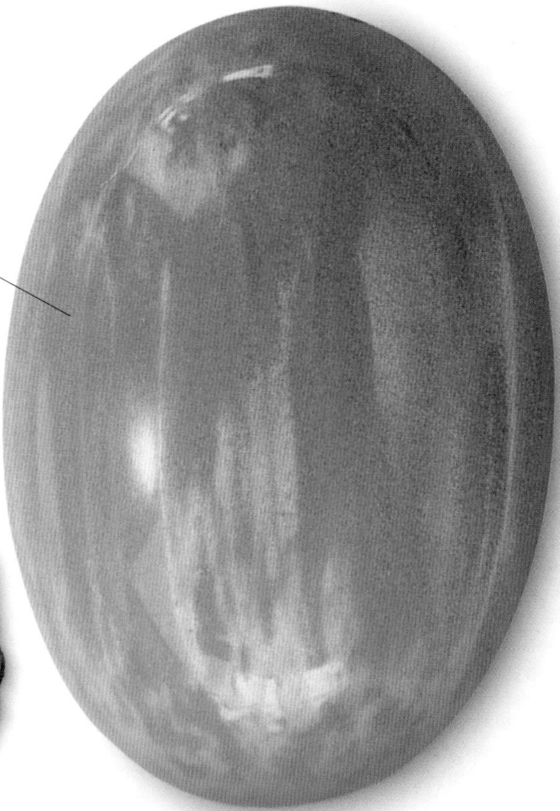

high
dome

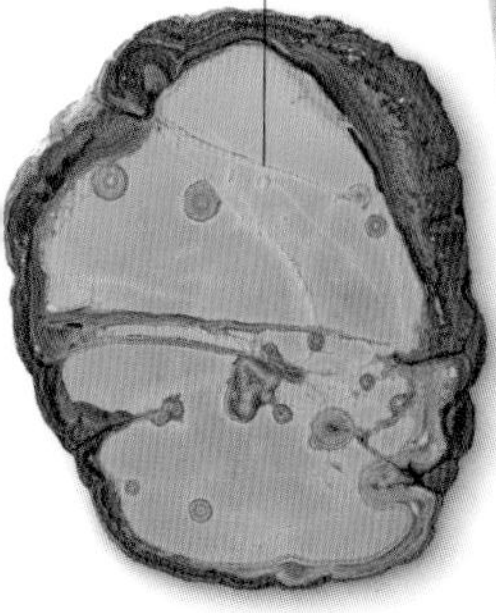

internal
pattern

SAWN VARISCITE NODULE

PROFILE

Cameo

Polished

Cabochon

Orthorhombic

4½

2.6

1.60–1.70

Vitreous to waxy

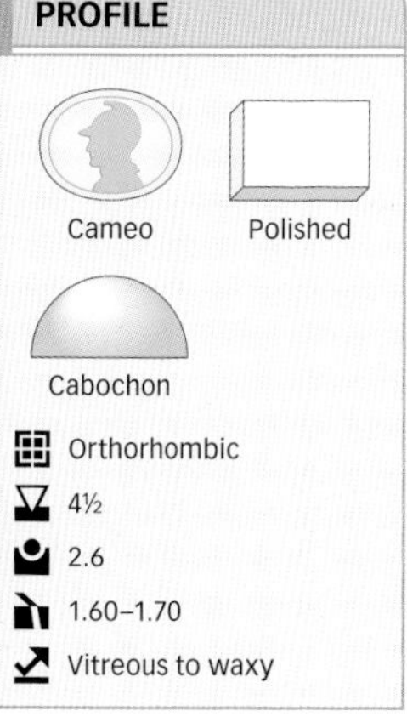

$AlPO_4 \cdot 2H_2O$

VARISCITE

A hydrated aluminum phospate, variscite is largely found as cryptocrystalline or fine-grained masses in veins, crusts, or nodules. It rarely forms crystals. Specimens can be pale to emerald green, blue-green, or colorless. Richly colored variscite is valued as a semiprecious gemstone, cut *en cabochon*, and is used for carvings and as an ornamental material. Variscite from Nevada, USA, often contains black spiderwebbing in the matrix and may be confused with green turquoise (pp.86–87), although variscite is usually much greener. Variscite that resembles turquoise in appearance is sometimes sold as "variquoise." Variscite is porous, so when worn next to the skin it tends to absorb body oils, which discolor it.

Variscite was named after Variscia, the old name for the German district of Voightland, where it was first discovered. It forms in cavities in near-surface deposits. Variscite is produced by the action of phosphate-rich waters on aluminous rocks. It is found in Austria, Australia, the Czech Republic, Venezuela, and the USA.

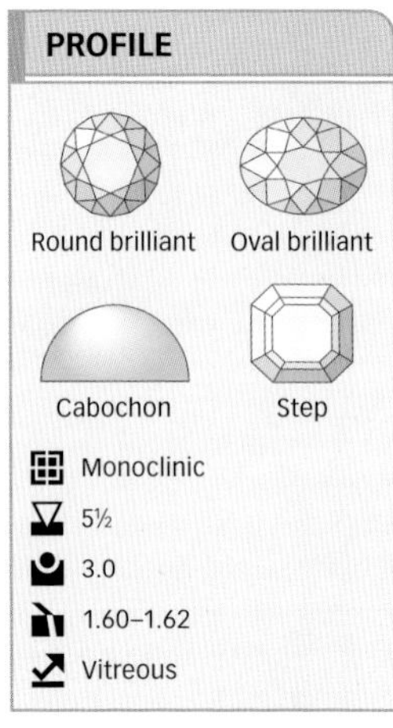

GROUP OF BRAZILIANITE CRYSTALS

Emerald-cut brazilianite This faceted gem exhibits brazilianite's typical greenish yellow color and shows a veil of bubblelike inclusions.

VARIANT

Kite-cut gem Faceted brazilianite in a darker yellow color than usual

$NaAl_3(PO_4)_2(OH)_4$

BRAZILIANITE

This mineral is named after Brazil, where it was first discovered and where gem-quality crystals measuring up to 6 in (15 cm) long have been found. Most brazilianite is pale yellow to yellowish green. A moderately hard gem, brazilianite would have been a popular gem but for its brittleness, fragility, and relative scarcity. It is only used as a collector's gem and is almost always faceted. Due to its fragility, brazilianite must be cut with great care. In addition to crystalline forms, brazilianite can occur in globular, radiating, or fibrous habits.

A sodium aluminum phosphate hydroxide, brazilianite forms in phosphate-rich granitic pegmatites. Gem-quality material is occasionally also found in New Hampshire and Maine in the USA. The New Hampshire deposit yielded gem-quality material even before brazilianite was identified as a distinct mineral.

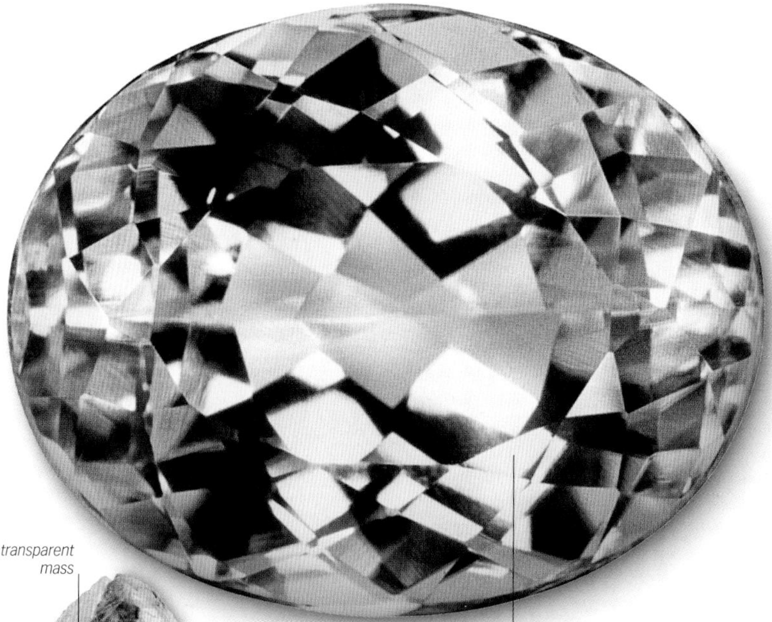

near colorless amblygonite

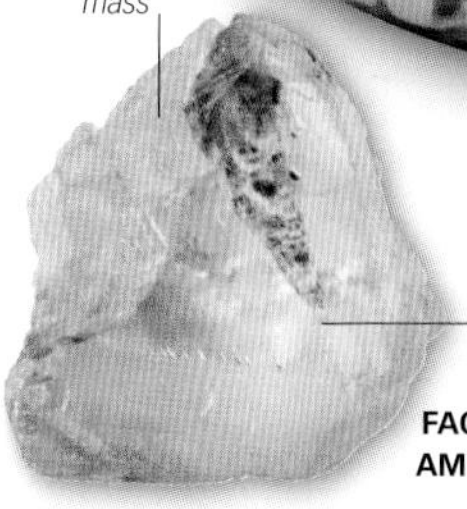

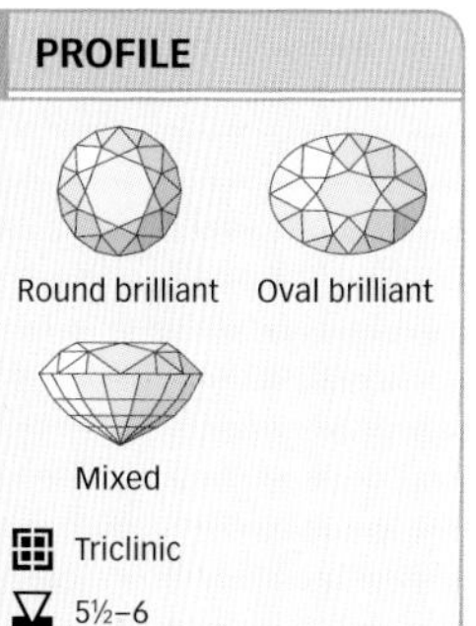

FACET-GRADE AMBLYGONITE

Oval brilliant amblygonite
Transparent amblygonite is often faceted in variations of the brilliant cut to emphasize its colorlessness.

PROFILE

Round brilliant

Oval brilliant

Mixed

Triclinic

5½–6

3.0

1.57–1.60

Vitreous to greasy or pearly

(Li,Na)$AlPO_4$(F,OH)

AMBLYGONITE

A lithium phospate, amblygonite is most commonly found in large, white, translucent masses. Transparent amblygonite has been faceted and set into jewellery, although it is a relatively soft and brittle stone and is vulnerable to breakage and abrasion. Yellow, greenish yellow, or lilac specimens are preferred for gems.

The name amblygonite comes from the Greek words *amblus* and *gõnia*, which mean "blunt" and "angle"—a reference to the shape of the mineral's crystals. Amblygonite occurs with other lithium-bearing minerals in pegmatite veins. Most gem-quality amblygonite comes from Brazil and the USA, where huge crystals are found in South Dakota and Maine. Some gem material is also found in Australia, France, Germany, Spain, and Norway. A pale mauve variety of amblygonite is found in Namibia. The largest documented single crystal of amblygonite had a volume of nearly 530 cubic feet (15 cubic meters) and weighed about 112 tons (102 tonnes).

PROFILE

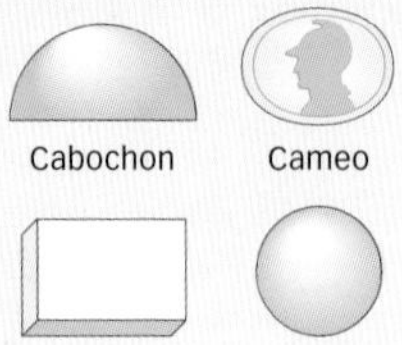

Cabochon Cameo

Polished Bead

Triclinic

5–6

2.6–2.8

1.61–1.65

Waxy to dull

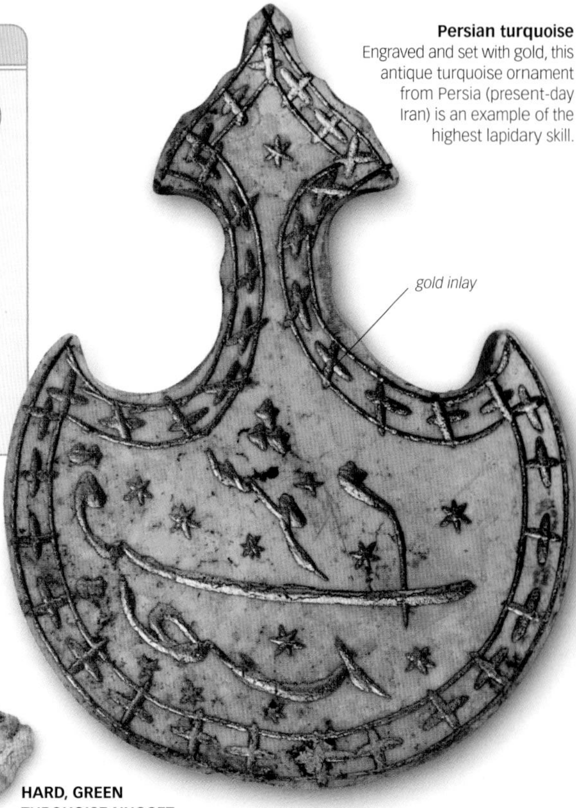

Persian turquoise
Engraved and set with gold, this antique turquoise ornament from Persia (present-day Iran) is an example of the highest lapidary skill.

gold inlay

rounded nugget shape

HARD, GREEN TURQUOISE NUGGET

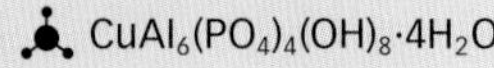
$CuAl_6(PO_4)_4(OH)_8 \cdot 4H_2O$

TURQUOISE

Being relatively soft and easily worked with primitive tools, turquoise was one of the first gemstones to be mined. Turquoise beads dating from about 5000 BCE have been found in Mesopotamia (present-day Iraq). Turquoise was first transported to Europe through Turkey. This probably accounts for its name, which is the French word for "Turkish."

Turquoise usually occurs in massive or microcrystalline forms, as encrustations or nodules, or in veins. It varies in color from sky-blue—a result of the presence of copper—to green. Much turquoise has greenish tints. As a result of its softness and porosity, the color of turquoise specimens may deteriorate if skin oils and cosmetics are absorbed during wear. Turquoise has embellished thrones, sword hilts, horse trappings, daggers, bowls, cups, and ornamental objects of all kinds. It has also been used extensively in jewelry.

Turquoise from Nishapur, Iran, is considered by many to be the finest. This variety, usually referred to as Persian turquoise, tends to be harder and of a more even color than North American turquoise. It is always sky-blue and never green. Despite this, most turquoise today is produced from the extensive copper mines in southwestern USA.

Turquoise diadem
Originally set with emeralds and replaced in the 1950s with turquoise, this diadem belonged to Empress Marie-Louise of France.

STABILIZED TURQUOISE

A significant portion of the turquoise sold in the North American market is stabilized turquoise. Stabilization is a process by which soft, chalky turquoise is impregnated with epoxy resin or plastic. This process hardens the stone and deepens its color, making it nearly impossible for the buyer to detect the artificial process.

Stabilized turquoise necklace
This necklace is strung with beads of stabilized turquoise and silver.

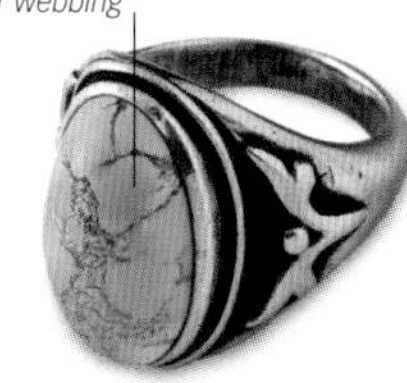

Turquoise ring
This sterling silver ring is set with an oval "spider web" turquoise cabochon.

thin layering

iron-oxide matrix

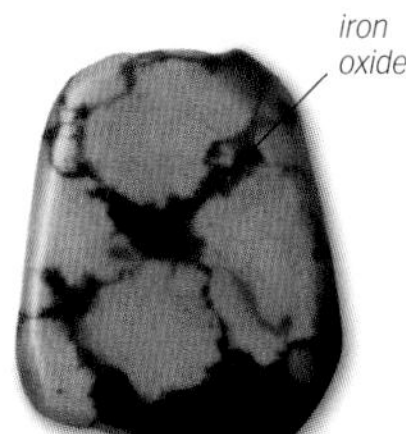

Layered turquoise
In this specimen, thin layers of turquoise are imbedded on a matrix.

Spiderweb rough
When sliced, the turquoise imbedded in this mass of iron oxides will show a "spider web" pattern.

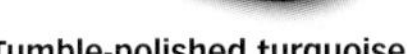

Tumble-polished turquoise
This piece of polished turquoise has a "spider web" pattern produced by interspersed iron oxides.

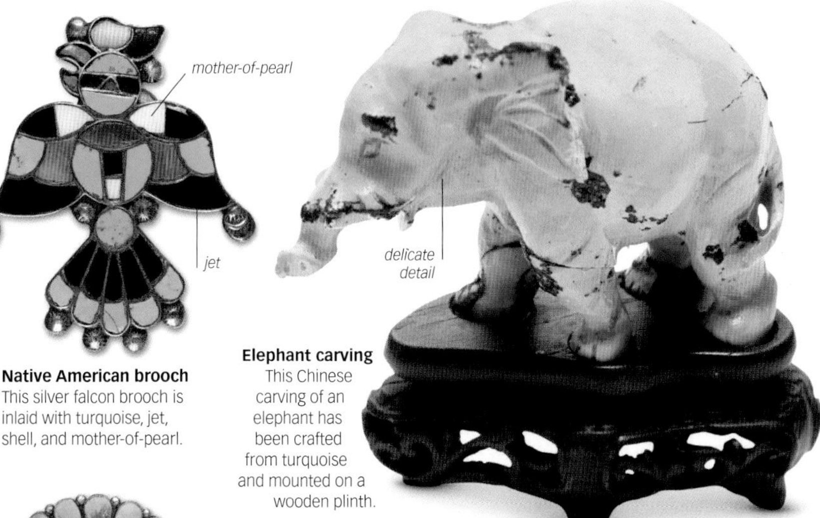

Native American brooch
This silver falcon brooch is inlaid with turquoise, jet, shell, and mother-of-pearl.

Elephant carving
This Chinese carving of an elephant has been crafted from turquoise and mounted on a wooden plinth.

Navajo turquoise
Set in silver, this North American turquoise bracelet is typical of the Navajo tribe of New Mexico, USA.

Arizona turquoise

Turquoise brooch
This 15-carat gold brooch features an oval turquoise cabochon and a freshwater pearl drop.

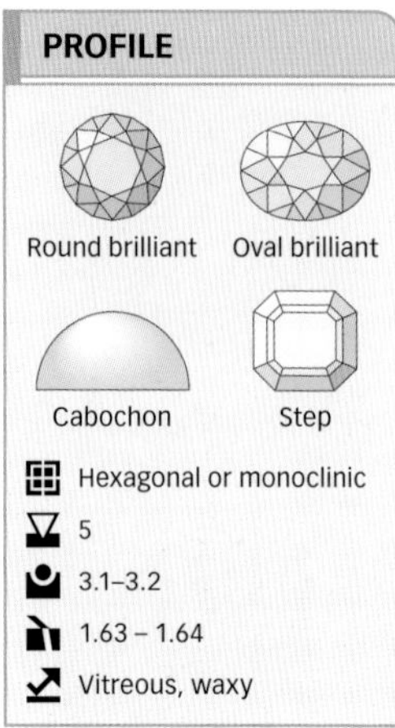

PROFILE

Round brilliant · Oval brilliant

Cabochon · Step

Hexagonal or monoclinic

5

3.1–3.2

1.63 – 1.64

Vitreous, waxy

MEXICAN YELLOW APATITE ROUGH

Emerald-cut apatite Faceted apatites are found in a number of different colors and cuts. This classic yellow apatite has been faceted in an emerald cut.

VARIANTS

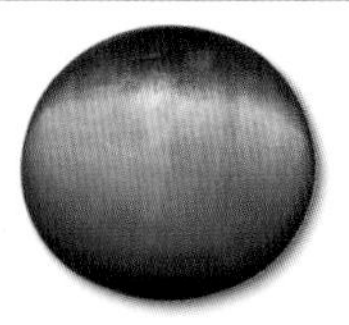

Apatite "eye" A bluish apatite cabochon showing a weak "cat's eye"

Cushion-cut apatite A specimen of typical cushion-cut apatite in its blue-green color

Brilliant-cut apatite A blue-green apatite in an oval brilliant-cut

$Ca_5(PO_4)_3(F,OH,Cl)$

APATITE

This series of structurally identical calcium phosphate minerals occurs as colored, glassy crystals that are well formed and transparent, or in masses or nodules. Apatite can be intensely colored, occurring as green, blue, violet-blue, purple, rose-red, flesh-colored, yellow, white, or colorless specimens. Faceted stones can be brightly colored. It is a soft stone and cut primarily for collectors. Recently, however, jewelry set with faceted apatites, some over 30 carats, has been marketed. A fibrous variety of apatite also yields cabochons with a cat's eye effect.

The name apatite is derived from the Greek *apate*, which means "deceit"—a reference to its similarity to crystals of aquamarine (p.164) and amethyst (pp.102–03). While gem-quality apatite is usually recovered from pegmatites, the mineral occurs in a wide range of igneous rocks. Madagascar, Mexico, Brazil, Pakistan, Namibia, Russia, and the USA all have notable deposits of apatite. Crystals weighing up to 440 lb (200 kg) have been found in Canada.

vitreous luster

mottled appearance

dipyramidal habit

SINGLE LAZULITE CRYSTAL

Lazulite cabochon
This low-domed lazulite cabochon exhibits the mottled color that is typical of most lazulite.

PROFILE

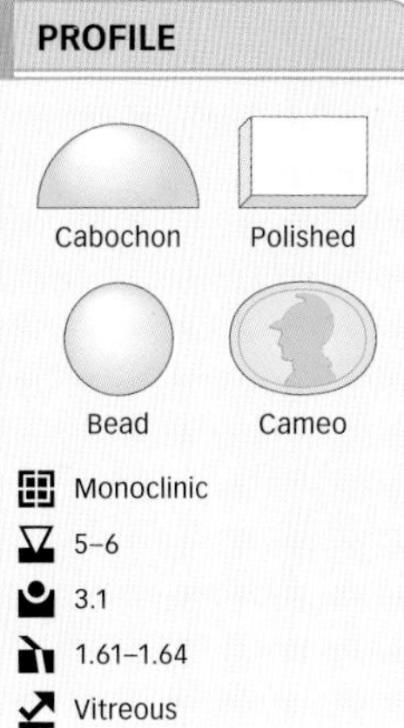

$(Mg,Fe)Al_2(PO_4)_2(OH)_2$

LAZULITE

This mineral takes its name from the old German word *lazurstein*, which means "blue stone." It can be azure-blue, sky blue, or bluish white to blue-green in color. Specimens can be massive or granular, or occur as pyramidal crystals. The granular variety of lazulite is cut *en cabochon* and is sometimes made into beads and other decorative items. It can also be carved and tumble-polished. Faceting material is rare. When found, it is pleochroic, showing blue and white colors when viewed from different angles. Lazulite gemstones are soft and can easily abrade in ordinary wear.

Lazulite occurs in aluminous metamorphic rocks, quartz veins, and granite pegmatites. Significant localities are Brazil, Switzerland, Austria, California in the USA, and Yukon in Canada. Lazulite is a magnesium aluminium hydroxophosphate, but its name can be confused with that of the silicate lazurite (p.130)—the principal mineral in lapis lazuli. Lazulite can appear similar to lapis lazuli, lazurite, and azurite (p.81) and is sometimes confused with these minerals.

Howlite carving
This charming frog is carved from howlite and shows the mineral veining typical of much material.

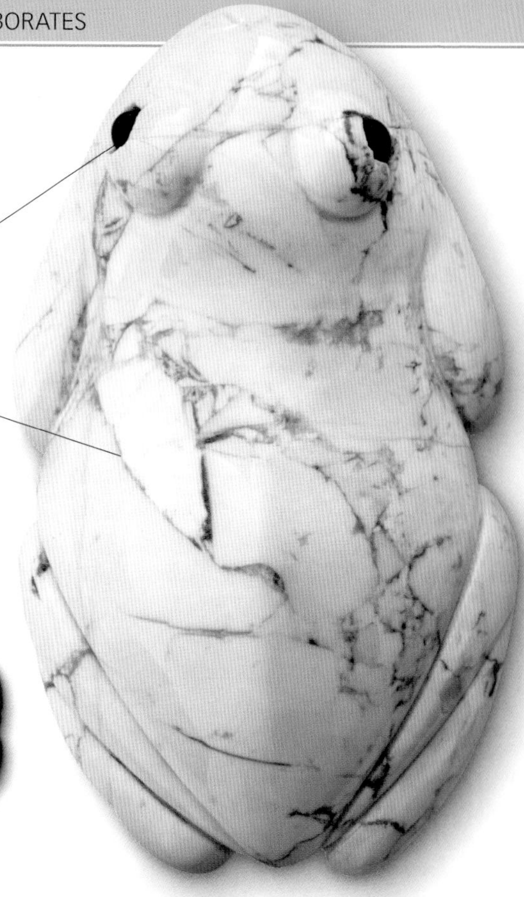

onyx eye

vein of other minerals

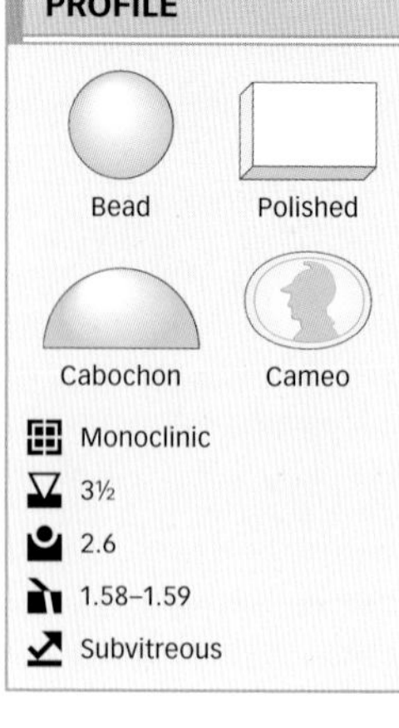

HOWLITE NODULE

PROFILE

Bead
Polished
Cabochon
Cameo

Monoclinic
3½
2.6
1.58–1.59
Subvitreous

$Ca_2B_5SiO_9(OH)_5$

HOWLITE

Named after Henry How, the Canadian mineralogist and chemist who discovered it, howlite is a calcium borosilicate hydroxide. It generally forms nodular masses, sometimes resembling cauliflowers. The nodules are white, with fine gray or black veins of other minerals in an erratic, often weblike pattern across them. Howlite is porous and can be dyed easily. Dyed howlite with dark veins of other minerals can resemble spiderweb turquoise (pp.86–87). It can be distinguished from turquoise by its inferior hardness and by turquoise's greater depth of color. Howlite is sometimes sold under the misleading trade names of "white buffalo turquoise" and "white turquoise," and turquoise-dyed howlite is marketed as turquenite. It takes a good polish and is commonly used to make carvings, beads, jewelry components, and other decorative items.

Howlite occurs in evaporite deposits with other boron minerals. Large quantities of howlite are found in California, USA, while smaller amounts come from Turkey, Canada, Mexico, Russia, and the Czech Republic.

Faceted barite Honey-colored barite, such as this emerald-cut stone, is the preferred color for faceting. Blue barite is sometimes faceted as well.

PROFILE

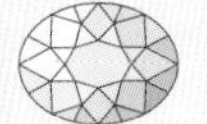
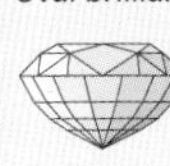

Oval brilliant | Round brilliant | Mixed | Step

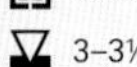

Orthorhombic

3–3½

4.5

1.63–1.65

Vitreous, resinous, pearly

BARITE CRYSTAL WITH AREAS OF FACET-GRADE MATERIAL

VARIANT

Polished barite A sawn and polished section of stalactitic barite

$BaSO_4$

BARITE

The most common barium mineral, barite is barium sulfate and is commonly well crystallized. Although colorless when pure, crystals are often tinged yellow, blue, or brown. A rare, much-prized golden variety occurs in Colorado and South Dakota, USA. Transparent blue crystals of barite can resemble aquamarine (p.164), but are distinguished by their softness, heaviness, and crystal shape. Barite is very soft and has several perfect cleavages, so it is faceted, with difficulty, purely as a collector's gem. Sections of stalatitic barite are sometimes polished and mounted on silver frames as pendants.

Barite takes its name from the Greek word *barys*, which means "heavy"—a reference to its high specific gravity. For the same reason, it is also called heavy spar. An important industrial mineral, barite is quite widespread, with deposits in England, Italy, the Czech Republic, Germany, Romania, and the USA. It is a common accessory mineral in lead and zinc veins.

Sky-blue celestine
Most faceted celestine, such as this modified brilliant-cut specimen, is light sky blue. Darker blue stones may be cut as well.

complex brilliant cut

light sky-blue celestine

granular habit

large, tabular crystal

DARK BLUE CELESTINE ROUGH

PROFILE

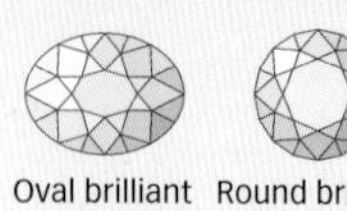

Oval brilliant Round brilliant

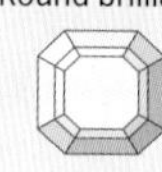

Mixed Step

Orthorhombic

3–3½

4

1.62–1.63

Vitreous, pearly on cleavage

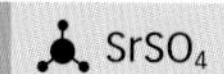

$SrSO_4$

CELESTINE

Also known as celestite, celestine is frequently light blue in color but can also be medium to dark blue, white, colorless, light red, green, or brown. Well-formed, transparent, light to medium blue crystals of celestine are common and have been known to be more than 30in (75cm) long. The mineral can also occur in massive, fibrous, granular, or nodular form. Soft and cleavable, celestine is faceted with great difficulty for collectors and museums. Single crystals are sometimes sold as pendants, but they are too fragile for general wear. Facet-grade celestine is found in Namibia, Madagascar, England, Italy, USA, and Canada.

Celestine takes its name from the Latin word *coelestis*, which means "heavenly"—an allusion to the color of the sky. Celestine is strontium sulfate. It is found in cavities within sedimentary rocks such as limestones, dolomites, and sandstones.

Alabaster bust
This bust of a young woman was carved from alabaster by the Italian artist Cipriani. It shows the detail possible in fine alabaster.

head made from lighter alabaster

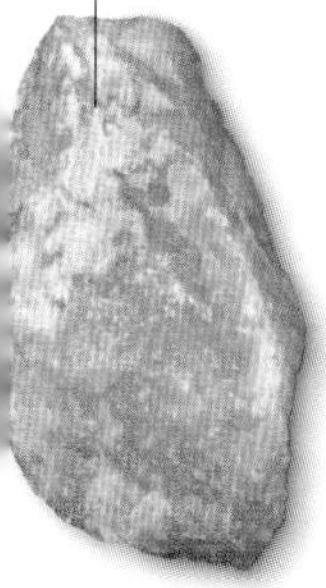

weathered surface

CARVING-GRADE ALABASTER ROUGH

PROFILE

Monoclinic
2
2.3
1.52–1.53
Subvitreous to pearly

$CaSO_4 \cdot 2H_2O$

ALABASTER

Fine-grained masses of gypsum, a hydrous calcium sulfate, are called alabaster. The name alabaster was previously applied to a fine-grained, massive form of calcite (p.76), and many ancient "alabaster" carvings are actually calcite. Modern carvings of alabaster can, however, be tested by applying a drop of acid—calcite effervesces, whereas gypsum does not. The word "alabaster" probably originates in Middle English, in turn derived from the Greek word *alabastos*—used to identify a vase made of alabaster. The use of alabaster vessels, called *a-labaste*, in the Ancient Egyptian cult of the deity Bast is well documented, and may also reflect the origin of its name.

Alabaster has been carved into ornaments and utensils for thousands of years. It is compact enough to even be turned on a lathe. Alabaster carvings are sometimes heat-treated to reduce their translucency and make them resemble marble. Alabaster treated like this is called *marmo di Castellina*. Alabaster is found in England, Italy, and the USA.

Satin spar cabochon
This satin spar gypsum cabochon has been cut with its fibers along the length, creating an eyelike effect.

fibrous structure

cat's eye effect

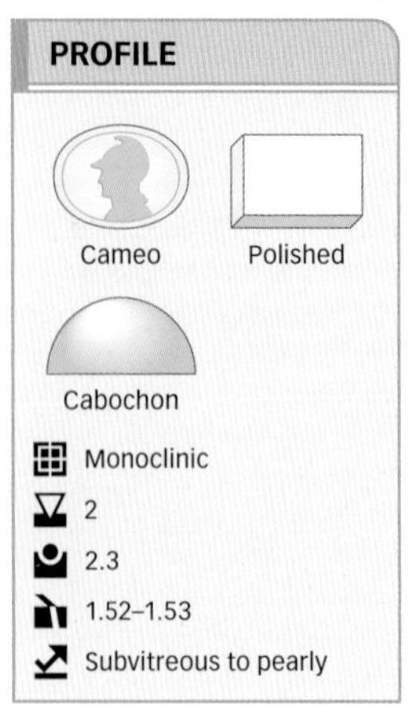

FIBROUS SATIN SPAR ROUGH

PROFILE

Cameo
Polished
Cabochon

Monoclinic
2
2.3
1.52–1.53
Subvitreous to pearly

$CaSO_4 \cdot 2H_20$

SELENITE (GYPSUM)

A transparent, crystalline variety of gypsum, selenite is named after the Greek word *selene*, which means "the moon." Besides the almost lunar luminescence of some selenite crystals, the name may be a reference to the ancient belief that certain selenite crystals waxed and waned with the moon. Swordlike selenite crystals that are 36 ft (11 m) or longer occur at the Cave of Swords at Naica in Mexico, creating possibly the most spectacular mineral deposit on Earth. Satin spar is a fibrous variety of selenite that exhibits a silky luster. When cut *en cabochon*, it can produce a cat's eye effect. Being too soft for general wear, satin spar is mainly used as collector's pieces.

A calcium sulfate hydrate, gypsum is colorless or white in color, but impurities can tint it light brown, gray, yellow, green, or orange. Gypsum occurs in extensive beds formed by the evaporation of ocean brine and as an alteration product of sulfides in ore deposits.

PROFILE

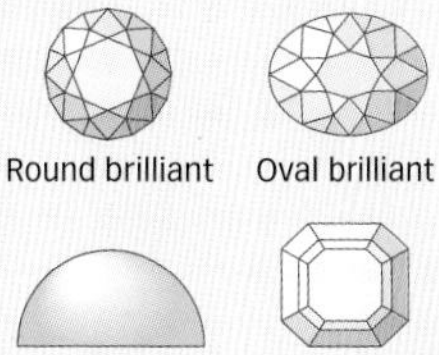

Round brilliant Oval brilliant

Cabochon Step

Tetragonal

4½–5

6.1

1.92–1.93

Vitreous to greasy

Faceted scheelite
Scheelite is rarely faceted as it is soft and easily scratched. The cutter of this stone was remarkably skilled.

typical yellow color

star facet

scheelite crystal

SCHEELITE CRYSTALS ON MATRIX

VARIANT

Colorless scheelite
A specimen of colorless, faceted scheelite

$CaWO_4$

SCHEELITE

A pale yellowish white to brown or bright orange mineral, scheelite is calcium tungstate. It was named in 1821 after the Swedish chemist C.W. Scheele. Relatively pure scheelite fluoresces vivid bluish white under short-wave ultraviolet light. Large crystals of scheelite are mostly opaque and yield very little transparent facet-grade material. Smaller transparent crystals are faceted, but being too soft to be worn they are cut only for collectors. Cut stones exhibit good dispersion of light, and synthetic colorless scheelite has been used as a diamond simulant. Synthetic specimens have also been colored by trace elements to simulate other gemstones.

Scheelite is commonly found in hydrothermal veins formed at high temperatures (1,065°F/575°C or above) and in contact metamorphic rocks. It occasionally occurs in granitic pegmatites. Gem-quality material comes from Brazil, Australia, Switzerland, France, Sri Lanka, and Arizona, USA.

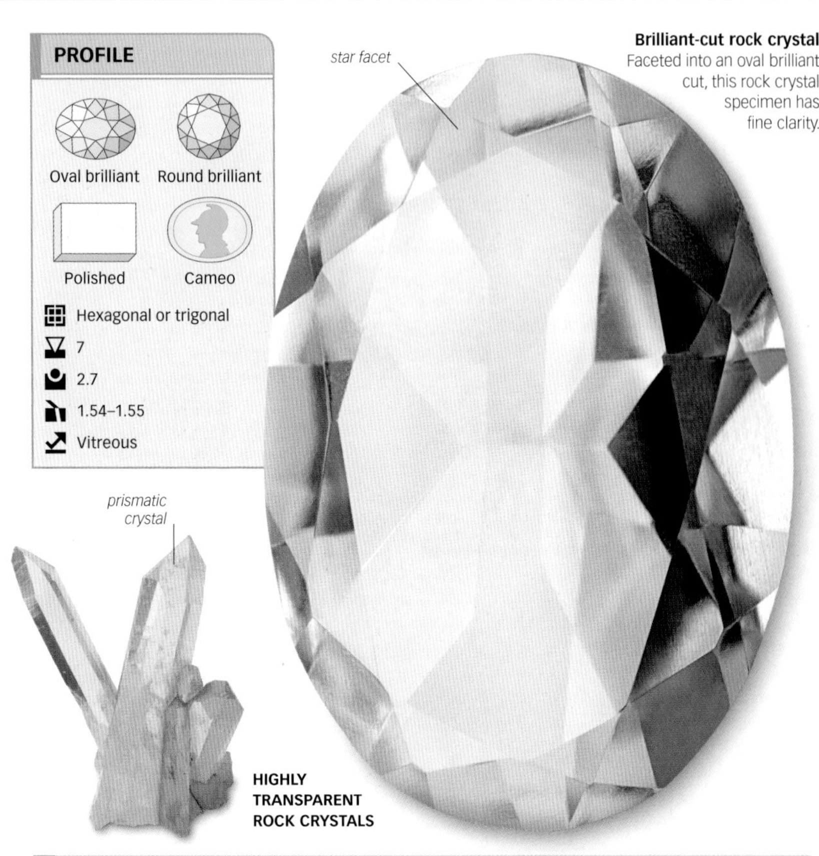

Brilliant-cut rock crystal Faceted into an oval brilliant cut, this rock crystal specimen has fine clarity.

HIGHLY TRANSPARENT ROCK CRYSTALS

SiO_2

ROCK CRYSTAL

A colorless and transparent variety of quartz, rock crystal is named after the Greek word *krystalos*, which means "water-clear crystals." The ancient Romans believed that rock crystal was ice that had frozen too hard to melt. The name rock crystal emerged in the late Middle Ages, to differentiate the mineral from the then newly perfected colorless glass, which came to be called crystal or crystal glass.

Quartz occurs in nearly all silica-rich metamorphic, sedimentary, and igneous rocks. Crystals weighing several tons are known. Brazil, Madagascar, and the USA have extensive deposits of rock crystal.

Rock crystal was traditionally used by Australian Aborigines and the Prairie Indians of North America as a talisman and to produce visions. In Europe, rhinestones were initially cut from the clear quartz pebbles found in the Rhine River. The optical properties of rock crystal led to its extensive use in lenses and prisms, and as an inexpensive gemstone. Natural rock crystal is still occasionally cut as a gemstone, although the colored varieties of quartz are much more popular. It is extensively mined for use in spheres, carvings, and a wide range of other lapidary products. Natural crystals are frequently mounted and worn as pendants. They are also artificially coated with various substances to produce different kinds of "aura" quartz. Synthetic quartz is now used in the electronics industry, but it is too expensive to be used as a gemstone.

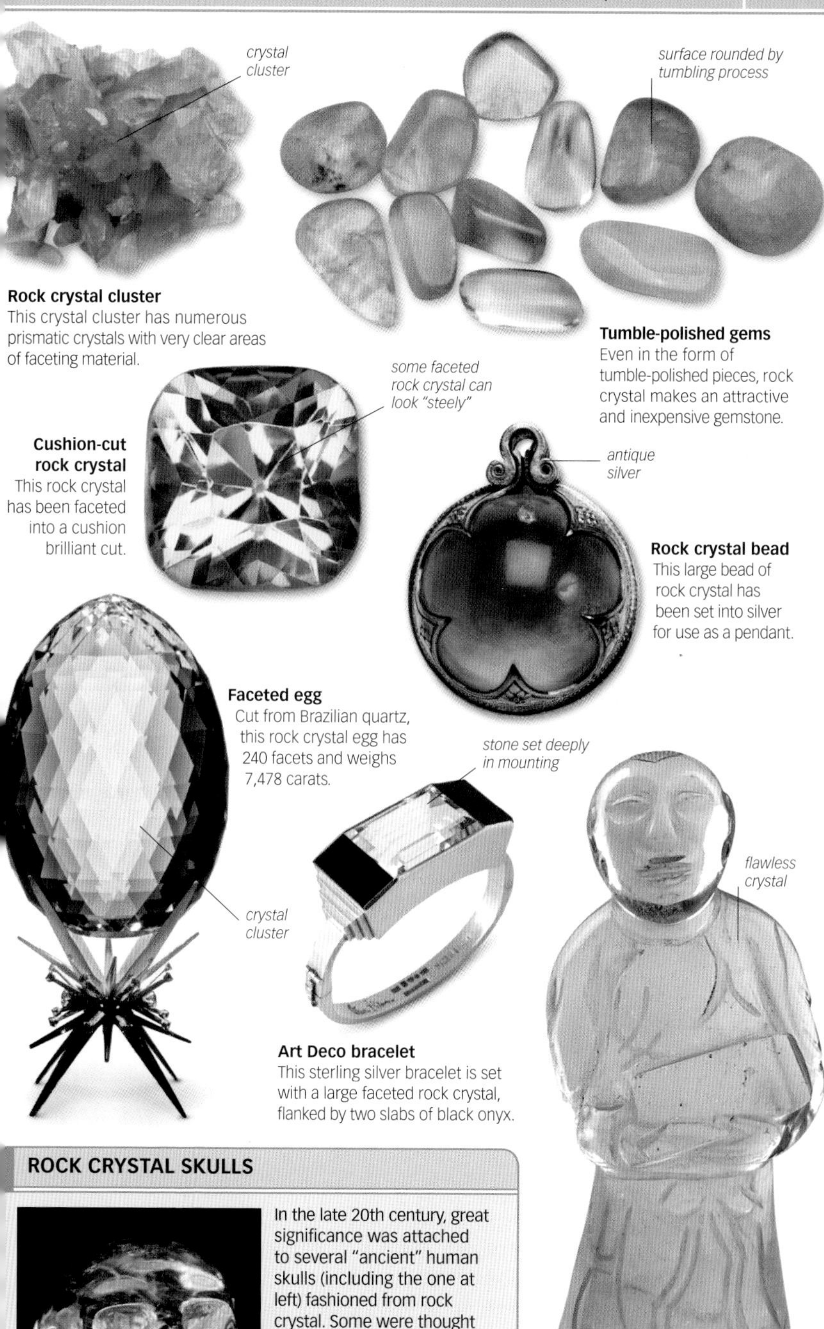

Rock crystal cluster
This crystal cluster has numerous prismatic crystals with very clear areas of faceting material.

Tumble-polished gems
Even in the form of tumble-polished pieces, rock crystal makes an attractive and inexpensive gemstone.

Cushion-cut rock crystal
This rock crystal has been faceted into a cushion brilliant cut.

Rock crystal bead
This large bead of rock crystal has been set into silver for use as a pendant.

Faceted egg
Cut from Brazilian quartz, this rock crystal egg has 240 facets and weighs 7,478 carats.

Art Deco bracelet
This sterling silver bracelet is set with a large faceted rock crystal, flanked by two slabs of black onyx.

Carved figure
This Chinese monk figure has been crudely carved from rock crystal.

ROCK CRYSTAL SKULLS

In the late 20th century, great significance was attached to several "ancient" human skulls (including the one at left) fashioned from rock crystal. Some were thought to have originated with past civilizations in present-day Mexico. Closer study of the skulls later revealed that they were, in fact, made by a notorious French faker of antiquities, Eugène Boban, in the 19th century.

PROFILE

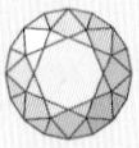

Round brilliant 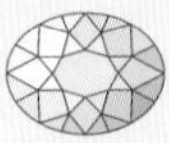 Oval brilliant

Bead 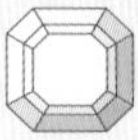 Step

Cabochon

Hexagonal or trigonal

7

2.7

1.54–1.55

Vitreous

brownish black color

dipyramidal smoky quartz crystal

SMOKY QUARTZ CRYSTAL ON MATRIX

Oval cushion cut
The combination of black and brown shades of smoky quartz is highlighted in this brilliant-cut, oval cushion gem.

VARIANTS

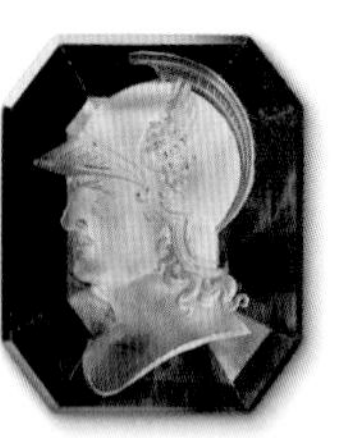

Cameo A rock crystal carving of a warrior set on a faceted smoky quartz background

Faceted bead A specimen faceted to produce a sphere

Pendeloque A light-colored smoky quartz in a pendeloque cut

SiO_2

SMOKY QUARTZ

The light brown to nearly black variety of crystalline quartz is called smoky quartz. Faceted crystals of light brown smoky quartz are sold as smoky topaz quartz in some countries. Black smoky quartz is often created by irradiating rock crystal (pp.96–97). Very dark, natural smoky quartz may be heated to give it a lighter, more attractive hue. The heat may turn it yellow so that it can be sold as the more valuable citrine (p.101).

In Germany, Spain, the Netherlands, and Poland, the dark brown to black variety of smoky quartz is known as morion—from *mormorion,* the name that the Roman naturalist Pliny the Elder gave it in the 1st century CE. Brown to yellow-brown smoky quartz is also called cairngorm or cairngorm stone—after the Cairngorm Mountains in Scotland. Smoky quartz is relatively abundant and, as such, it is worth less than amethyst (pp.102–03) or natural citrine. It is found in pegmatites cutting through naturally radioactive rocks such as granite. Fine crystals come from Brazil, the Swiss Alps, and Colorado, USA.

Oval brilliant stone
Although milky quartz is usually near-opaque, translucent specimens are occasionally found and faceted, yielding a stone of very good quality.

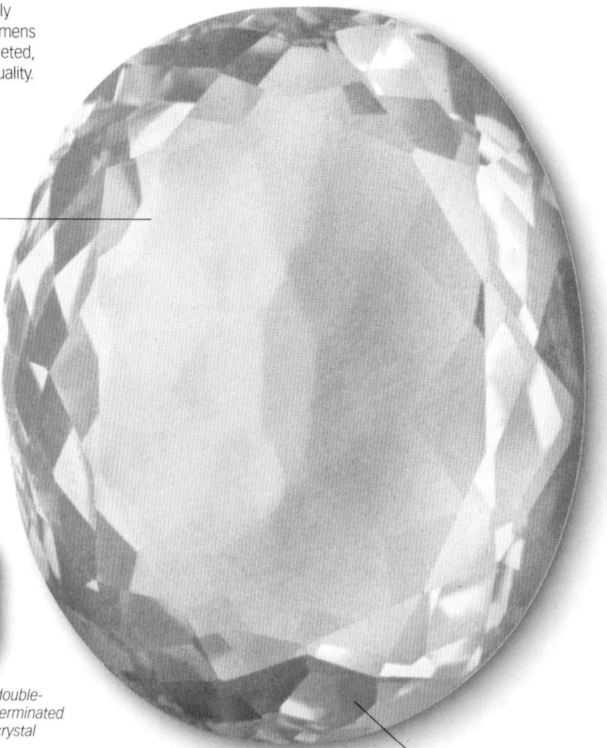

cloudy appearance
complex oval brilliant

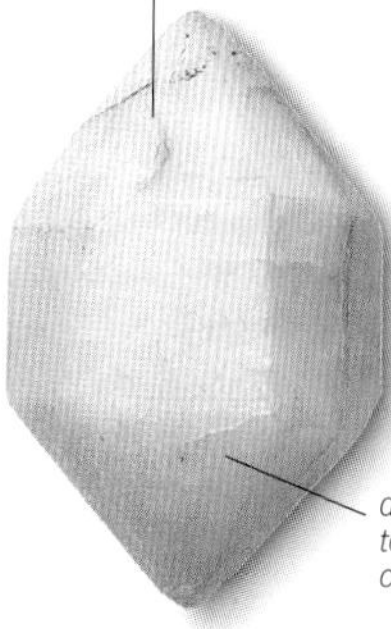

vitreous luster
double-terminated crystal

MILKY QUARTZ CRYSTAL

PROFILE

Cabochon

Cameo

Step

Hexagonal or trigonal
7
2.7
1.54–1.55
Vitreous

SiO_2

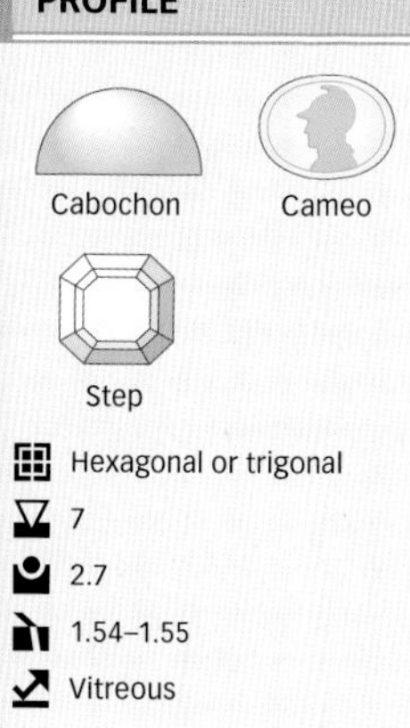

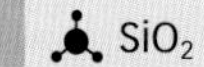

MILKY QUARTZ

By far the most common variety of quartz, milky quartz is translucent to nearly opaque and white to greyish white to cream in color. Milky and transparent areas can occur within the same crystal of milky quartz. The milkiness is caused by the presence of minute gas bubbles trapped inside the crystal. Translucent milky crystals are sometimes faceted, while translucent to opaque crystals are sometimes cut *en cabochon*. Some cabochon-cut stones may be mistaken for opal. Both forms of cutting may yield stones with an opalescent glow.

Based on a Native American tradition, milky crystals are designated "female" to create a market for them among the spiritually oriented. Crystals of milky quartz are identical to rock crystal (pp.96–97) in all respects except color and transparency, and often occur in the same deposit. Large quantities of milky quartz are recovered from major quartz mining areas such as Brazil, and Arkansas, USA, where crystals weighing hundreds of pounds are sometimes found.

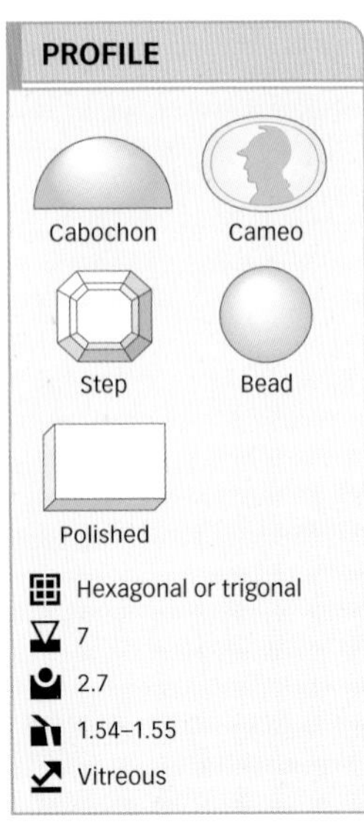

Faceted drop This rose quartz drop shows unusually skillful faceting, with each facet perfectly aligned to the next.

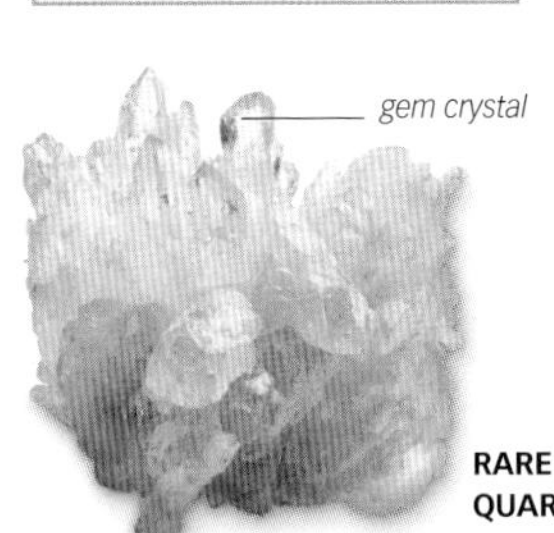

RARE ROSE QUARTZ CRYSTALS

VARIANT

Brilliant cut A brilliant-cut rose quartz with better-than-average clarity

SiO_2

ROSE QUARTZ

A silicon dioxide, rose quartz is the translucent or transparent pink to rose-red variety of crystalline quartz. It is rarely found as crystals and is far more common in massive form. Near-transparent stones are sometimes faceted. Rose quartz is also carved and cut *en cabochon*. When rose quartz containing microscopic fibrous mineral inclusions from localities such as Madagascar is cut *en cabochon* with proper orientation, it exhibits a starlike effect like that of sapphires (p.59, pp.62–63).

Rose quartz has been carved since ancient times and is used today by crystal healers, who attribute unconditional love and emotional healing to the stone. It is generally found in pegmatites, sometimes in large masses. Significant localities are Sweden, Brazil, Madagascar, Namibia, Scotland, Russia, Spain, and the USA.

Rose quartz beads The color-matched rose quartz beads in this necklace are well faceted on all sides.

PROFILE

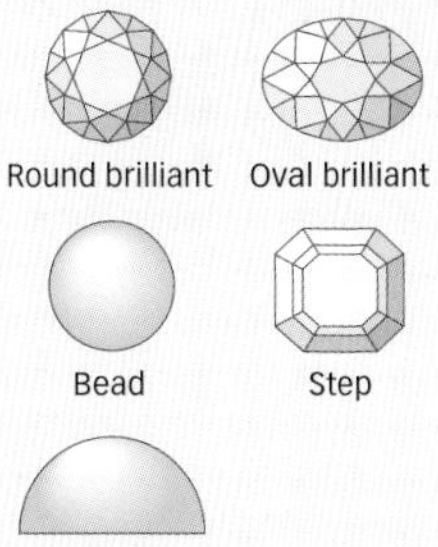

Round brilliant Oval brilliant

Bead Step

Cabochon

Hexagonal or trigonal

7

2.7

1.54–1.55

Vitreous

Light yellow citrine Citrine varies in color, from the light yellow of this oval mixed cut to a dark honey color.

yellow color due to traces of iron

orange tinge

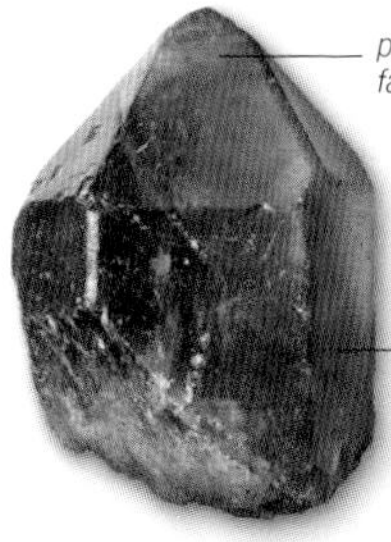

pyramid face

prism face

GEM-QUALITY CITRINE CRYSTAL

VARIANTS

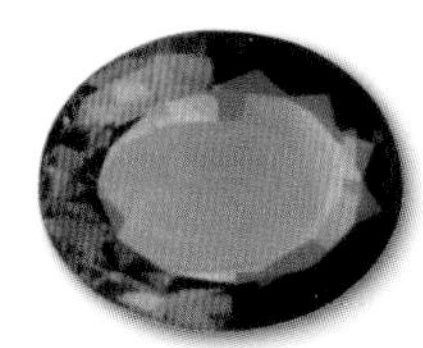

Honey color A mixed-cut citrine showing its dark honey color

Pendeloque citrine A pendeloque-cut citrine in its middle range yellow color

SiO_2

CITRINE

A variety of crystalline quartz, citrine resembles yellow topaz (pp.198–99) in appearance. Crystals are hexagonal, ranging from pale yellow to yellow-brown. Almost exclusively faceted, citrine is often marketed under names that confuse it with topaz to inflate its price. However, topaz can be distinguished from citrine by its superior hardness.

The name citrine is derived from the Latin word *citrina*, which means "yellow." Citrine is mainly found in either pegmatite veins or their weathering products. Gem-quality citrine is found in Russia, India, France, Brazil, and on the Isle of Arran in Scotland. Natural citrine is much less common than amethyst (pp.102–03) or smoky quartz (p.98), both of which can be heat-treated to turn their color to that of citrine. Much of the material marketed as citrine is actually heat-treated amethyst or, in lesser quantities, smoky quartz. When citrine is found as color-zones in amethyst, it is known as ametrine. Faceted ametrines are cut to display colors of both citrine and amethyst in the same stone.

Oval mixed-cut amethyst This gem has triangular facets on the top half and rectangular facets below it.

BRAZILIAN AMETHYST CRYSTAL

SiO_2

AMETHYST

The purple, violet, or red-purple variety of vitreous quartz, amethyst derives its name from the Greek word *amethustos*, which means "not drunk"—a reference to the belief that it guards against drunkenness. Amethyst has a long history as a gemstone. In the ancient civilizations of Mesopotamia and Egypt, it was used in jewelry and carved into ornaments. Egyptian amethyst came principally from Nubia (modern Sudan). In the early Christian church, an amethyst ring was part of a bishop's regalia. Even today, gem cutters refer to the highest grade of amethyst as "Bishop's Grade."

The most valued shades of amethyst are deep, rich purple and deep purple with a reddish tinge, the coloration caused by traces of iron and natural radiation. Amethyst is sometimes strongly color-zoned. Nowadays, it is faceted, carved, and cut *en cabochon*. Thin crystals are capped with silver and worn as pendants. Clusters of amethyst crystals and amethyst geodes are popular decorative items.

Amethyst is found in most countries where granitic rocks are exposed. Its crystals can be little more than pyramids, like those from Brazil and Uruguay, or slender prisms like those from Mexico. Major commercial sources are Uruguay, Brazil, Siberia, and North America. Brazilian and Uruguayan amethysts are often heat treated to change the color to a yellow-brown citrine (p.101). Where amethyst and citrine occur naturally in the same stone, the name ametrine is used.

AMETHYST IN MYTHOLOGY

According to Greek mythology, amethyst was created by Dionysus—the god of wine and fruitfulness. He tried to kill a young woman called Amethyst, but the goddess Diana turned her into white quartz. Dionysus, shedding tears of remorse, spilled his goblet of wine over the quartz, turning it purple.

Dionysus
Dionysus is the central figure on this vase contemporary with the Greek myth.

Silver brooch
A central square amethyst is flanked by two other amethysts in this silver brooch.

diamonds around central amethyst

Edwardian brooch
A magnificent 96-carat amethyst is surrounded by old European-cut diamonds in this brooch that dates back to the Edwardian era.

Amethyst geode
A mass of pyramid-shaped crystals can be seen in this broken section of a Brazilian amethyst geode.

color most intense on certain faces

Color zoning
This polished amethyst section shows preferential absorption of coloring material.

Square-cut amethyst
This square step-cut amethyst is of excellent quality.

Prismatic crystal
Uncut prismatic amethyst crystals, such as this one from Colorado, USA, are often worn as pendants.

Unusual cut
This amethyst is faceted in an unusual hexagonal mixed cut.

PROFILE

Cabochon 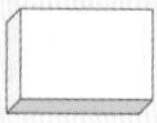 Polished

Cameo

Hexagonal or trigonal

7

2.7

1.54–1.55

Vitreous

granular texture

massive form

GEM-QUALITY GREEN AVENTURINE ROUGH

Oval cabochon
The internal sparkles of aventurine are highlighted in this deep-domed, oval cabochon.

orange-brown cabochon

bright speckles

VARIANT

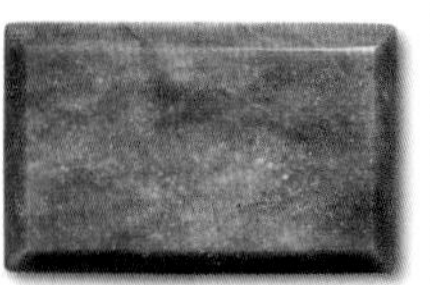

Rectangular cabochon
A flat-cut, rectangular cabochon showing typically green aventurine color

SiO_2

AVENTURINE QUARTZ

A form of quartz, aventurine is characterized by its translucency and its spangled appearance due to sparkling internal reflections from minute inclusions of other minerals. Aventurine occurs in several colors: it can be colored brown by the presence of pyrite (p.55), reddish brown by hematite (p.57), or green by fuchsite mica. Other inclusions can color the mineral orange, yellow, bluish white, or bluish green. Aventurine is always massive and is generally carved, cut *en cabochon*, or sliced and polished.

The name aventurine is derived from the Italian term *a ventura*, which means "by chance." This is a reference to the chance discovery of goldstone—a glass with uniformly dispersed flecks of metallic copper that is somewhat similar in appearance to aventurine. Goldstone can be distinguished from aventurine by its unnaturally uniform flecks and inferior hardness. The term aventurine feldspar refers to a variety of plagioclase feldspars that exhibit flecks of colored inclusions, although the gold variety is usually called sunstone (p.128).

PROFILE

Cabochon

Hexagonal or trigonal

7

2.7

1.54–1.55

Vitreous

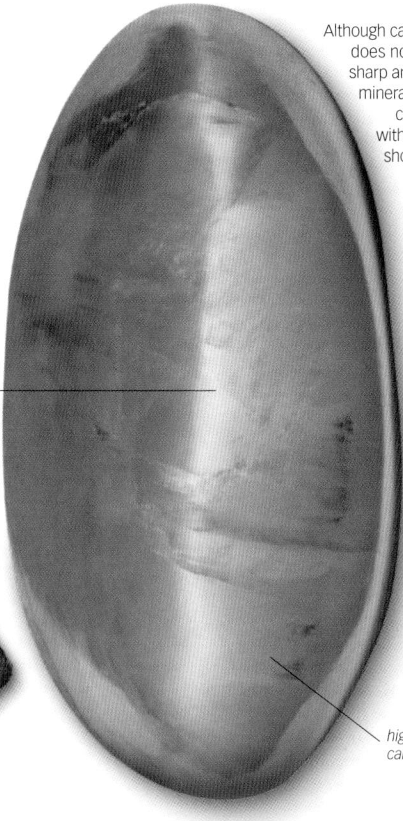

Quartz eye
Although cat's eye quartz does not produce as sharp an eye as other mineral species, this cabochon, cut with a high dome, shows the "eye."

single white line along stone ("eye")

fibrous structure

high-domed cabochon

FIBROUS CAT'S EYE QUARTZ ROUGH

VARIANTS

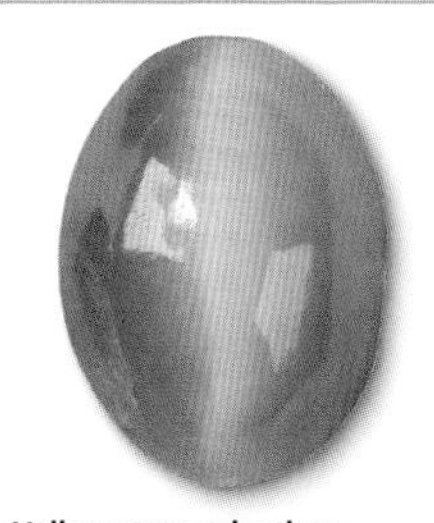

Yellow-gray cabochon
A translucent specimen cut *en cabochon*

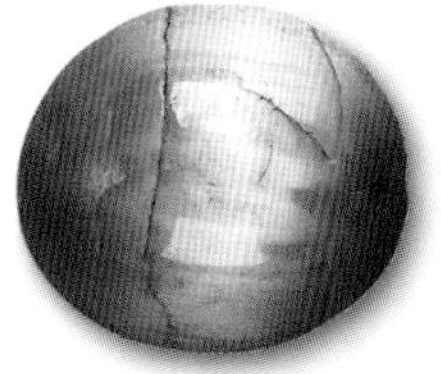

Fibrous cabochon
A cabochon-cut specimen with a fibrous structure

SiO_2

CAT'S EYE QUARTZ

This variety of quartz is also called Occidental cat's eye to differentiate it from the more valuable but similar looking cat's eye chrysoberyl (p.69). Cat's eye quartz can be distinguished from cat's eye chrysoberyl by its lower specific gravity.

When cat's eye quartz is cut *en cabochon,* it shows a single shimmering white line across the stone. This cat's-eye effect, or chatoyancy, is due to the presence of parallel fibers of crocidolite, a form of asbestos. Crocidolite also gives specimens a grayish green or greenish color. A more reddish or golden color comes from minute fibers of rutile (p.71). A chatoyant golden-brown stone from South Africa is called tiger's eye quartz (p.106), and the blue variety is hawk's eye quartz (p.107). The main source of cat's eye quartz is the gem gravels of Sri Lanka. It is also found in India and Australia, while inferior green stones are obtained from Bavaria, Germany.

PROFILE

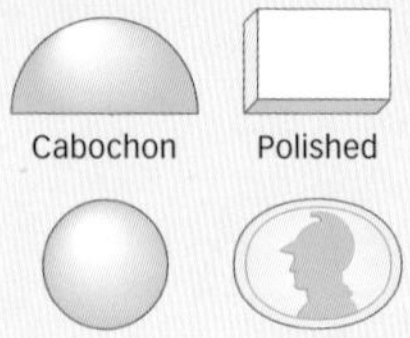

Cabochon Polished

Bead Cameo

Hexagonal or trigonal

7

2.7

1.54–1.55

Vitreous

banding due to iron staining

SLICED SECTION OF LIGHT TIGER'S EYE

VARIANT

Polished piece A small, tumble-polished piece of tiger's eye

Tiger's eye sphere
Veins of tiger's eye are usually only a couple of inches thick. Spheres such as this one are made from rare thicker material.

yellow-brown stripes

fibrous crocidolite

SiO_2

TIGER'S EYE

A semiprecious variety of quartz, tiger's eye exhibits a luminescent band that resembles a tiger's or cat's eye when cut *en cabochon*. However, unlike cat's eye quartz (p.105), tiger's eye quartz is more opaque and has a rich yellow to brown color owing to its iron-oxide content. Tiger's eye is sometimes treated with heat or acid to alter its color. Gentle heat treatment results in a red variety of tiger's eye. Acid treatment yields a honey-colored variety, which can superficially resemble the much more highly valued cat's eye chrysoberyl (p.69).

Tiger iron, which is composed of tiger's eye, red jasper, and black hematite in undulating, contrasting bands, is used as a gem and ornamental stone. Griqualand West in South Africa is a major source of tiger's eye.

Tiger's eye beads
This bracelet is made up of beads of tiger's eye and rock crystal. It is secured by a gold clasp.

Hawk's eye cabochon
This specimen of hawk's eye has been cut *en cabochon* and shows a cat's eye effect.

cat's eye effect

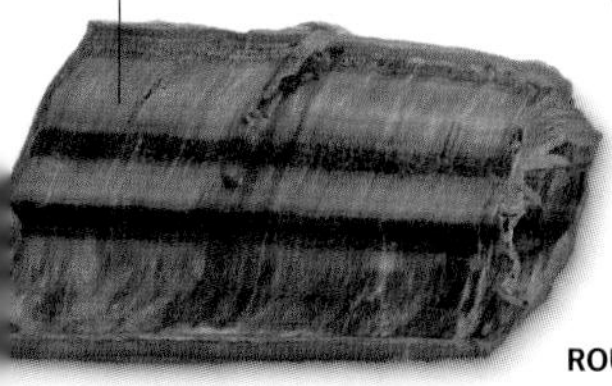

visible fibers

ROUGH HAWK'S EYE

PROFILE

Cameo

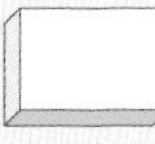
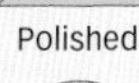
Polished

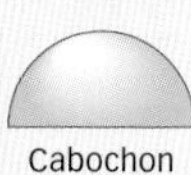
Cabochon

Bead

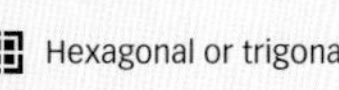
Hexagonal or trigonal

7

2.7

1.54–1.55

Vitreous

SiO_2

HAWK'S EYE

A chatoyant gemstone, hawk's eye is a semiprecious variety of quartz and is closely related to tiger's eye (p.106). Both are formed when parallel veins of crocidolite (blue asbestos) grow simultaneously with silica. In tiger's eye, the crocidolite is completely altered into iron oxides, giving it a golden color. However, in hawk's eye, the crocidolite is unaltered and retains its natural blue color. Like tiger's eye, hawk's eye, when cut *en cabochon*, exhibits a luminescent band as light reflects off the enclosed fibers. Gemstones cut into cabochons have a fine luster. Hawk's eye is less common than tiger's eye, but it is used for the same lapidary purposes and cut into cabochons, beads, spheres, and carved objects.

The major sources of hawk's eye are for the most part the same as tiger's eye. Hawk's eye comes from the portions of the deposit in which the crocilodite has been less altered. It is found at Griqualand West, South Africa, and Wittenoom Gorge, Western Australia.

Rutilated quartz cabochon
Within this quartz cabochon is an attractive, regular arrangement of golden needles of rutile.

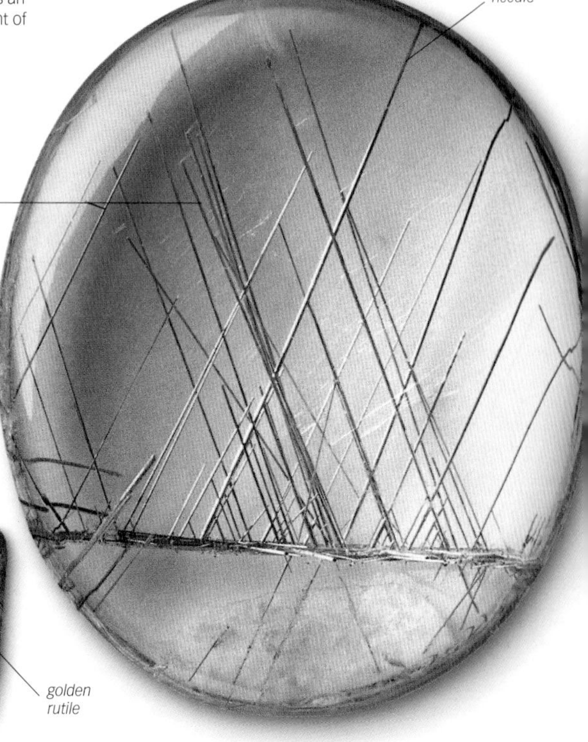

slender rutile needle

regular arrangement of needles

vitreous luster

golden rutile

RUTILATED QUARTZ ROUGH

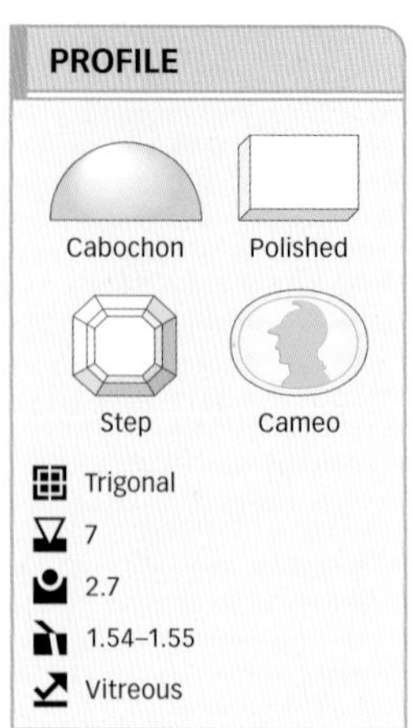

SiO_2

RUTILATED QUARTZ

Enclosed needles of rutile give this quartz its name. Unlike other gemstones, where inclusions of other minerals are considered undesirable, rutilated quartz is valued for its inclusions of rutile, or titanium dioxide. These rutile crystals occur randomly or as sprays and vary from a few to many. Although usually golden, the needles can range from red to deep red to black. Depending on the density of the needles, the stone can range from translucent to nearly opaque. Cut into gemstones, cabochons, beads, and large spheres, rutilated quartz has been used for ornamental and religious objects for centuries.

The quartz in which the rutiles are enclosed is usually rock crystal (pp.96–97), but natural radiation can cause it to turn brown, creating rutilated smoky quartz.

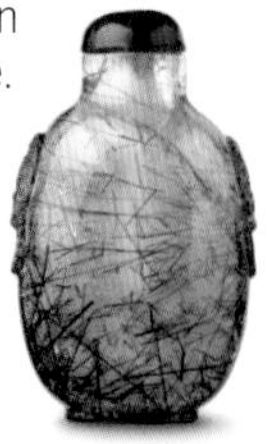

Chinese snuff bottle
Rutilated quartz is often used to make carved items, such as this Chinese snuff bottle.

fine gold enameling

intricate decorations on handles

waxy appearance

Chalcedony cup
Made from waxy grey chalcedony, this antique cup shows fine gold work and exhibits the best of the lapidary and enameling arts.

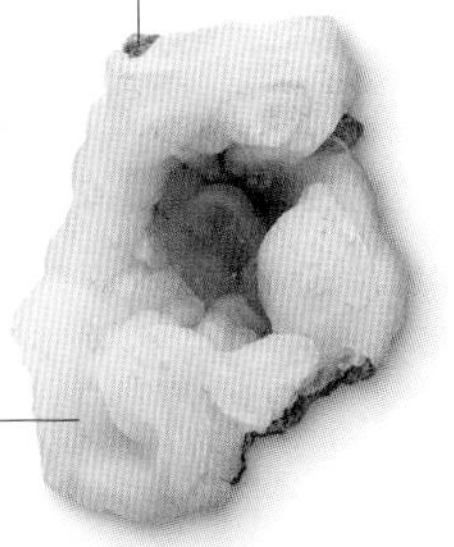

rock matrix

grapelike aggregates of chalcedony

GLOBULAR AGGREGATES OF PINK CHALCEDONY

PROFILE

- Hexagonal or trigonal
- 7
- 2.7
- 1.54–1.55
- Vitreous

SiO_2

CHALCEDONY

A compact variety of microcrystalline quartz, chalcedony is composed of thin layers of microscopic quartz fibers. It is extremely tough and has been used for centuries as an excellent carving material. Although it is white when pure, chalcedony may contain traces of other minerals that give it a range of colors. Many of these colored chalcedonies have their own names.

Chalcedony can occur in rounded, grapelike, or stalactitic forms. It is porous and much of it is dyed to alter or enhance its color before it is sold. Many chalcedonies are semiprecious gems. The mineral is found in veins, geodes, and concretions. It forms in cavities and cracks when silica-rich waters at low temperatures (up to 400°F/200°C) percolate through existing rocks.

Chalcedony fob seal
Cut from chalcedony, this fob seal features an intaglio portrait of an 18th-century Georgian gentleman.

Australian chrysoprase
This cabochon of chrysoprase has been cut from material discovered in Australia in the 1960s.

high dome

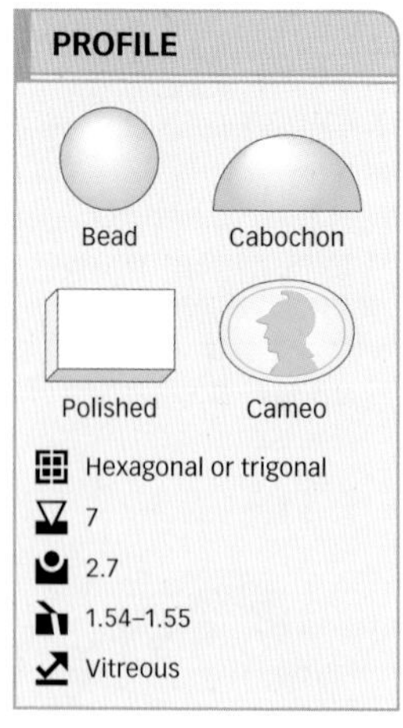

POROUS AUSTRALIAN CHRYSOPRASE ROUGH

PROFILE

Bead | Cabochon | Polished | Cameo

- Hexagonal or trigonal
- 7
- 2.7
- 1.54–1.55
- Vitreous

SiO_2

CHRYSOPRASE

Also spelled chrysophrase, chrysoprase is a translucent, apple-green gemstone variety of chalcedony (p.109). It derives its color from the presence of nickel. Unlike other chalcedonies, it is the color rather than any pattern of markings that makes chrysoprase desirable. Lighter-colored cut stones may be confused with fine jade. Chrysoprase was used by the ancient Greeks and Romans and is still the most valued chalcedony. Prase is another green chalcedony with less intense color.

Chrysoprase results from the deep weathering of nickel-bearing rocks. The best-quality material currently comes from Queensland, Australia. Lesser amounts are found in Brazil; California, USA; and the Ural Mountains, Russia.

Chrysoprase jewelry
This pair of half-hoop ear clips by Van Cleef & Arpels is set with dark chrysoprase and diamonds.

PROFILE

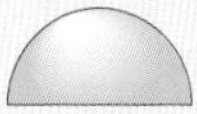

Cabochon  Polished

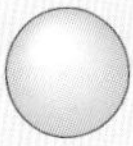

Bead  Cameo

Hexagonal or trigonal

7

2.7

1.54–1.55

Vitreous

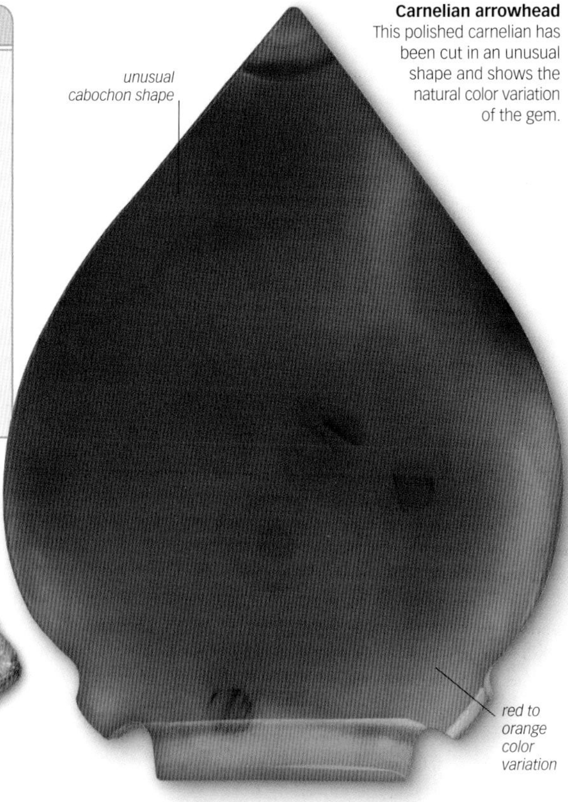

unusual cabochon shape

Carnelian arrowhead
This polished carnelian has been cut in an unusual shape and shows the natural color variation of the gem.

red to orange color variation

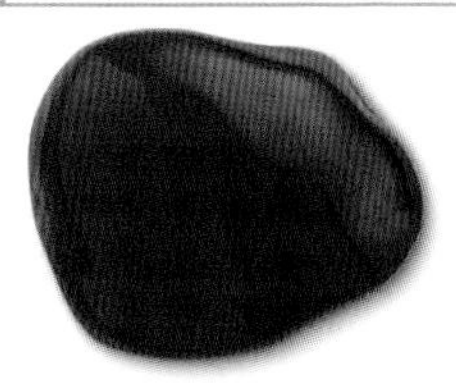

FRAGMENT OF CARNELIAN ROUGH

VARIANT

Dark red carnelian
A tumble-polished carnelian pebble in a darker shade than usual

SiO_2

CARNELIAN

Also spelled "cornelian," carnelian has been used as a gemstone and talisman since the 4th millennium BCE. Worked carnelian has been found from ancient Mesopotamia, Crete, Egypt, Phoenicia, and Greece. The Romans used engraved carnelian gems widely in jewelry. The stone was once thought to still the blood and calm the temper. Conversely, it was also believed to give the owner courage in battle and to make timid speakers eloquent.

Carnelian is a translucent, blood-red to reddish orange variety of chalcedony (p.111). Specimens can be uniformly colored, exhibit various shades of red, or show banding. Strongly banded material is known as carnelian agate. Much of the material that is sold as carnelian today is, in fact, dyed material from Brazil and Uruguay.

Carnelian bracelet
This carnelian bracelet is made from 10 beads that are well matched in size and color.

Bloodstone and jasper carving
This deeply carved cameo of a Roman emperor is composed of a red jasper figure set on a bloodstone background.

bloodstone background

red jasper figure

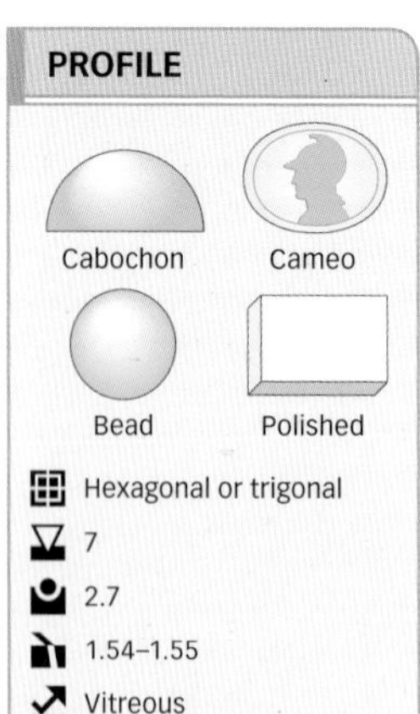

PIECE OF ROUGH BLOODSTONE

PROFILE

Cabochon
Cameo
Bead
Polished

Hexagonal or trigonal
7
2.7
1.54–1.55
Vitreous

SiO_2

BLOODSTONE

Also called heliotrope, bloodstone was one of the first gems and talismans to be used by humans. In the 1st century BCE, it was believed to protect against deception and preserve health. During the Middle Ages in Europe, it was used in sculptures that represented flagellation and martyrdom. It was also thought to be a remedy for hemorrhages and inflammatory diseases, to prevent nosebleeds, and to remove anger and discord.

A dark green variety of chalcedony (p.109), bloodstone is colored by traces of iron silicates and has patches of bright red jasper (p.113) throughout its mass. The name bloodstone is a reference to the blood-red spots that can be seen on polished and rough specimens. Sometimes the color spots are yellow, in which case the mineral is called plasma. Bloodstone is deposited as silica-rich waters at low temperatures (up to 400°F/200°C) percolate through cracks and fissures. The ancient source of bloodstone was the Kathiawar Peninsula of India. Brazil and Australia are the modern sources.

Picture jasper
The layering in this sandy-looking jasper sometimes gives the appearance of a desert scene.

"sandy" appearance

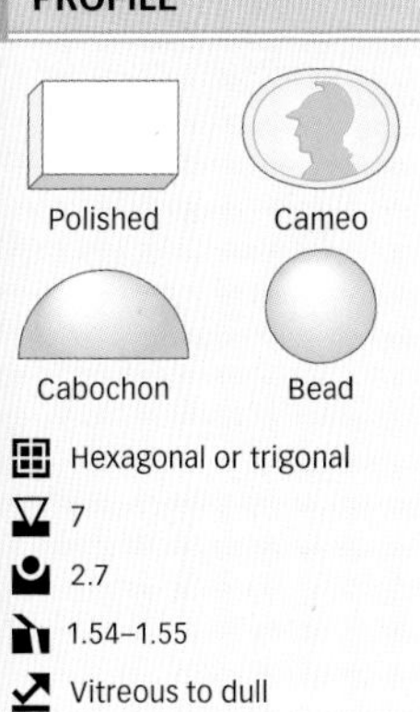

MOTTLED RED JASPER ROUGH

PROFILE

Polished | Cameo
Cabochon | Bead

- Hexagonal or trigonal
- 7
- 2.7
- 1.54–1.55
- Vitreous to dull

SiO_2

JASPER

A quartz mineral, jasper consists of a mass of minute, randomly arranged, interlocking quartz crystals. It has large amounts of impurities that impart opacity and color to it. Brick-red to brownish red jasper contains hematite (p.57), the presence of clay results in yellowish white or gray specimens, and goethite produces brown or yellow material. Jasper has been used in jewelry and for ornamentation since the Stone Age. The Babylonians considered it to be a symbol of childbirth. It is still widely used in jewelry, carvings, and as polished pieces.

The name jasper originates in the Greek name for the stone, *iaspis*, which in turn is probably of Semitic origin. Jasper often has local names based on its source or color, but only a few of these are recognized mineralogical names. It forms through deposition when silica-rich waters at low temperatures (up to 400°F/200°C) percolate through cracks and fissures in rocks. In the process, jasper picks up the impurities that give rise to its color. Jasper is found worldwide wherever cryptocrystalline quartz occurs.

PROFILE

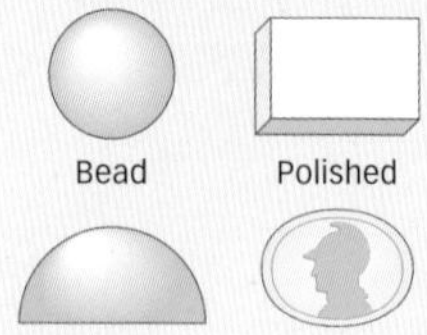

Bead | Polished | Cabochon | Cameo

Cubic
6½–7
3.6
1.69–1.73
Vitreous

lacelike pattern

MEXICAN LACE AGATE ROUGH

inclusions of other minerals

Moss agate cabochon
As in all moss agates, the "moss" in this oval cabochon is formed by inclusions of other minerals.

SiO_2

AGATE

A semiprecious chalcedony (p.109), agate is the compact, microcrystalline variety of quartz. Agate is generally characterized by concentric color bands in shades of white, yellow, gray, pale blue, brown, pink, red, or black, and less often by mosslike inclusions. Most agates form in cavities in ancient lavas or other extrusive igneous rocks, and the color bands usually follow the outline of the cavity in which the mineral formed.

The word agate is often preceded by other names that refer to the locality where the mineral is found or to a particular type of color or pattern. Fortification agate is a general term for agates with angularly arranged bands that resemble an aerial view of an ancient fortress. Brazilian agate is a fortification agate with banding in angled concentric circles like the fortifications of a castle. Mexican lace agate—sometimes called "crazy lace"—is a multicolored fortification agate with highly convoluted layering.

Moss agate is another variety of agate. It does not have bands and is commonly white or gray with brown, black, or green moss- or treelike inclusions of other minerals—mostly iron or manganese oxides or chlorite. Moss agate with brown inclusions is sometimes called mocha stone. Indian moss agate often has green, mosslike dendrites (treelike markings) in a near-transparent chalcedony. Sweetwater agate from the Sweetwater River area of Wyoming, USA, is known for its fine black dendrites.

IDAR-OBERSTEIN

Idar-Oberstein is a city in Rhineland, southwest Germany. Agates were abundant in this area for at least 700 years, and an agate-working industry was well established by 1548. The sandstone cutting and polishing wheels were driven by the motion of the local river.

Gem-polishing location
This engraving from 1650 shows Idar-Oberstein on the local river, which was the source of the power for its gem-polishing wheels.

Unusual cabochon
The "image" of a tree has formed naturally in this moss agate cabochon as a result of inclusions of oxide minerals.

Agate brooch
Scottish Montrose blue agate has been used to create the interlaced panels of this silver-set brooch.

Brown agate
The color of this circular agate cabochon is close to that of carnelian.

Agate cameo
Dating back to the 17th century, this three-layered agate cameo depicts the Roman god of wine.

Green moss agate rough
This specimen of moss agate has tendrils of green "moss"—probably chlorite—winding through it.

Chinese snuff bottle
This 19th-century agate snuff bottle has ornamentation that has been carved from an outer layer of carnelian.

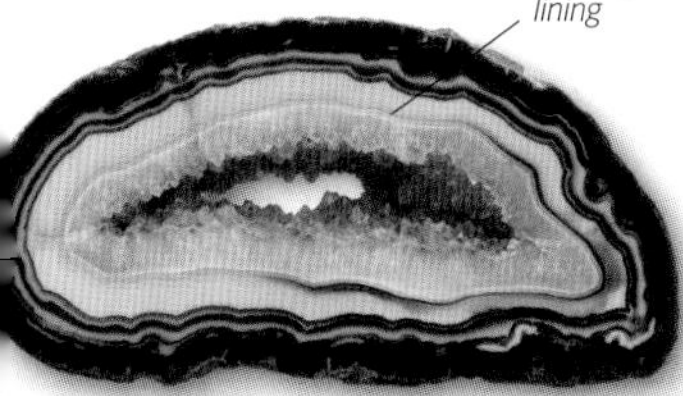

Dyed agate slice
Dark blue is not a naturally occurring color in agate. This agate slice with a lining of quartz crystals has been dyed blue.

PROFILE

Cabochon

Hexagonal or trigonal

7

2.7

1.54–1.55

Vitreous

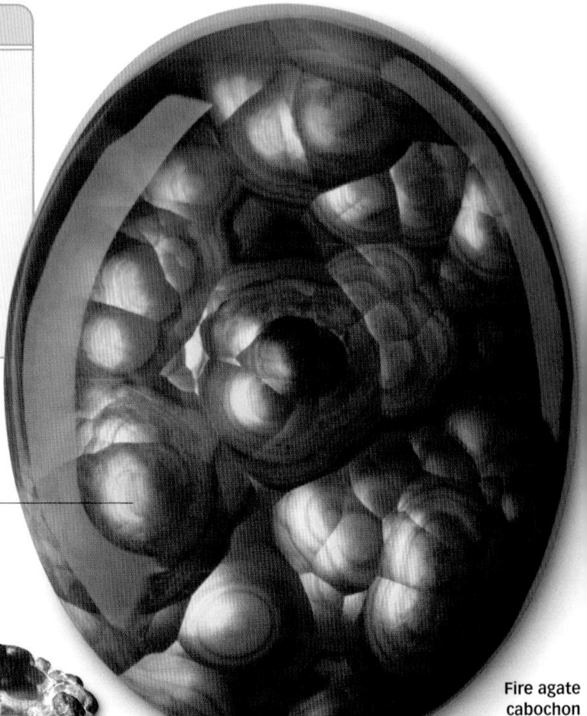

chalcedony "bubble"

weathered surface

ROUGH FIRE AGATE

Fire agate cabochon This fine-quality cabochon of Arizona fire agate shows well-developed bubbles of "fire."

VARIANT

Good "fire" A specimen of fire agate with unusually fine yellow and green "fire"

SiO_2

FIRE AGATE

This gem is an unusual occurrence of chalcedony (p.109), a variety of quartz. The base material is usually a brown to honey-colored botryoidal chalcedony—a chalcedony whose surface appears as a mass of grapelike bunches. These form in layers, and within some of the layers platelike crystals of iron oxides originally coated the surfaces. Later deposition of transparent chalcedony sealed these surfaces within the stone. It is these iridescent surfaces within the chalcedony that produce the "fire" in fire agate—the red, gold, green and, occasionally, blue-violet colors.

Fire agate gems are always cut *en cabochon* and seldom exceed 1 in (2.5 cm) across. Cutting fire agate is a meticulous process. It involves following the natural contours of the stone and removing only enough stone to reveal the "fire," but taking care not to cut through it. Fire agate is found only in certain areas of northern Mexico and southwestern USA.

PROFILE

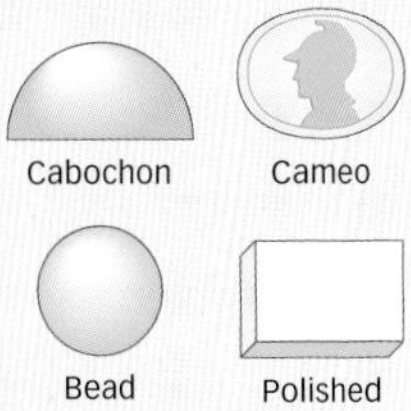

Cabochon Cameo

Bead Polished

Hexagonal or trigonal

7

2.7

1.54–1.55

Vitreous

characteristic straight banding

Onyx cabochon This cabochon has the alternate straight black and white bands typical of onyx.

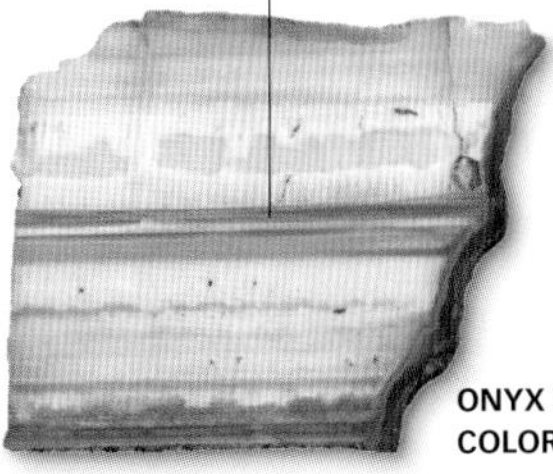

multiple layering

ONYX WITH LIGHT COLORED BANDS

VARIANT

Polished onyx A specimen of onyx with a polished face that reveals its banding

SiO_2

ONYX

The striped, semiprecious variety of chalcedony (p.109), onyx is usually characterized by alternating bands of black and white. The name onyx comes from the Greek word *onux*, which means "nail" or "claw"—a reference to the mineral's typical black and white color. However, onyx can also have white and red bands, as in carnelian onyx; or white and brown bands, as in sardonyx (p.118). As its layers can be cut to show a color contrast, onyx is popular for cameos and intaglios. Some of the most impressive ones were carved by the Romans in the 1st century CE.

Onyx forms through deposition when silica-rich waters at low temperatures (up to 400°F/ 200°C) percolate through cracks and fissures in rocks. Onyx is relatively uncommon in nature. Natural onyx comes from India and South America.

Onyx seal This Georgian seal has a finely shaped handle of attractively banded onyx.

PROFILE

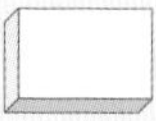

Polished
Cabochon 
Cameo 

Hexagonal or trigonal
7
2.6
1.54–1.55
Vitreous

Stunning cameo This sardonyx cameo, exhibiting remarkable detail and finish, is cut to the very highest standard of hardstone engraving.

layer of sard

intricate carving

vitreous lustre

sard

chalcedony

LAYERED SARDONYX ROUGH

VARIANTS

Circular cabochon A circular, flat-topped specimen of sardonyx, cut *en cabochon*

Oval cabochon A reddish, carnelian-like, oval cabochon of sard

SiO_2

SARD AND SARDONYX

Used since ancient times for making cameos and intaglios, both sard and sardonyx are among the earliest gemstones used by man. Sard is named after Sardis, the Greek capital of ancient Lydia, but it was used much earlier as a gemstone by the Harappans, Mycenaeans, and Assyrians. Wearing sard jewelry has always had mystical or medical connotations, and it was believed to protect against sorcery.

Sard is a light to dark brown to brownish red chalcedony (p.109), while bands of sard and white chalcedony are called sardonyx. Both are cut *en cabochon*, but sardonyx is especially popular for cameos. Both are also often artificially treated to enhance or even change their colour. Ratnapura in Sri Lanka is a famous source of sard. Other sources include Uruguay, India, and Brazil.

Victorian ring This 19th-century Victorian gold ring is set with a beautiful stone of sard.

Green opal cabochon
This high-domed cabochon has been cut from translucent green opal, one of the many colors of common opal.

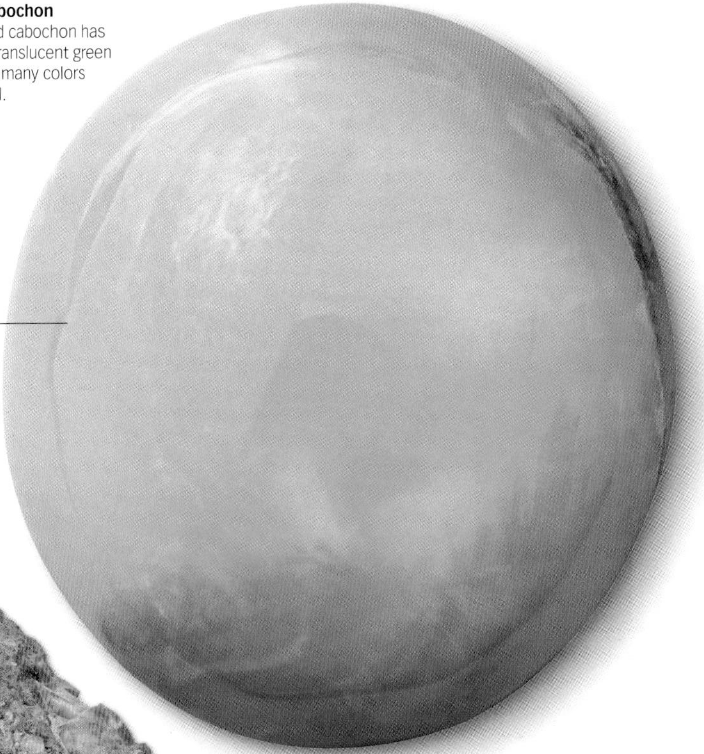

translucent cabochon

broken surface

PINK OPAL ROUGH

PROFILE

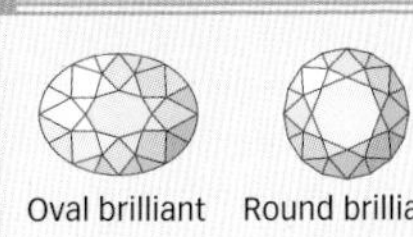

Oval brilliant Round brilliant

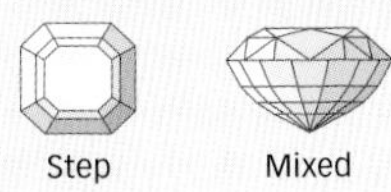

Step Mixed

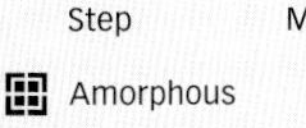

Amorphous

5–6

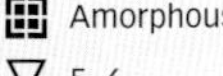

1.9–2.3

1.37–1.47

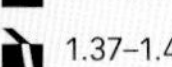

Vitreous

$SiO_2 \cdot nH_2O$

COMMON OPAL

As the name suggests, common opal is the most widespread form of opal. It occurs in a number of sedimentary rock types and is also found filling hollow spaces in silica-rich igneous rocks. However, the term common implies more than abundance: it refers to opal that, unlike precious opal (p.120), exhibits no color play, and, unlike fire opal (p.121), it shows no transparency. The internal structure of common opal is less ordered than the other forms: precious opal has a highly ordered internal structure, in which microscopic quartz spheres diffract light; fire opal's structure is moderately ordered, but the spheres may not be of the correct size to produce diffraction.

Common opal is found in virtually all colors: white, gray, red, orange, yellow, green, blue, magenta, rose, pink, slate, olive, brown, and black. Potch opal is common opal that has a milky, turbid appearance. This does not, however, make it valueless—opaque opal in a number of colors is cut *en cabochon* and mounted in jewelry.

PROFILE

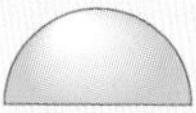

Cabochon

Amorphous
5–6
1.9–2.3
1.37–1.47
Vitreous

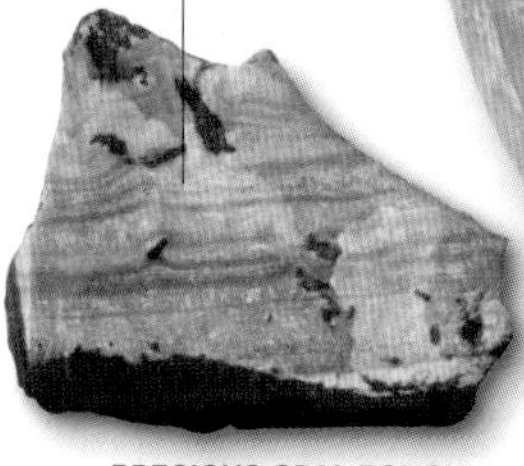

iron oxides

layering of "fire"

PRECIOUS OPAL ROUGH

Boulder opal
This fine specimen of boulder opal is from Yowah field in Queensland, Australia.

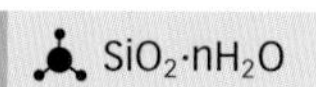

$SiO_2 \cdot nH_2O$

PRECIOUS OPAL

Known since antiquity, opal derives its name from the Roman word *opalus*, which means "precious stone." In the Middle Ages, opal was considered a lucky stone. In 1829, Sir Walter Scott published the novel *Anne of Geierstein, or The Maiden of the Mist*, in which the protagonist owns a magical opal talisman that causes the death of its owner when it accidentally comes into contact with holy water. Within a year of its publication, the sales of opal plummeted in Europe. Many still consider the stone unlucky.

Opal is hardened silica gel and usually contains 5 to 10 percent water in submicroscopic pores. Precious opal consists of a regular arrangement of tiny silica spheres. When the spheres are the correct size, they diffract light and give rise to color play. Precious opal can have a white, colorless, or very dark gray or blue-to-black base color. Cabochons are often capped with a harder stone, such as quartz, and are called opal doublets. Slices of precious opal sandwiched between two layers of quartz make opal triplets.

Opal is deposited at low temperatures (up to 400°F/200°C) from silica-bearing, circulating waters, most often in sedimentary rocks. In ancient times the primary source of precious opal was present-day Slovakia, but the chief producer of precious opal today is Australia. Fossil bones and seashells replaced by precious opal have been discovered in Australia.

COOBER PEDE

An Australian aboriginal phrase, "coober pede" means "white man's hole." It is the name of one of the world's most prolific opal fields. The largest cut stone from the mine weighs as much as 17,000 carats. The Coober Pede opal field is located in South Australia where, because of the heat, many miners live underground.

Coober Pede
Mounds of excavated material dot the landscape in the opal mining region of Coober Pede in South Australia.

Chocolate opal
This brown base opal from a recently discovered Ethiopian deposit is called "chocolate opal."

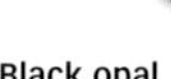

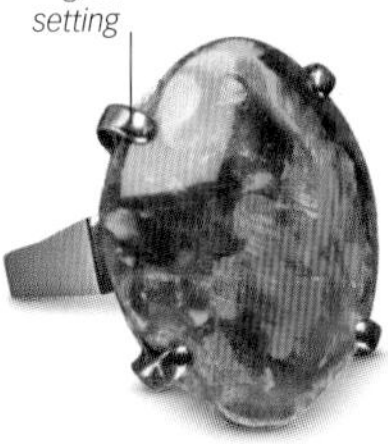

Black opal
The 26.9-carat black opal in this gold ring is from Lightning Ridge, Australia.

Opal necklace
This necklace by Louis Comfort Tiffany features black opals accented with rare, brilliant green demantoid garnets.

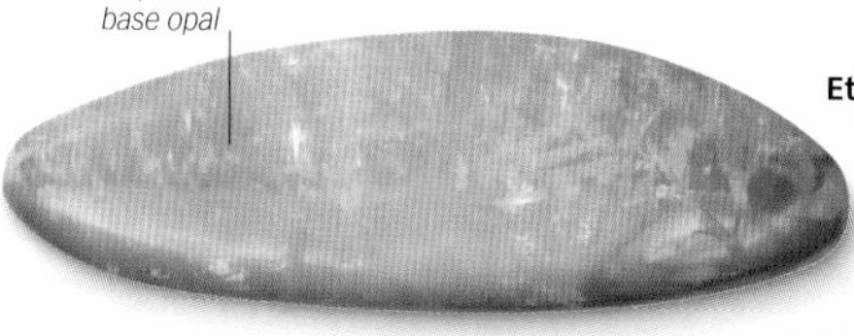

Ethiopian opal
This 3.26-carat crystal opal is from a relatively new opal find in Ethiopia.

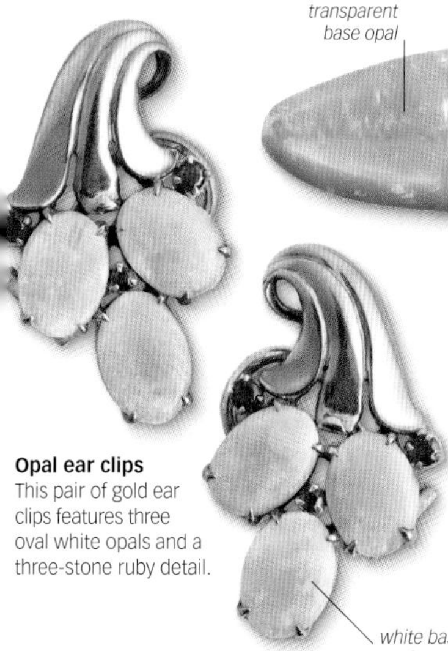

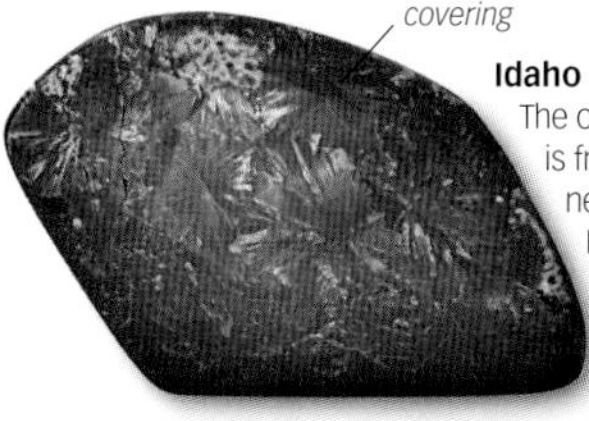

Idaho opal
The opal in this triplet is from a deposit near Spencer in Idaho, USA. It is 2 in (5.1 cm) long.

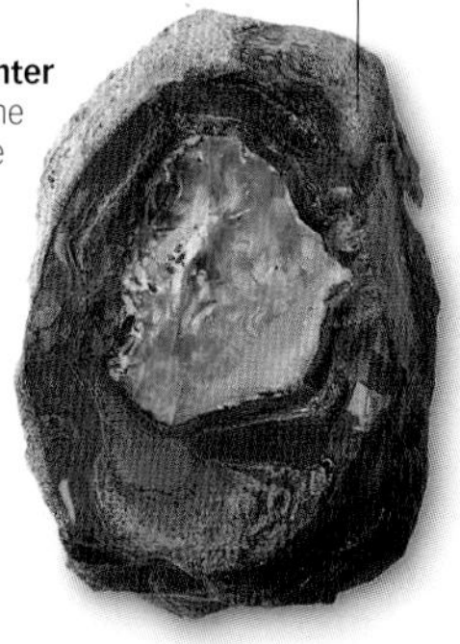

Opal ear clips
This pair of gold ear clips features three oval white opals and a three-stone ruby detail.

Opal center
The blue opal in the center of this ironstone concretion shows good color play.

White base opal
This white base opal has layers of yellow potch opal and shows color play.

Cushion-cut gem
This nearly transparent, orange fire opal has been faceted in a modified brilliant cushion cut.

star facet

vitreous luster

FIRE OPAL ROUGH

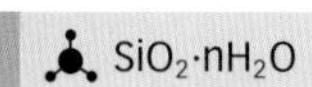

PROFILE

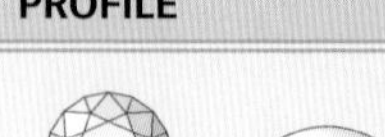

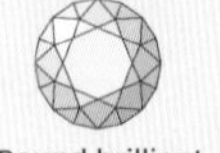

Round brilliant 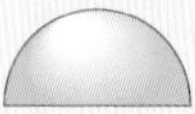 | Cabochon

 Amorphous

 5–6

 1.9–2.3

 1.37–1.47

Vitreous

$SiO_2 \cdot nH_2O$

FIRE OPAL

Like precious and common opal (pp.119–21), fire opal is hardened silica gel and usually contains 5 to 10 percent water in submicroscopic pores. A transparent to translucent variety of opal, fire opal usually does not exhibit color play—unlike precious opal. For this reason, it is sometimes called jelly opal. However, a few Mexican stones show a bright green flash. Fire opals are prized for their rich colors, such as yellow, orange, orange-yellow, and red. Transparent specimens are usually faceted and are often set into silver jewelry.

Fire opal is found in sedimentary rocks such as sandstone and ironstone. In Mexico, a prime source of fire opal, it is found filling cavities in rhyolite. Fire opals from Mexico are sometimes sold as Mexican fire opals. Mexican opals are sometimes cut *en cabochon* with the opal resting in the center of its rhyolite host. Colorless Mexican water opal exhibits either a bluish or a golden internal sheen when cut.

PROFILE

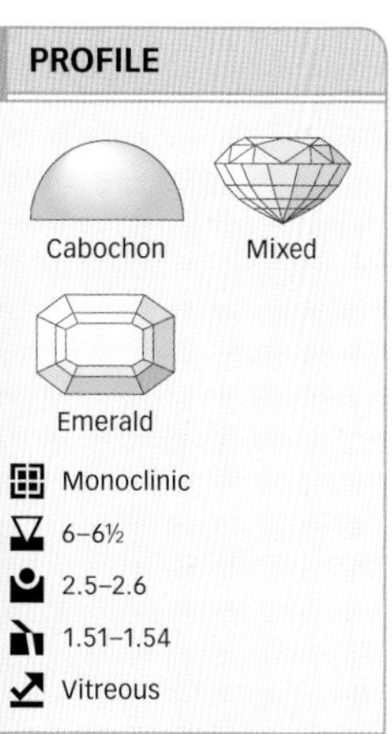

Monoclinic

6–6½

2.5–2.6

1.51–1.54

Vitreous

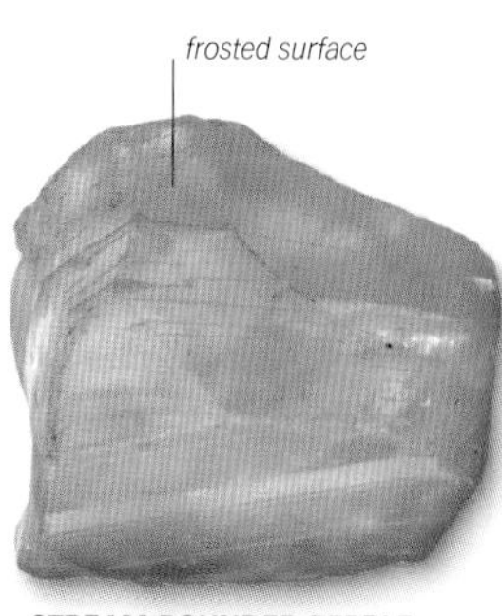

STREAM-ROUNDED PEBBLE OF ORTHOCLASE

Brittle stone The corners of this typical yellow orthoclase specimen are cut at an angle due to the brittleness of the stone.

VARIANTS

Brilliant cushion cut A colorless, faceted orthoclase with slight moonstonelike sheen

Yellow stone An emerald-cut, bright yellow orthoclase with good color and clarity

$KAlSi_3O_8$

ORTHOCLASE

One of several alkali (or potassium) feldspars, orthoclase is an important rock-forming mineral that also yields gemstones. It derives its name from the Greek words *orthos* and *klassis*, which mean "straight" and "fracture" respectively—a reference to its perpendicular planes of breakage. Transparent yellow and colorless orthoclase is faceted for collectors. Some yellow and white specimens are occasionally cut *en cabochon* to produce a cat's eye effect. A variety of orthoclase that exhibits a schiller effect is called moonstone (p.129).

Orthoclase is a major component of granite—its crystals give common granite its characteristic pink or white color. The largest documented crystal of orthoclase was found in the Ural Mountains, Russia, and weighed about 112 tons (102 tonnes). Gem-quality star orthoclase is found in the gem gravels of Sri Lanka and Myanmar. Other gem material is found in Madagascar and Germany. The Madagascar orthoclase and much of the sunstone (p.128) variety of the mineral occur in pegmatites.

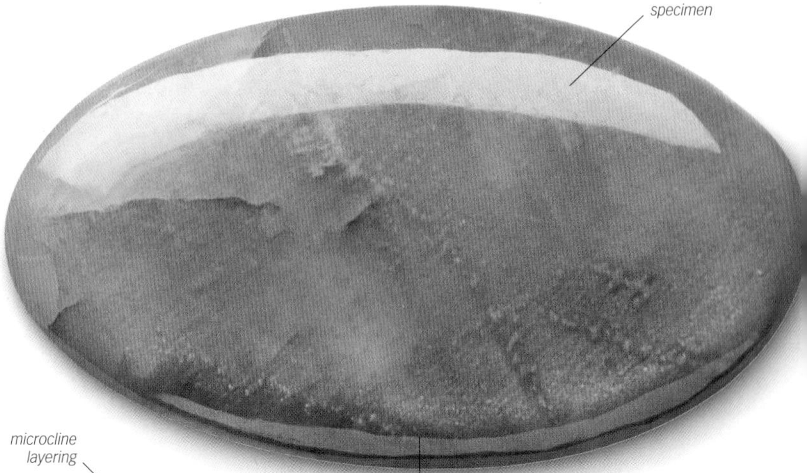

translucent specimen

microcline layering

blue-green color

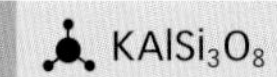

UNCUT AMAZONITE CRYSTAL SHOWING PINK MICROCLINE

Oval cabochon
Amazonite is the main gemstone variety of microcline. This oval cabochon of amazonite has unusually fine translucence.

PROFILE

Polished | Cabochon

- Triclinic
- 6–6½
- 2.6
- 1.50
- Vitreous, dull

$KAlSi_3O_8$

MICROCLINE

A common feldspar, microcline is a colorless, white, cream to pale yellow, salmon-pink to red, or bright green to blue-green mineral. The bright green variety of microcline is called amazonite or amazonstone, and is prized as a gemstone. Although deep blue-green is the most sought-after color, amazonite varies from yellow-green to blue-green and may also exhibit fine white streaks. Specimens are usually opaque and, as such, cut *en cabochon*. Being relatively brittle, amazonite is rarely used for carvings or beads.

Amazonite crystals often have two sets of fine lines set at right angles to each other, an effect called cross-hatch twinning that creates a "plaid" effect. This distinguishes them from other feldspars and from green jade. Single crystals from granite pegmatites can weigh several tons and be tens of yards long. Although named after the Amazon River, no deposits of amazonite have been found there. The Pikes Peak district of Colorado, USA, is the prime source of amazonite.

good transparency

complex faceting

vitreous to pearly luster

multiple crystals

TYPICALLY OPAQUE ALBITE CRYSTALS

Faceted oval gem
This albite gem is colorless and transparent, and faceted in a complex, brilliant oval form.

PROFILE

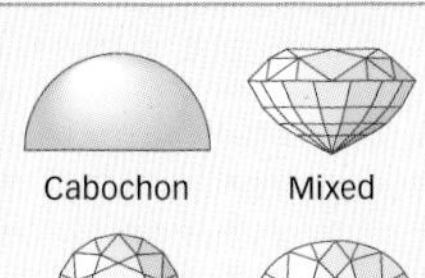

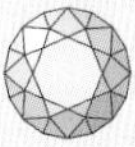

Round brilliant 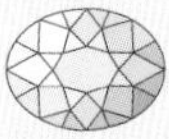 Oval brilliant

 Triclinic

 6–6½

2.6

 1.54–1.55

Vitreous to pearly

$NaAlSi_3O_8$

ALBITE

A sodium aluminosilicate, albite is one of six types of plagioclase feldspar. It is named after the Latin word *albus*, which means "white"—a reference to the usual color of albite. Specimens can also be colorless, yellowish, pink, or green. Albite is sometimes found as well-formed, glassy crystals. Because it is relatively soft and brittle, albite is faceted exclusively for collectors. An intergrowth of albite and oligoclase, called peristerite (p.127), produces a bluish, moonstonelike sheen when cut *en cabochon*.

Albite is an important rock-forming mineral. It occurs widely in pegmatites and in most feldspar- and quartz-rich igneous rocks. The best peristerite is from Canada, with facet-grade material coming from Brazil and Norway. Lesser amounts come from a number of localities worldwide.

pavilion facets visible through table cut

broken surface

MASSIVE BYTOWNITE ROUGH

Step-cut bytownite
This uncommonly transparent bytownite is faceted in an unusual step-cut square cushion.

PROFILE

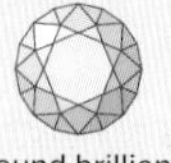

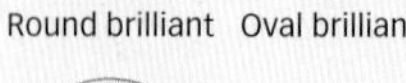

Round brilliant Oval brilliant

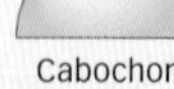

Cabochon

Triclinic

6–6½

2.7

1.57–1.59

Vitreous to pearly

$NaAlSi_3O_8–CaAl_2Si_2O_8$

BYTOWNITE

The rarest of the plagioclases, bytownite is a calcium-rich sodium and calcium aluminosilicate. Well-developed crystals of bytownite are uncommon, but when found they are short prismatic to tabular. Crystals are mostly gray to white. Transparent specimens varying in color from pale straw yellow to light brown are usually faceted.

Bytownite is named after Bytown (now Ottawa), Canada—the locality where it was first recognized. It occurs in igneous rocks with medium to low silica content as part of the structure of the rock itself. Gem-quality material is found at Nueva Casas Grandes in the state of Chihuahua, Mexico, and Lakeview, Oregon, USA. Other localities include Rhum Island, Scotland; Fiskenaesset, Greenland; Chester and Lebanon counties, Pennsylvania, USA; and Ottawa, Canada. A Mexican variety has been marketed under the name Golden sunstone, but it is different from the gemstone varieties of sunstone (p.128), which are other forms of plagioclase or orthoclase (p.122).

play of color

natural inclusions

iridescent surface

vitreous luster

IRIDESCENT LABRADORITE ROUGH

Translucent labradorite
This cabochon cut from highly translucent labradorite shows the shimmering blue iridescence at the top of its dome.

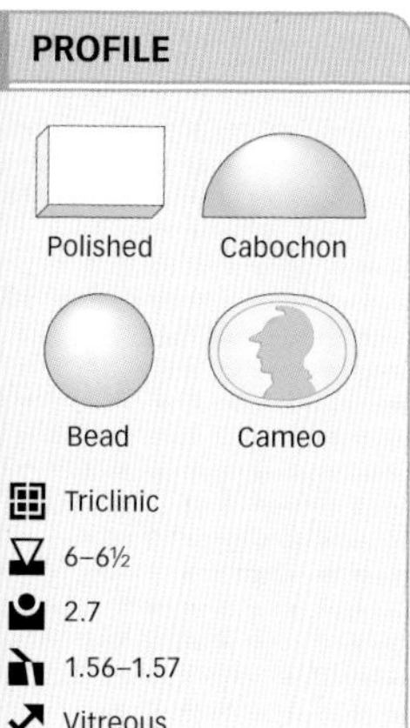

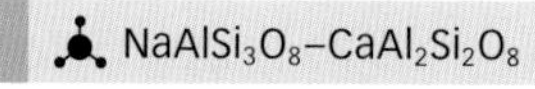
$NaAlSi_3O_8–CaAl_2Si_2O_8$

LABRADORITE

A middle-range member of the plagioclase feldspars, labradorite is a calcium-rich mineral. It is characterized by and valued for its schiller effect—a rich play of iridescent colors, mainly blue, on cleavage surfaces. This effect is caused by the scattering of light from alternating thin layers of calcium- and sodium- rich feldspar that develop as the mineral cools. The base color is generally blue or dark gray but can also be colorless or white. It can also be transparent and can then be yellow, orange, red, or green. Iridescent labradorite is either cut *en cabochon* or carved, and transparent material is faceted for collectors.

Well-formed crystals of labradorite are rare. It mostly occurs in crystalline masses that can be up to 3ft (1m) or more wide. Iridescent material is mainly found in ancient crystalline rocks that formed deep in Earth's crust.

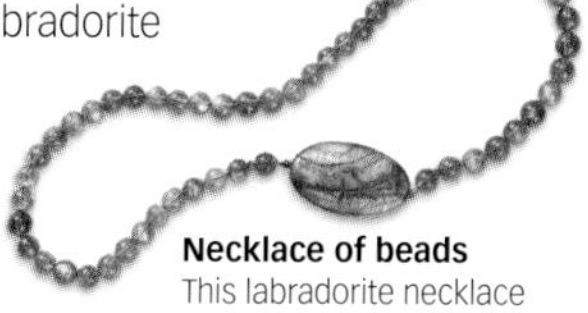

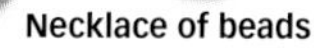

Necklace of beads
This labradorite necklace has a finely matched set of near-transparent beads and a cabochon clasp.

internal hematite flakes

Marquise-cut sunstone
This orthoclase sunstone, faceted in an unusual marquise cut, shows the platy inclusions that give it its sparkle.

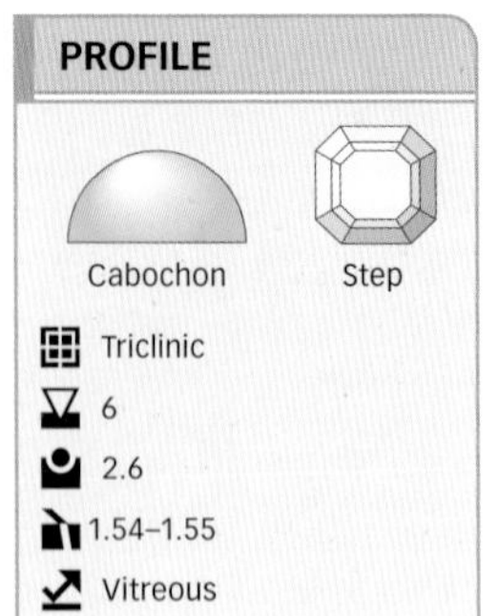

UNCUT OLIGOCLASE SUNSTONE SHOWING PLATY INCLUSIONS

PROFILE

Cabochon | Step

Triclinic

6

2.6

1.54–1.55

Vitreous

$(Na,Ca)Al_2Si_2O_8$

SUNSTONE

Two feldspar minerals—oligoclase and orthoclase—produce the gems known as sunstone. Oligoclase is a plagioclase feldspar and orthoclase is an alkali feldspar. Other plagioclases, such as albite (p.124) and labradorite (p.126), also produce sunstone in small quantities. Sunstone is sometimes called aventurine feldspar. It is characterized by minute, platelike inclusions of iron oxide (hematite, p.57; goethite; or copper) oriented parallel to one another. This gives it a spangled appearance and often a reddish glow. Sunstone is usually cut *en cabochon*, but transparent orange oligoclase can be faceted and sold as sunstone.

Oligoclase occurs in silica-rich igneous rocks and in some metamorphic rocks. Oligoclase sunstone is found in Oregon and other places in the USA. It also comes from Norway, India, Canada, and Russia.

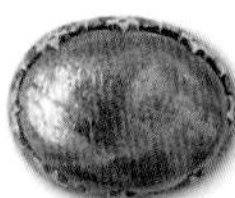

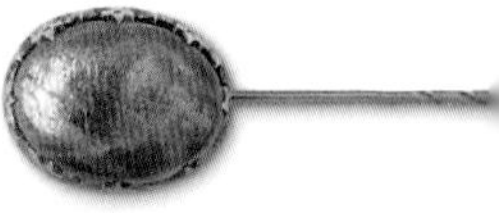

Gold pin
This Edwardian gold pin set with an oligoclase sunstone cabochon shows off the gemstone's internal sparkles.

PROFILE

Cabochon  Cameo

Monoclinic

6–6½

2.5–5.6

1.54

Vitreous

frosted surface

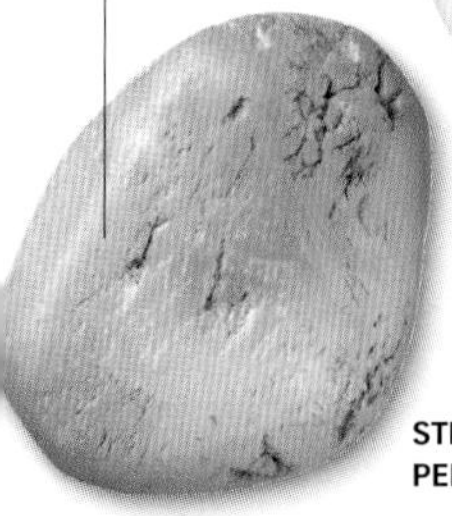

STREAM-ROUNDED PEBBLE OF MOONSTONE

intricate carving

Cameo cut
This cameo-carved portrait of a lady in moonstone shows a distinct blue sheen, called schiller.

VARIANTS

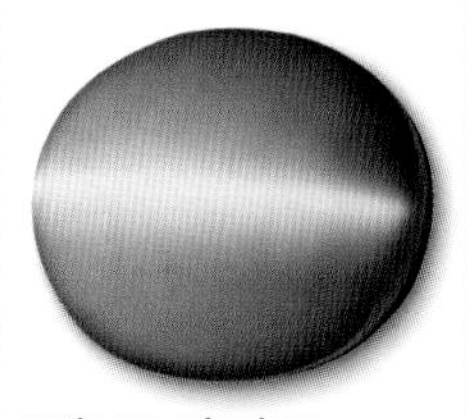

Cat's eye cabochon
A moonstone specimen showing a cat's eye effect

Orthoclase cabochon
An orthoclase moonstone cut *en cabochon*

$KAlSi_3O_8$

MOONSTONE

A variety of orthoclase and other feldspars, moonstone has a blue or white sheen or schiller—a result of the microscopic interlayering of orthoclase (p.122) with albite (p.124). When light is diffracted by these minute intergrowths, a soft schiller or bright iridescence may be seen. Moonstone is mainly cut *en cabochon* to emphasize its full sheen, but it is also carved and cut as cameos, which bring out its ethereal glow. The French goldsmith René Lalique and others of the Art Nouveau movement created moonstone jewelry toward the turn of the 19th century.

Ancient Greeks and Romans linked moonstone to their lunar deities. The Romans believed that it formed from the solidified rays of the Moon. Indians once believed that a moonstone placed in the mouth during a full moon would foretell the future for lovers.

Ornate brooch
A fine moonstone cabochon is surrounded by enameled leaves in this silver brooch.

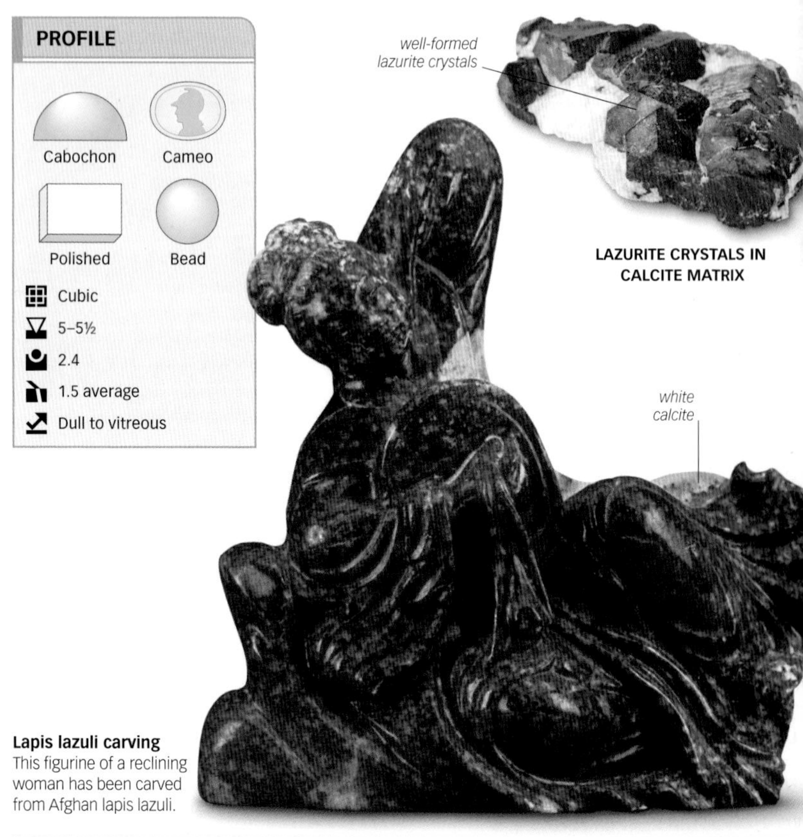

Lapis lazuli carving
This figurine of a reclining woman has been carved from Afghan lapis lazuli.

$Na_3Ca(Al_3Si_3O_{12})S$

LAZURITE AND LAPIS LAZULI

Lapis lazuli objects, such as scarabs, pendants, and beads, dating back to at least 3100 BCE, have been found in Egypt. The Egyptians also used powdered lapis lazuli as a pigment, medicine, and cosmetic (the first eye shadow). The Chinese and Greeks carved lapis as early as the 4th century BCE. At various times, it has been carved, fashioned as beads and cabochons, and used in inlays and mosaics.

The Roman term *sapphirus,* and other ancient references to "sapphire," probably referred to lapis lazuli. The modern name is derived from the Arabic word *lazaward*, which means "heaven" or "sky." The main component of lapis lazuli is the intense blue mineral lazurite, which accounts for its color. Lapis lazuli also contains pyrite (p.55) and calcite (p.76), and usually some sodalite (p.134) and haüyne (p.135). The best-quality lapis lazuli is intense dark blue, with minor patches of white calcite and brassy yellow pyrite.

Lapis lazuli is relatively rare and usually forms in crystalline limestones as a product of metamorphism. Mines in Afghanistan were an ancient source and remain a major source today. Some lapis is also found in Italy, Argentina, the USA, and Tajikistan. Lighter blue material is found in Chile.

Lazurite is a sodium calcium aluminosilicate sulfate. Distinct crystals of lazurite were considered very rare until large numbers were brought out of the mines of Badakhshan, Afghanistan, in the 1990s.

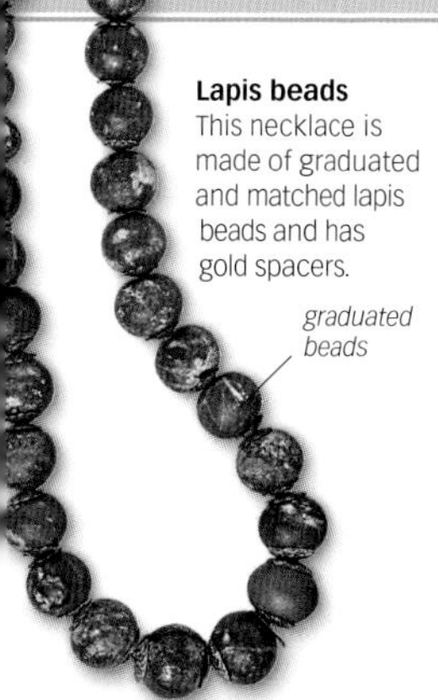

Lapis beads
This necklace is made of graduated and matched lapis beads and has gold spacers.

THE STANDARD OF UR

Dating back to 2600–2400 BCE, the Standard of Ur was found in the royal cemetery of Ur in present-day Iraq. Probably the sound box of a musical instrument, the "Standard" is 8.4 in (21.6 cm) high and 19.3 in (49.5 cm) long, with depictions in lapis, red limestone, and shell.

Detail of the Standard
In this detail, a musician plays a bull-headed harp.

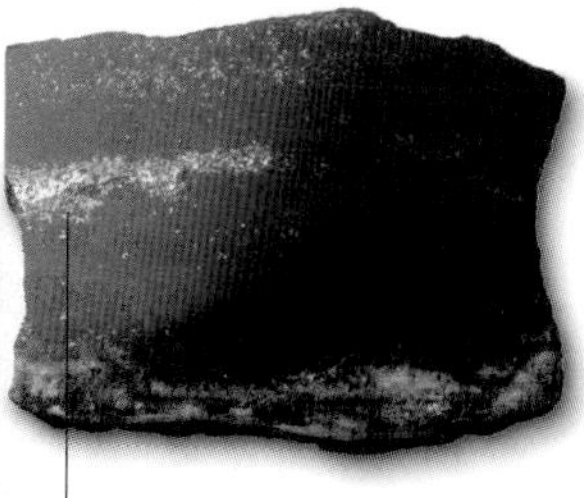

pyrite flecking

Lapis slice
This polished slice of lapis lazuli shows characteristic and desirable pyrite flecking.

carnelian finial

calcite veining

Low-grade lapis
Even lapis with less intense color, such as this cabochon of Afghan material, has a pleasing pale blue hue.

white calcite

Powdered lapis
Powdered lapis lazuli was once used as a pigment.

Lapis lazuli vase
This lapis lazuli and gold vase is on display at the Museo Degli Argenti in Florence, Italy. It is 3¼ in (8.3 cm) tall.

the best lapis takes a high polish

Afghan lapis lazuli
This carving made of Afghan lapis lazuli features an adult and two infant tortoises.

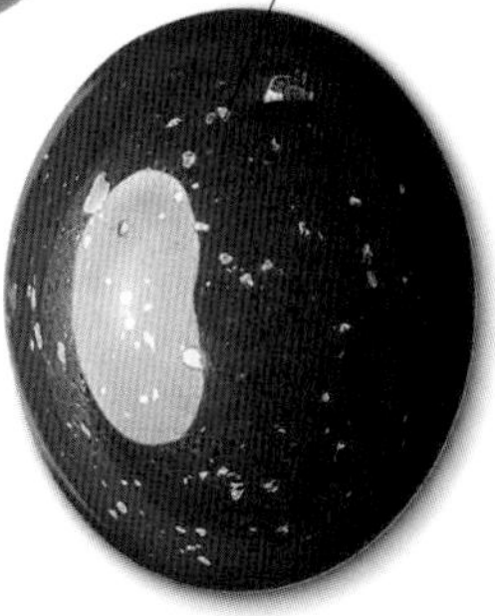

simulated pyrite flecking

Imitation lapis
This bright blue imitation lapis lazuli gemstone has golden flecks.

ANCIENT GEM MINING

For as long as people have been adorning themselves with gems, mines have been excavated for gemstones. At first it involved just picking up pretty pebbles, but within a short time—about 6,000 years ago—mining from gravels and rocks was underway.

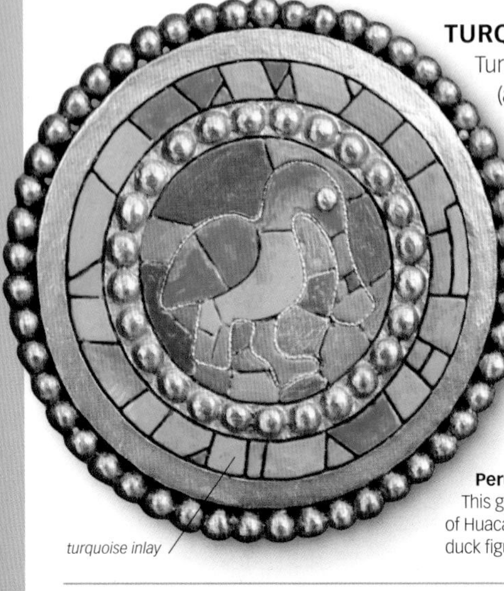

TURQUOISE

Turquoise has been highly prized in Iran (ancient Persia) since antiquity. It was found in the mines of Neyshabur, in the Khorasan region of Iran. Widely traded, it was in use in the Indus Valley Civilization of India as far back as the 2nd millennium BCE. Turquoise was found in Egypt during the same period at Wadi Hamamat, Tura, Aswan, and various other Nubian sites. Native Americans have worked deposits in the southwestern USA since 1000 CE.

Peruvian ear spool
This gold-beaded earspool from the Site Museum of Huaca Rajada, Lambayeque, Peru, has a spoonbill duck figure and a border of turquoise inlay.

DIAMOND

Diamonds are believed to have been first recognized and mined in India, where they have been known for at least 3,000 years, possibly even more. Golconda was the world center of the diamond trade at the time. The mines in the immediate vicinity of Golconda were themselves not very productive, but mines in the area around Golconda—in the modern-day districts of Guntur and Krishna—were highly productive. A number of large and famous diamonds were found in the region. Until diamonds were discovered in Brazil in 1725, India was the only known source of diamonds.

Golconda Fort
The Golconda fort was a stronghold for the diamond trade. It is thought that the Koh-i-noor and the Hope Diamond were once stored here.

LAPIS LAZULI

Afghanistan was the source of lapis lazuli for the ancient Egyptian and Mesopotamian civilizations. It was mined in Badakhshan province as early as the 3rd millennium BCE. In about 2000 BCE, the Harappans of the Indus Valley established a colony around the mines to exploit them. The same mines supplied lapis lazuli to the ancient Greeks and Romans more than a thousand years later.

Sar-e-sang mine
Miners empty rubble from an entrance to Sar-e-sang, a lapis lazuli mine in the mountains above Madan, Afghanistan, in May 2001.

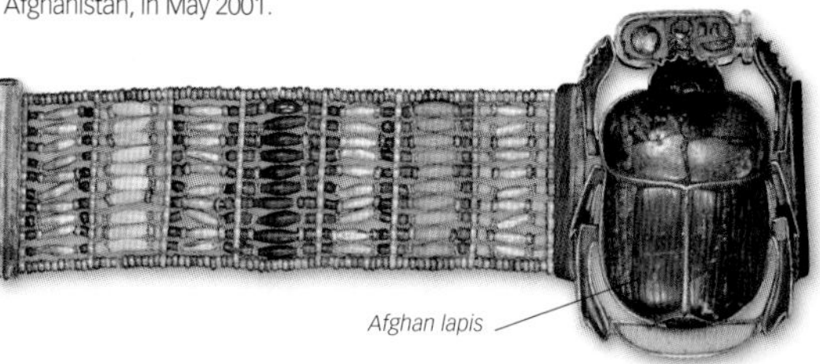

Egyptian bracelet
This gold and beaded bracelet from the tomb of Tutankhamen features a scarab made from Afghan lapis lazuli and a turquoise inlay at the bottom.

JADE

Nephrite jade was mined in China as early as 6000 BCE, where it was found as stream-rounded pebbles and quarried. In Mesoamerica, jadeite was mined from a single source located in the Motagua River valley, Guatemala, which supplied the Mayas and Aztecs. The Maoris of New Zealand used nephrite for tools, weapons, and ornaments.

Chinese comb
This comb, decorated with a feline figure, is made of nephrite jade and dates back to the late Shang Dynasty (11th–10th century BCE). It is an example of classic early jade work.

EMERALD

As early as 1300 BCE, emeralds were being mined in Upper Egypt at Jabal Sukayt and Jabal Zabgrah near the Red Sea coast. Most emeralds used in ancient jewelry came from these mines, which, after the conquest of Egypt by Alexander the Great, became known as "Cleopatra's Mines." Another ancient source was Habachtal in Austria.

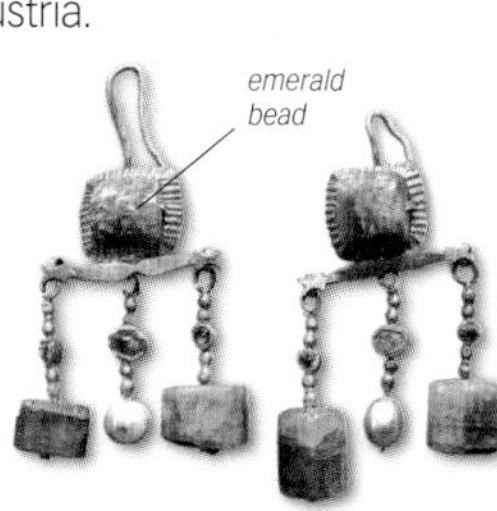

Roman earrings
These gold-and-emerald earrings dating back to the 3rd–4th century CE were discovered near Lyon in modern France.

Cleopatra's Mines
A modern Ababda tribesman sits by the temple entrance at Cleopatra's Mines in Wadi El Gemal National Park, Red Sea, Egypt.

PROFILE

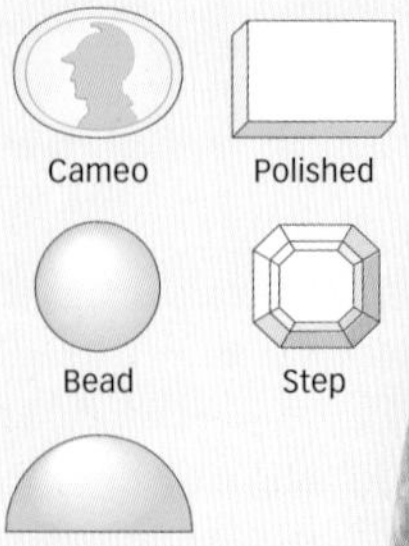

Cameo
Polished
Bead
Step
Cabochon

Cubic
5½–6
2.1–2.3
1.45
Vitreous to greasy

Intermixture of colors This cabochon of sodalite shows the intermixture of blue and white that is characteristic of this mineral.

mottling due to other minerals

white calcite

fractured surface

BROKEN PIECE OF SODALITE ROUGH

VARIANT

Rose-cut sodalite A rose-cut specimen of unusual blue and solid-color sodalite

$Na_4Al_3Si_3O_{12}Cl$

SODALITE

Named for its high sodium content, sodalite is a sodium aluminum silicate chloride. Rarely found as crystals, it usually forms massive aggregates or disseminated grains. Single specimens can weigh several pounds. Sodalite is sometimes veined with calcite—this material is favored by some carvers for the interesting patterns it creates. Mainly used as a gemstone, most sodalite is cut into cabochons or beads. Rare transparent material from Mont Saint-Hilaire, Canada, has been faceted for collectors.

A blue mineral, sodalite is sometimes mistaken for lapis lazuli (pp.130–31). However, it can be distinguished by its color, which is a less intense blue than lapis. Sodalite is also less dense and chemically different. Unlike some lapis, it does not contain pyrite crystals. However, it can be one of the constituents of lapis lazuli. Massive sodalite is found in the Kola Peninsula, Russia; Eifel, Germany; Rajasthan, India; Ontario, Canada; and Maine, Arkansas, and New Hampshire in the USA.

Brilliant-cut haüyne
Haüyne is a very fragile gem and is rarely found as crystals that are large enough to be cut. This brilliant-cut oval specimen shows areas of excellent clarity.

internal flaws

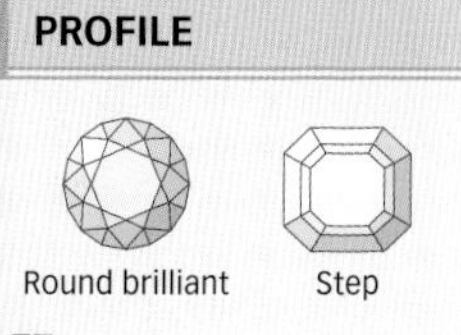

SMALL, GEM-QUALITY CRYSTALS OF HAÜYNE

PROFILE

Round brilliant | Step

Cubic
5½–6
2.5
1.49–1.51
Vitreous to greasy

$Na_3Ca(Al_3Si_3O_{12})(SO_4)$

HAÜYNE

A feldspathoid mineral, haüyne is named after one of the pioneers of crystallography, the French mineralogist René Just Haüy. It can be blue, white, gray, yellow, green, or pink in color. It is usually found as small, rounded grains in volcanic rock. Haüyne crystals are octahedral or dodecahedral. Individual crystals are sometimes found and are faceted for collectors. Haüyne's perfect and easily set-off cleavage makes it one of the more difficult materials to facet. Faceted stones tend to weigh 5 carats or less.

Haüyne is a sodium calcium aluminosilicate that contains a sulfate radical. It is one of the components of lapis lazuli (pp.130–31), along with lazurite, calcite (p.76), pyrite (p.55), and sodalite (p.134). Haüyne is primarily found in silica-poor volcanic rocks, although it has also been found in a few metamorphic rocks. Its sources are Morocco, Germany, Italy, Serbia, Russia, China, and New York and Colorado in the USA.

PROFILE

Cabochon 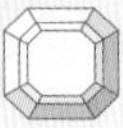 Step

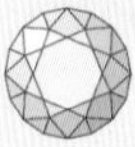

Round brilliant

Tetragonal

5–6

2.5– 2.7

1.53–1.60

Vitreous

multiple small facets

Oval mixed-cut gem
The many small facets of this highly transparent scapolite specimen bring out its brilliance.

scapolite crystal

SCAPOLITE CRYSTALS IN ROCK MATRIX

VARIANTS

Scapolite cabochon
A light purple, high-domed scapolite cabochon

Colorless scapolite
A bright and flawless mixed-cut scapolite

$Na_4(Al_3Si_9O_{24})Cl – Ca_4(Al_6Si_6O_{24})(CO_3SO_4)$

SCAPOLITE

A silicate mineral, scapolite can be colorless, white, yellow, orange, gray, pink, or purple. Specimens may exhibit chatoyancy, creating a cat's eye effect when cut *en cabochon*. Scapolite is distinctly pleochroic: violet stones appear dark or light blue and violet when viewed from different directions; yellow stones look pale yellow or colorless. Scapolite crystals can be up to 10 in (25 cm) long. Faceted stones are cut mainly for collectors and are usually colorless, yellowish, or lavender.

Originally believed to be a single mineral, scapolite is now defined as a compositional series with a calcium aluminosilicate at one end and a sodium aluminosilicate at the other end. Most gemstones are of a composition somewhere between the two. The name scapolite is still used in the gem trade to refer to any member of the scapolite group that is cut as a gemstone. Scapolites are mainly found in metamorphic rocks. Faceting material was first found in Myanmar, and large crystals occur in Quebec and Ontario, Canada; Tanzania; and New York, USA.

Transparent pollucite
Although perfectly transparent pollucite is uncommon, this pendaloque-cut specimen shows reasonable clarity for the gem.

BROKEN FRAGMENT OF POLLUCITE

PROFILE

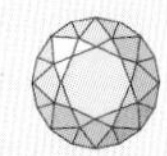 

Round brilliant Cabochon

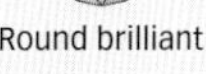

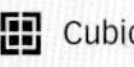 Cubic

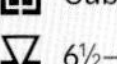 6½–7

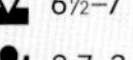 2.7–3.0

1.51

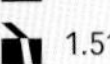 Vitreous to greasy

$(Cs,Na)(AlSi_2)O_6H_2O$

POLLUCITE

Pollucite is one of the two minerals discovered in 1846 and named after the Gemini twins—Pollux and Castor—of Greek mythology. The other mineral, castorite, was named after Castor, but is now called petalite (p.141). Pollucite is usually colorless or white, but can also be pink, blue, or violet. With a hardness of 6.5–7, it is not often used in jewellery.

A zeolite mineral, pollucite is a complex hydrous aluminosilicate containing cesium, sodium, rubidium, and lithium. It is only found in rare-earth-bearing granitic pegmatites, where it occurs with gem minerals such as spodumene, petalite, quartz, and apatite (p.88). A deposit at Bernic Lake, Canada, has an estimated 386,000 tons (350,000 tonnes) of mostly massive pollucite, accounting for more than 80 percent of the world's known reserves. Crystals up to 24 in (60 cm) wide have been found at Kamdeysh, Afghanistan, although facet-grade material is much smaller. Gem-quality pollucite is also found in Italy and the USA.

Serpentine cabochon
This round cabochon of serpentine shows the wide range of color variation and texture that this mineral can exhibit.

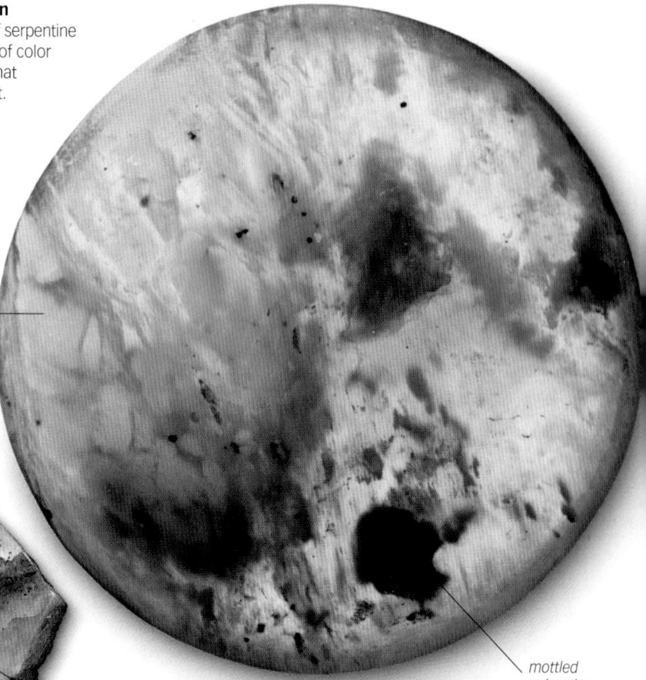

partly translucent cabochon

no cleavage

mottled coloration

greasy luster

GREEN SERPENTINE ROUGH

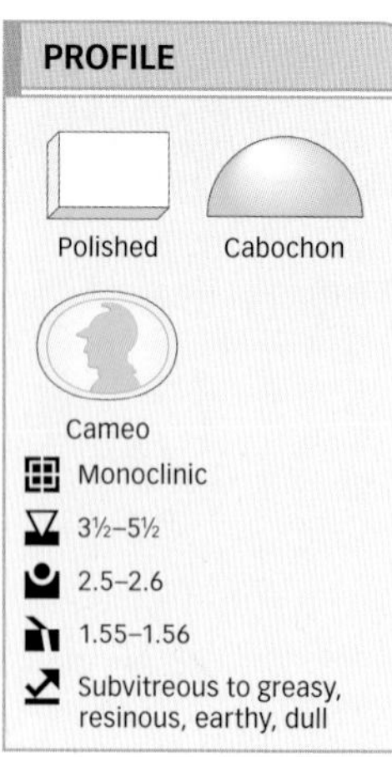

PROFILE

Polished Cabochon

Cameo

Monoclinic

3½–5½

2.5–2.6

1.55–1.56

Subvitreous to greasy, resinous, earthy, dull

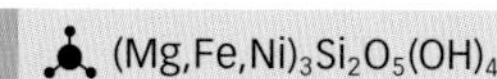

$(Mg,Fe,Ni)_3Si_2O_5(OH)_4$

SERPENTINE

Serpentine is a group of at least 16 white, yellowish, green, or gray-green magnesium silicate minerals with complex chemistries and similar appearances. There are four major serpentine materials: chrysotile, a fibrous material used as asbestos; antigorite, which occurs in corrugated plates or layers; lizardite, which is fine-grained and platy; and amesite, which occurs in platy or columnar crystals. Serpentine gets its name from the snakeskinlike appearance of some specimens.

Relatively soft and tough, serpentine is extensively used by gem cutters. Gem-quality serpentine, often with a jadelike appearance, is cut *en cabochon.* Soft enough to engrave, the mineral is also used to carve seals. Serpentines quarried as ornamental stones are sometimes called serpentine marble.

Bowenite serpentine
This intricately carved pendant is made from bowenite—a hard, compact variety of antigorite.

PROFILE

Cameo | Polished

- Triclinic or monoclinic
- 1
- 2.8
- 1.54–1.62
- Pearly to greasy

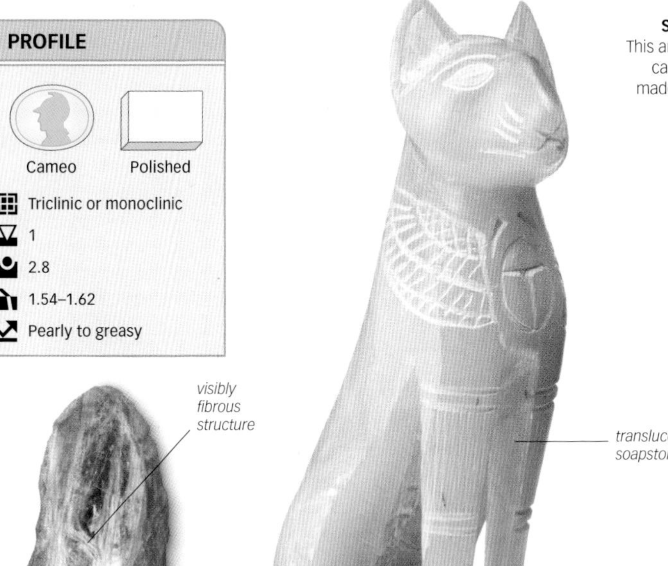

Soapstone cat This ancient Egyptian carving of a cat is made of soapstone.

FIBROUS SOAPSTONE ROUGH

VARIANT

Pink soapstone A carving of a rhinoceros in pink soapstone from Kenya

$Mg_3Si_4O_{10}(OH)_2$

SOAPSTONE (TALC)

The name soapstone is given to compact masses of talc and other minerals due to their soapy or greasy feel. Soapstone can be colorless, white, pink, pale to dark green, or yellowish to brown. Used since ancient times for carvings, ornaments, and utensils, it may also be humanity's oldest lapidary material other than flint. It has been carved into Assyrian cylinder seals and Egyptian scarabs dating back to the 2nd millennium BCE.

The most common soapstone is entirely or mainly talc, a hydrous magnesium silicate. Dense, high-purity talc called steatite is used by the Inuit people of Canada for sought-after carvings of birds and animals. Soapstone can be distinguished from jade and serpentine (p.138) by its extreme softness. Translucent, light green talc soapstone carvings are widely sold in China and are lacquered to improve their hardness and color. Talc is a metamorphic mineral found in veins, magnesium-rich rocks, and as an alteration product of silica-poor igneous rocks. Localities include China, Canada, and the USA.

PROFILE

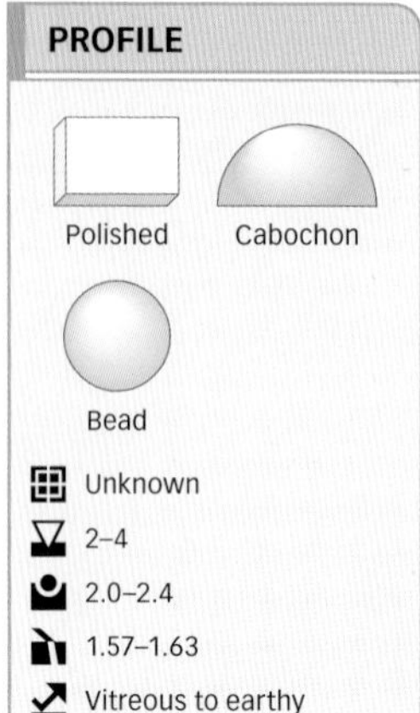

Unknown
2–4
2.0–2.4
1.57–1.63
Vitreous to earthy

ROUGH PIECE OF OPALIZED CHRYSOCOLLA

Chrysocolla cabochon
This rectangular-cut cabochon shows blue-green chrysocolla set into a matrix of a reddish copper ore.

VARIANTS

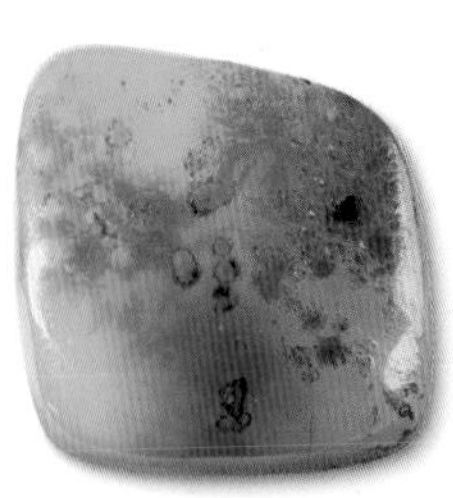

Opalized cabochon
A bright blue cabochon of opalized chrysocolla

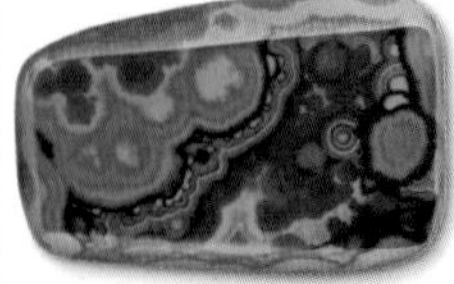

Chrysocolla in malachite
A cabochon with blue-green chrysocolla in malachite

$Cu_2H_2(Si_2O_5)(OH)_4 \cdot nH_2O$

CHRYSOCOLLA

An otherwise soft mineral, chrysocolla is frequently naturally intergrown with other minerals, such as quartz, chalcedony (p.109), or opal (p.119), to yield a harder and more resilient gemstone variety. In gemstone terminology, the word chrysocolla is applied to this intermixture rather than to the pure mineral. A copper aluminum silicate, chrysocolla is generally blue green in color. It is commonly very fine-grained and massive. Gemstone pieces can exceed 5 lb (2.3 kg) in weight.

Translucent, rich blue-green chrysocolla is highly prized as a gemstone. Chrysocolla intergrown with malachite (p.82) and turquoise (pp.86–87) from Israel is called Eilat stone and was reputedly a stone from King Solomon's mines. Eilat stone is almost exclusively cut as beads and cabochons.

Oval cabochon
This silver bracelet, crafted in the Native American style, features a rich, blue-green, oval chrysocolla cabochon.

PROFILE

Cabochon Mixed

Round brilliant Cushion

Monoclinic

6½

2.4

1.50–1.51

Vitreous

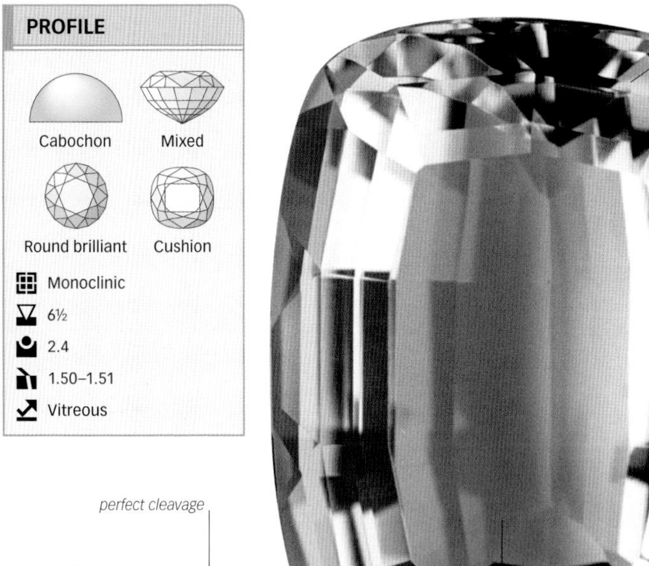

SEMITRANSPARENT GEM-QUALITY, PETALITE ROUGH

Step-cut petalite
This specimen of colorless petalite has been faceted in a cushion cut.

VARIANT

Triangular-cut petalite
A faceted gem with squared corners to prevent breakage

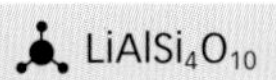

$LiAlSi_4O_{10}$

PETALITE

Formerly known as castorite, petalite is a lithium aluminum silicate. Its name comes from the Greek word for "leaf"—a reference to its perfect cleavage, which allows it to peel off in thin, leaflike layers. It is colorless to grayish white, and occasionally light pink, yellow, or green. Petalite is rarely found as individual crystals and commonly occurs as aggregates. Relatively rare, colorless, transparent material is sometimes faceted, but only for collectors as it is brittle and easily cleaved and requires extreme care while faceting. Because of this it is too fragile to be worn as jewelry. The massive form of petalite is cut *en cabochon*.

Petalite forms in granitic pegmatites along with albite (p.125), quartz, and lepidolite. Facet-grade petalite is found mainly in Brazil, yielding collectors' stones of up to 50 carats. It is also found in Canada, Sweden, Italy, Russia, Australia, Zimbabwe, and California and Maine, USA. The chemical element lithium was first discovered in petalite, and petalite is still an important ore of lithium.

intricate carving

weathered surface

RAW MEERSCHAUM

Carved beads
The meerchaum beads used in this necklace show the fine detail that can be achieved in carving this material.

PROFILE

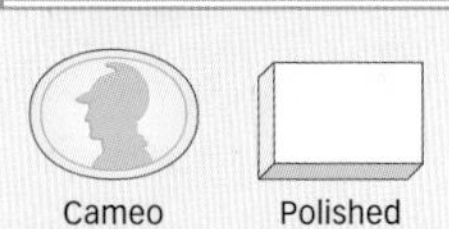

Cameo Polished

- Orthorhombic
- 2–2½
- 2.1–2.3
- Opaque
- Dull to earthy

$Mg_4Si_6O_{15}(OH)_2.6H_2O$

MEERSCHAUM

A variety of the mineral sepiolite, meerschaum is compact, earthy, and claylike, and can be porous. Meerschaum is usually found in nodules with interlocking fibers, which give it a toughness greater than that suggested by its mineralogical softness. It is soft when first extracted, but hardens on exposure to the sun or when dried in a warm room. It is usually white or gray, but it may be tinted yellow, brown, or green.

Meerschaum is considered the perfect material to make tobacco pipes, as it is porous and draws moisture and tobacco tar. Some art objects are also carved from it. The major source of meerschaum is Turkey, but it has banned its exports since the 1970s. Tanzania is the current alternative source.

Smoking pipe
Meerschaum is favored for carving smoking pipes, such as this one with an amber stem.

pavilion facets show through table facets

fine blue color

PHOSPHYLLITE ROUGH

Fine blue stone
This fine blue specimen of phosphophyllite, faceted in an emerald cut, shows excellent cutting and clarity.

PROFILE

Step
Monoclinic
3–3½
3.08
1.59–1.62
Vitreous

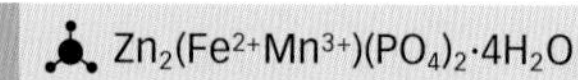

$Zn_2(Fe^{2+}Mn^{3+})(PO_4)_2 \cdot 4H_2O$

PHOSPHOPHYLLITE

A rare mineral and an even rarer gemstone, phosphophyllite is composed of hydrated zinc phosphate. Specimens can range from colorless to a deep bluish green, with delicate bluish green being the most sought-after color. Phosphophyllite gems are highly prized by museums and collectors. It is rare as a gemstone, partly because crystals large enough to be cut are too valuable to be broken up, and also because they are faceted only with the greatest difficulty due to their brittleness and fragility.

Phosphophyllite derives its name from its chemical composition (phosphate) and the Greek word for leaf, *phyllon*—a reference to its cleavage, or its tendency to readily break into thin plates. The finest crystals and the ones that provided most of the existing faceted stones originally came from Potosí, Bolivia, but that deposit is now exhausted. Current sources include New Hampshire, USA; Broken Hill, Australia; and Hagendorf, Germany.

PROFILE

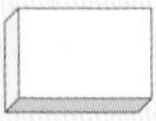

Polished Cabochon

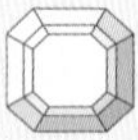

Step

Orthorhombic

6–6½

2.9

1.61–1.64

Vitreous

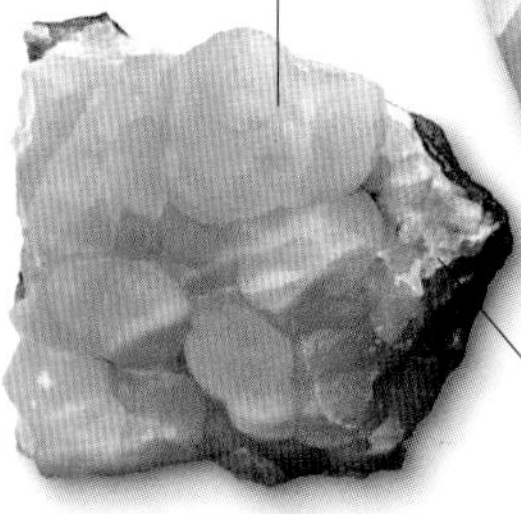

typical milkiness

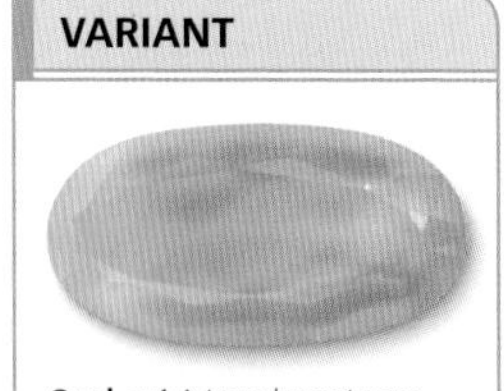

GRAPELIKE PREHNITE ON MATRIX

Good transparency Although milky compared to other faceted gems, this cushion-cut stone shows good transparency for prehnite.

VARIANT

Oval cut A translucent gem cut as an elongated oval

$Ca_2Al_2Si_3O_{10}(OH)_2$

PREHNITE

A calcium aluminum hydroxysilicate, prehnite is named after its discoverer, Hendrik von Prehn, a Dutch military officer. It is usually found as globular, spherical, or stalactitic aggregates of fine to coarse crystals, and rarely as individual crystals. Prehnite often has an oily luster and is usually pale to mid-green, but it can also be tan, pale yellow, gray, or white. Some of the pale yellowish brown fibrous material is cut *en cabochon* and shows a cat's-eye effect. Prehnite is occasionally faceted, but the stones are usually translucent rather than transparent. Faceted stones are cut exclusively for collectors and tend to be small.

Prehnite is often found lining cavities in volcanic rocks and in mineral veins in granite. Semitransparent material comes from Australia and Scotland, with the occasional near-transparent piece. Crystals several inches long come from Canada. Prehnite is also found in India, Pakistan, Portugal, Germany, Japan, and the USA. Cut green prehnite from South Africa has been marketed under the name Cape Emerald.

PROFILE

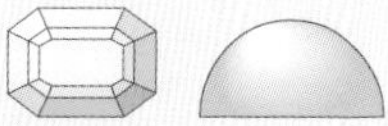

Emerald Cabochon

Orthorhombic

5–6

3.1–3.9

1.65–1.68

Vitreous

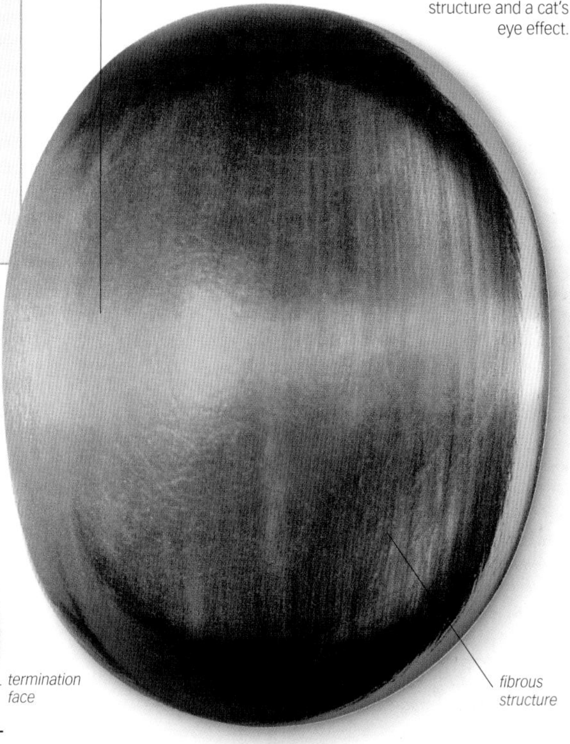

cat's eye effect

Cat's eye cabochon This high-domed cabochon of enstatite shows its fibrous structure and a cat's eye effect.

fibrous structure

prism face

termination face

ROUGH ENSTATITE CRYSTAL

VARIANT

Faceted stone An oval cut specimen with good clarity and color

$Mg_2Si_2O_6$

ENSTATITE

A common mineral in the pyroxene family, enstatite is a magnesium silicate. It is colorless, pale yellow, or pale green, and becomes darker with increasing iron content, turning greenish brown to black. Emerald-green enstatite, called chrome enstatite, is the most popular color, especially when it is cut as a gemstone. Enstatite owes its green color to traces of chromium. Although enstatite occurs in colors other than yellow and green, these are rare in gem-quality specimens. Gemstones are either faceted or cut *en cabochon*.

Enstatite takes its name from the Greek word *enstates*, which means "opponent"—a reference to its use as a refractory "opponent" of heat in the lining of ovens and kilns. It is a widespread mineral, commonly occurring in silica-deficient igneous rocks. Gem-quality star-enstatite comes from India and iridescent enstatite from Canada. Myanmar and Sri Lanka produce good-quality, facet-grade material, while Arizona, USA, is a source of enstatite for colorless, light green, and brown faceted stones.

PROFILE

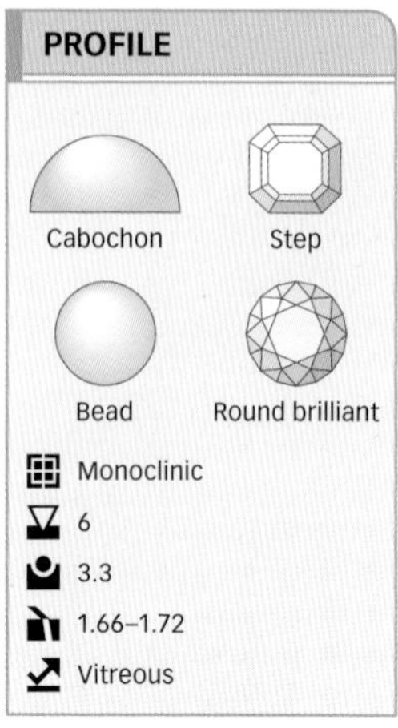

Monoclinic

6

3.3

1.66–1.72

Vitreous

DIOPSIDE CRYSTAL IN ROCK MATRIX

Chrome diopside
This emerald-cut specimen of chrome diopside is in the most desirable green color.

VARIANTS

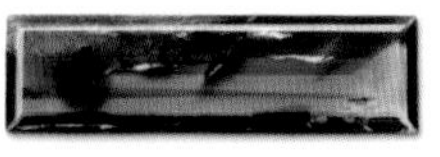

Step-cut diopside
A rectangular step-cut diopside with fractures

Emerald-cut diopside A fine green, emerald-cut diopside

$CaMg(Si_2O_6)$

DIOPSIDE

A calcium magnesium silicate, diopside is a member of the pyroxene family of minerals. It is found as crystals, fibrous masses, or masses of large, blocky crystals. It can be dark bottle-green, light green, brown, blue, or colorless. A high iron content can cause darker colors and increased density. A rich green variety known as chrome diopside is colored by chromium and is faceted as a prized collectors' gem. Violet-blue crystals colored by manganese are sometimes called violane. These are found in Italy and the USA and are also prized by collectors. Cloudy or fibrous material can be cut *en cabochon* to show a cat's eye or star effect. Massive diopside is carved into beads.

Chrome diopside has been found in Siberia, Myanmar, the Hunza Valley of Pakistan, and the Kimberley diamond mines in South Africa. Facet-grade diopside is found in Austria and Italy. Other localities include the gem gravels of Sri Lanka and Brazil, and some regions in Canada and the USA. Dark green to black material used to make stars is found in southern India.

Navette-cut hiddenite
This flawless, 4.69-carat hiddenite gem is faceted in a type of fancy cut called a navette cut. Its faces are cut with a mixture of triangular and rectangular faces.

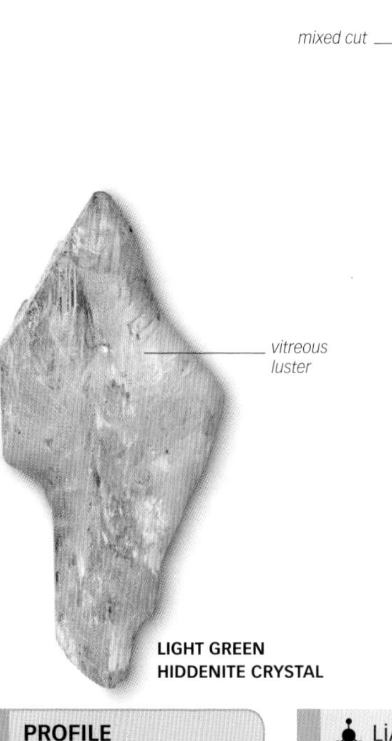

LIGHT GREEN HIDDENITE CRYSTAL

PROFILE

Mixed | Step | Round brilliant

Monoclinic
6½–7
3.0–3.2
1.66–1.67
Vitreous

$LiAl(Si_2O_6)$

HIDDENITE

A pale to emerald-green variety of spodumene, hiddenite is a lithium aluminosilicate. Although single crystals of spodumene as long as 47 ft (14.3 m) have been found, hiddenite crystals, paradoxically, are small and seldom more than 1 in (25 mm) long. Hiddenite is strongly pleochroic and appears green, bluish green, and yellowish green when viewed from different directions. This makes it essential to orient the rough correctly when faceting. Natural hiddenite is colored by traces of chromium, but green spodumene from Afghanistan and Pakistan is believed to be irradiated (p.32). It is debated whether this is true hiddenite.

Hiddenite is named after the geologist William Earl Hidden, who first recognized it. The first specimens were recovered in North Carolina, USA, in about 1879. They occurred with emerald and were called "lithia emerald" for some time. Mining was undertaken at the discovery site in the 1890s. In addition to North Carolina, hiddenite occurs in Brazil, China, and Madagascar.

PROFILE

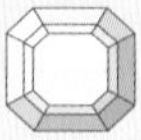

Step

Mixed

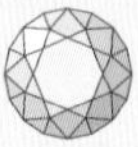

Round brilliant

Monoclinic

6½–7

3.0–3.2

1.66–1.67

Vitreous

natural inclusions

striations

GEM-GRADE KUNZITE CRYSTAL

Emerald-cut kunzite This kunzite gem has been faceted in an emerald cut with a deep pavilion to deepen its color.

VARIANT

Heart-shaped gem A large, heart-shaped, light-colored faceted kunzite specimen

$LiAl(Si_2O_6)$

KUNZITE

The pink variety of the mineral spodumene, kunzite was named after G.F. Kunz, the American gemologist who first described it in 1902. It is a member of the pyroxene mineral group. Gem-quality kunzite is strongly pleochroic, exhibiting two different shades when viewed from different angles. As a result, gemstones are carefully cut to show the best color through the top surface of the stone. Kunzite and other spodumene gems are almost always faceted. They tend to be splintery, with slivers likely to fall off during the cutting process if the stone is not oriented correctly.

Kunzite is typically found in lithium-bearing granitic pegmatites. Source localities include Afghanistan, Brazil, Madagascar, and the USA.

The Picasso necklace A 396.30-carat kunzite from Afghanistan adorns this necklace designed by Paloma Picasso.

thick girdle

slightly rounded corners to prevent chipping

crystal striations

HYPERSTHENE ROUGH

Step-cut hypersthene
As in this step-cut specimen, faceted hypersthene shows good color but often lacks clarity and brilliance.

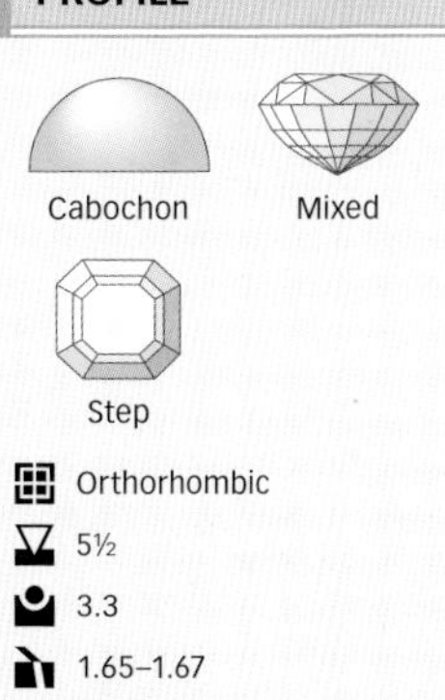

PROFILE

Cabochon

Mixed

Step

Orthorhombic

5½

3.3

1.65–1.67

Vitreous

$Mg,Fe(Si_2O_6)$

HYPERSTHENE

The name hypersthene comes from the Greek words *hyper* and *stenthos*, meaning "over" and "strength" respectively, an allusion to hypersthene's greater hardness than the mineral hornblende, with which it was often confused. Hypersthene is usually gray, brown, or green. It is noted for its copper-red iridescence, partly caused by hematite and goethite inclusions. It is often cut *en cabochon*, as it can be too dark to facet. When stones are faceted, they are intense in color but often cloudy.

As well as being a gemstone name, "hypersthene" also used to be applied to a mineral belonging to the pyroxene group of silicates. It formed part of a chemical series between the minerals enstatite (p.145) and ferrosilite. Bronzite, another member of this series, is greenish brown, opaque to translucent, and has a bronzelike luster. Gem-quality bronzite is cut *en cabochon*. Hypersthene occurs in igneous and metamorphic rocks. Most gem-quality material comes from India, Norway, Germany, and Greenland.

VARIANT

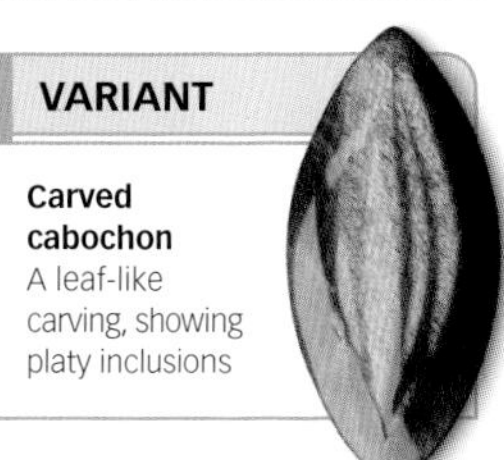

Carved cabochon
A leaf-like carving, showing platy inclusions

PROFILE

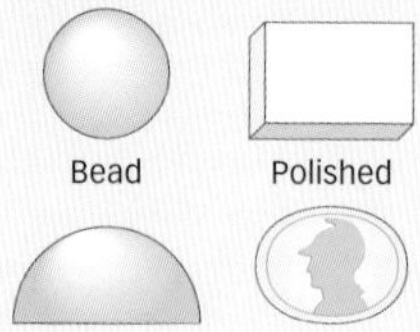

Bead
Polished
Cabochon
Cameo

Monoclinic
6–7
3.2–3.4
1.66–1.68
Vitreous to greasy

granular broken surface

BROKEN PIECE OF LILAC JADEITE

highly polished surface

Jadeite Buddha
This smiling Buddha has been carved from a specimen of mottled green jadeite.

$Na(Al,Fe)Si_2O_6$

JADEITE

A member of the pyroxene mineral group, jadeite is one of two minerals that are called "jade." The other jade is nephrite (p.153)—a variety of tremolite or actinolite and a member of the amphibole mineral group. Whereas jadeite has interlocking, blocky, granular crystals that give it a sugary or granular texture, nephrite is fibrous. This difference in textures can sometimes help distinguish between the two minerals. Also, jadeite is found in a number of colors, but nephrite has a much more limited color range.

Jadeite is white when pure. It can be colored green by iron; lilac by manganese and iron; and pink, brown, red, blue, black, orange, or yellow by inclusions of other minerals. Emerald-green specimens called imperial jade are the most valuable and result from the presence of chromium. When weathered, jadeite typically develops a brown skin that is frequently incorporated into carvings.

Jadeite most often occurs in metamorphic rocks formed under high pressure. It is usually recovered as alluvial pebbles and boulders but is also found in its place of origin. Myanmar is a major source of jadeite, especially imperial jade. Other sources are in Japan and Guatemala.

Jadeite snuff bottle
This delicately carved jadeite snuff bottle has a darker area that is carved to depict a duck among lotus flowers.

Green jadeite
White and cream streaks can be seen in this slice of dark green jadeite.

Lavender jadeite
This polished piece of jadeite has a highly desirable lavender color.

Polished rough
This piece of partly polished lavender jadeite rough has a rim of weathered material.

Mexican mask
This mask made of gray-green jadeite is from Mexico.

Jadeite ball
This ball is fashioned from green jadeite.

Jadeite necklace
Color-matched beads of translucent jadeite have been used to make this necklace.

Dragon vase
Carved from rare lavender jadeite from Myanmar, this jade vase from the Smithsonian Institution collection stands 12 in (50 cm) tall.

OLMEC JADEITE

Using jadeite from Guatemala and Costa Rica, the Olmecs were the first Mesoamericans to carve jade, perhaps 3,000 years ago. Across Mexico and Central America, jade was more valued than gold and was used in the most precious objects—masks, depictions of the gods, and ritual items.

Olmec axhead
This Olmec votive axhead was cut from jadeite in 1200–400 BCE.

black manganese oxide veins

rich color

uneven fracture

vitreous luster

SOLID-COLOR RHODONITE ROUGH

Rhodonite cabochon
This oval cabochon of rhodonite exhibits good red color and the black veining that is popular among many cutters and buyers.

PROFILE

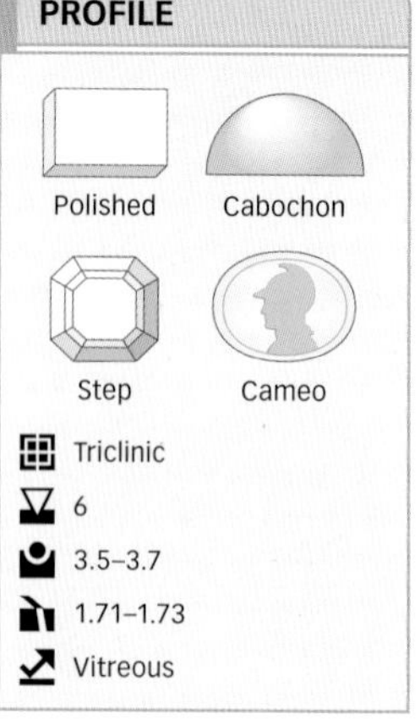

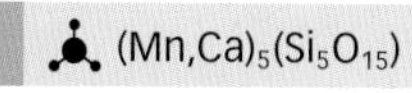

RHODONITE

Often mined as a semiprecious gem and ornamental stone, rhodonite is found as rounded crystals, masses, or grains. It takes its name from the Greek word *rhodon*, which means "rose"—a reference to its typical rose color. Black manganese-oxide veins or coatings are common. Gem cutters prefer the streaked variety of rhodonite over the featureless pink variety. Relatively tough, massive rhodonite is primarily cut *en cabochon* or as beads and is often used as a carving material. The mineral is sometimes found as crystals, some of which are transparent. Crystals are extremely fragile and care must be taken during faceting. These rare faceted stones are cut strictly for collectors.

Rhodonite is found in various manganese ores and is a relatively widespread mineral.

Carved box
This finely carved oblong box of rhodonite shows the desirable dark veins on the surface of the stone.

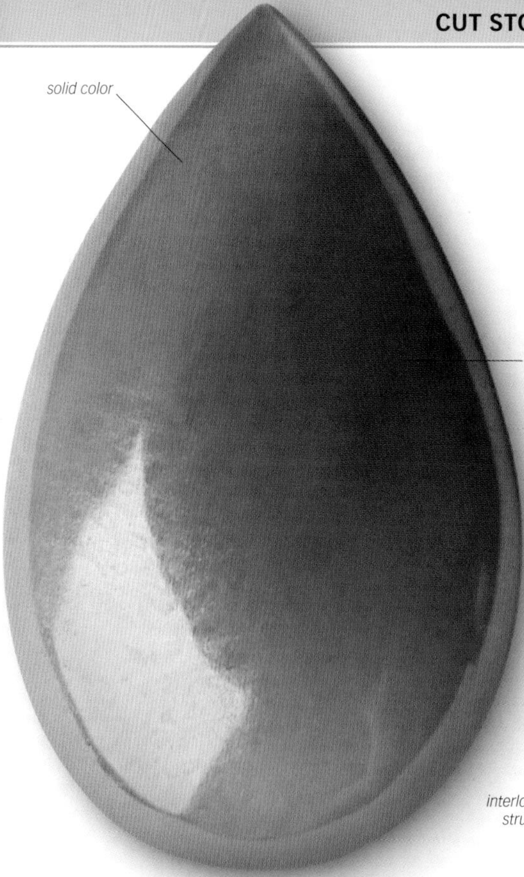

solid color

"orange peel" surface

Teardrop cabochon
This near-translucent cabochon of nephrite is cut in the shape of a teardrop and shows the slight "orange peel" finish characteristic of much polished nephrite.

sawn surface

interlocking structure

ROUGH JADE CUT TO REVEAL INTERIOR QUALITY

PROFILE

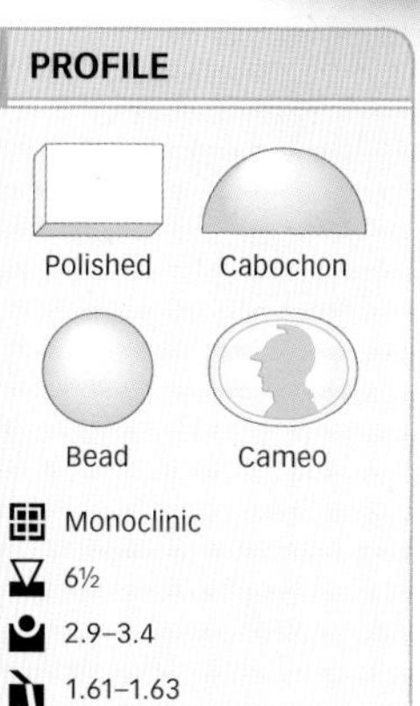

- Monoclinic
- 6½
- 2.9–3.4
- 1.61–1.63
- Dull to waxy

$Ca_2(Mg,Fe)_5(Si_8O_{22})(OH)_2$

NEPHRITE

One of two minerals called "jade," nephrite is not a mineral in its own right but the name applied to the tough, compact form of either tremolite or actinolite, both of which are structurally identical calcium magnesium silicate hydroxides. Jadeite (pp.150–51) is the other jade mineral. Nephrite varies in color with its composition: it is dark green when rich in iron, and cream-colored when rich in magnesium. A white variety composed of pure tremolite is called "mutton-fat jade." The crystalline texture of nephrite is a mat of tightly interlocking fibres. This creates a stone tougher than steel.

The Chinese perfected jade carving in the 1st millennium BCE, and Maoris have been making jade weapons and ornaments for many centuries.

Nephrite figurine
This Hei Tiki figure has been carved out of nephrite jade by Maoris from New Zealand.

CHINESE JADE

Jade has been carved in China since the late Stone Age (*c.*6000 BCE). It was initially worked into relatively crude ritual objects, but as skills developed, Chinese jade objects soon began to take on the beauty and complexity that is associated with them today.

CULTURAL CONNECTION

Jade holds the same position in Chinese culture that gold and silver have occupied in European cultures. Imbued with mystical significance, jade was thought to prevent fatigue and delay the decomposition of the body. It was also associated with important human virtues due to its beauty, hardness, and durability. Six jade objects were even made a part of the Chinese burial ritual.

Jade pi disk
Pi disks such as this one made of jade from the late Zhou Dynasty (*c.*300 BCE) were thought to symbolize the sky and represent the Sun.

ANCIENT ROOTS

Nephrite, produced from sources along the Yangtze River, was the first type of jade to be worked by the Chinese. By the start of the 4th millennium BCE, nephrite carving had spread to the whole of China. As in other cultures, such as the Maori of New Zealand, the toughness of nephrite made it the material of choice for axes and other cutting implements. By the start of the 2nd millennium BCE, elaborately ornamented and finely finished ritual objects were being carved.

Jade samples used for burial
These jade plaques are representative of the various colors and patterns of nephrite used to make up a burial suit.

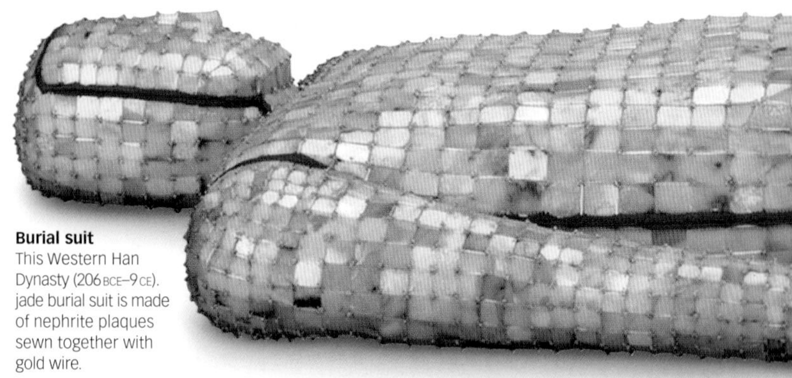

Burial suit
This Western Han Dynasty (206 BCE–9 CE). jade burial suit is made of nephrite plaques sewn together with gold wire.

STYLES AND MOTIFS

The first jade objects were ritual representations of objects used in daily life. By the 18th century BCE, jade objects came to be ornamented with cultural motifs characteristic of the period—a trend that was continued by the later dynasties. Jadeite, introduced from Myanmar around 1800 CE, makes up the pastel jade carvings for which China is well known.

stylized foliage

Jade deer
This jade carving of a deer and her fawn dates back to the 18th century.

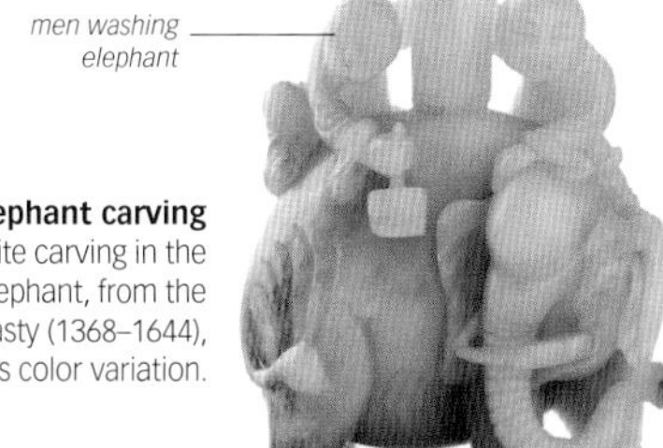

Elephant carving
This nephrite carving in the shape of an elephant, from the late Ming Dynasty (1368–1644), shows color variation.

Taoist god
This figurine made of carved green jade shows a Taoist god or sage depicted as a venerable old man nurturing a child at his feet.

natural color variation

detailed carving

Ming Dynasty vase
This 4.75-in (12-cm) tall jade vase from the Ming Dynasty (1368–1644) has an elaborately carved surface.

Qing Dynasty carving
This Chinese white nephrite carving from the late Qing Dynasty (*c.*1880) depicts a garden scene with figures under pine trees and a pavilion.

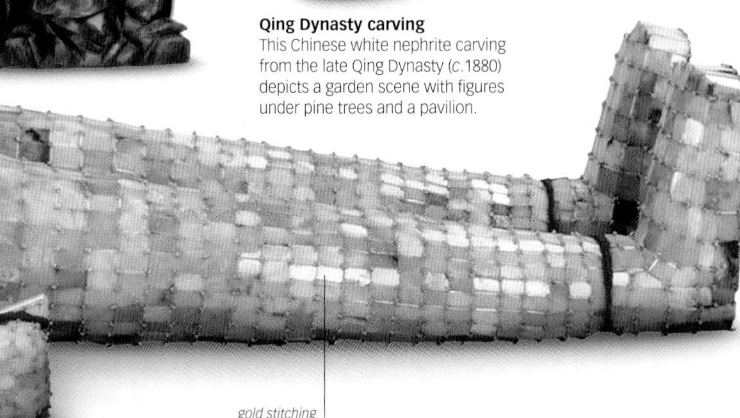

Emerald-cut dioptase
Dioptase is a fragile gemstone that is frequently flawed. This superbly colored emerald-cut specimen has many inclusions.

excellent crystals

GEM-QUALITY DIOPTASE CRYSTALS

PROFILE

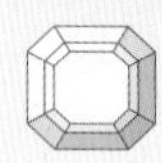
Step

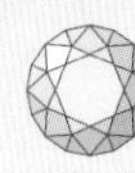
Round brilliant

- Hexagonal or trigonal
- 5
- 3.3
- 1.67–1.72
- Vitreous to greasy

$CuSiO_2(OH_2)$

DIOPTASE

The bright green crystals of dioptase can superficially resemble emerald (p.169)—so much so that crystals mined from a rich deposit in Kazakhstan were wrongly identified as emerald when they were sent to Czar Paul of Russia in 1797. Its prismatic crystals can be highly transparent, and transparent specimens can be weakly pleochroic. Intensely colored dioptase can also be translucent. Dioptase would make a superb gemstone to rival emerald in color, were it not for the fact that it is soft and fragile with easily set-off cleavages—even mineral specimens must be carefully handled. Although it is very fragile, it is a popular mineral with collectors and cut only for gemstone collections. These gems are very susceptible to mechanical shock and shatter if they are exposed to ultrasonic cleaning.

Dioptase forms where copper veins have been altered by oxidation. It derives its name from the Greek words *dia* and *optazein*, which mean "through" and "visible" respectively—a reference to the cleavage planes often visible inside unbroken crystals.

PROFILE

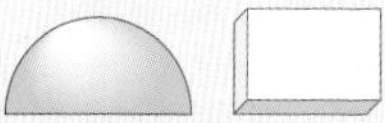

Cabochon Polished

Hexagonal

5½–6½

2.7–2.8

1.60–1.61

Vitreous

Oval cabochon
This rich purple specimen of sugilite has been cut into a high-domed oval cabochon.

high-domed cabochon

purple coloration

massive material

deep, rich color

LAYER OF SUGILITE IN ROCK MATRIX

VARIANT

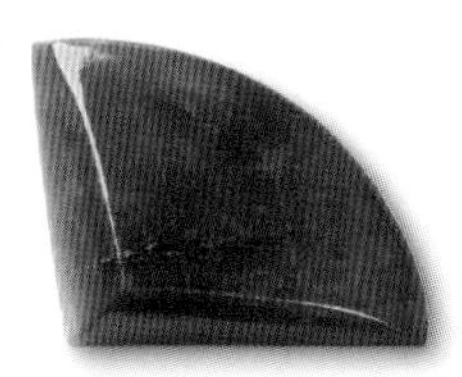

Quarter cabochon
A richly colored cabochon of sugilite in an unusual shape

$KNa_2(Fe,Mn,Al)_2Li_3Si_{12}O_{30}\cdot H_2O$

SUGILITE

Discovered in 1944 but recognized as a mineral only in 1976, sugilite is named after Ken-ici Sugi, a Japanese petrologist. Sugilite contains variable amounts of iron, aluminum, and manganese. It can be pale to deep pink, brownish yellow, or purple. Specimens are pink to purple due to the presence of manganese, purple when rich in iron, and pink when rich in aluminum. The mineral usually occurs in massive or granular form. Crystals are rare, but when found they are prismatic and small, being less than ¾ in (2 cm) wide. Sugilite is relatively new to the gemstone market. It is always cut *en cabochon* when used as a gemstone. Sugilite pebbles are valued for their vivid purple color and are sometimes polished in rock tumblers. Some massive sugilite has been sold under the name lavulite.

A sodium potassium lithium silicate hydrate, sugilite forms in metamorphosed manganese deposits and in marble. It is found at Mont St.-Hilaire, Canada; Iwagi Island, Japan; Kuruman, South Africa; and Faggiona, Italy.

PROFILE

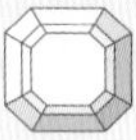

Step

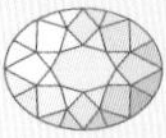

Oval brilliant

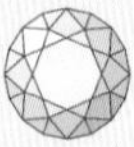

Round brilliant

Orthorhombic

7–7½

2.6

1.53–1.55

Vitreous to greasy

uniform faces

Checkerboard-cut iolite This iolite is faceted in an unusual and difficult chequerboard cut.

prismatic iolite crystal

GEM-QUALITY IOLITE CRYSTAL IN MATRIX

VARIANTS

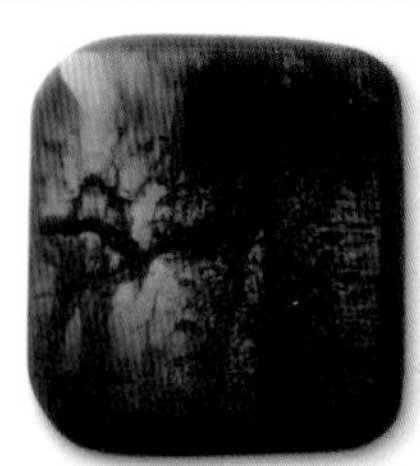

Iolite cabochon A rounded square cabochon of deep blue iolite

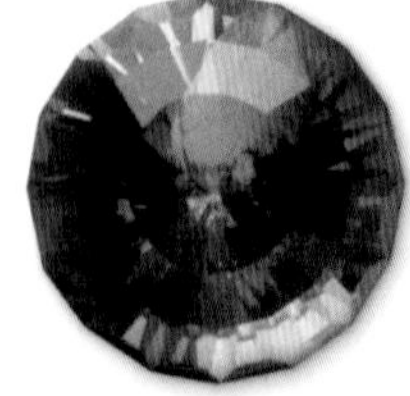

Brilliant-cut iolite A faceted, complex brilliant-cut specimen of iolite

$(Mg,Fe)_2Al_4Si_5O_{18}$

IOLITE

Gem-quality blue cordierite is known as iolite, a name derived from a Greek word meaning violet—a general reference to its color. Iolite is noted for its pleochroism and appears intense blue from one direction, yellowish gray or blue from another, and almost colorless as the stone is turned to a third direction. Iolite is informally referred to as "water sapphire" because of its color. Its crystals are prisms, and the best blue color is seen when they are viewed along their long axes. Iolite is usually faceted, with the cutter taking careful note of the orientation of the stone to get the best color.

A magnesium iron aluminum silicate, iolite most often occurs in alumina-rich rocks metamorphosed by intense heat. Although it can occur as crystals up to 2 in (5 cm) wide, it is more often found as rolled pebbles in the gem gravels of Sri Lanka, Myanmar, and Madagascar. There is a major source of iolite near Chennai, India. Fine crystals are found on Garnet Island, Northwest Territories, Canada.

PROFILE

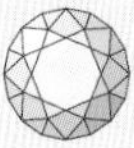

Round brilliant Step

- Hexagonal
- 6½
- 3.7
- 1.76–1.80
- Vitreous

good clarity and brilliance

crystal face

GEM-QUALITY BENITOITE CRYSTAL WITH BROKEN BASE

Fine blue benitoite This brilliant-cut specimen of benitoite exhibits the fine blue color for which this rare gem is known.

VARIANT

Multiple facets A brilliant-cut multifaceted benitoite gem

$BaTiSi_3O_9$

BENITOITE

The official state gem of California, benitoite was discovered in 1906 near the San Benito River, from which it takes its name. It is a very rare barium titanium silicate. Benitoite was supposedly found by a prospector looking for mercury and copper mineralization, who came across some brilliant blue crystals that he mistook for sapphires. It is this bright blue color that benitoite is best known for, although the California deposit occasionally produces colorless and pink crystals.

Benitoite has exceptionally strong dispersion—its "fire" is similar to that of diamond (pp.50–51), although this is often masked because of the intensity of its color. The best color is seen through the side of its crystals rather than from top to bottom. This, in turn, imposes a size limitation on cut stones, which are usually faceted. Gems tend to be small, seldom exceeding 3 carats, and are cut principally for collectors. In addition to California, benitoite is found in small amounts in Japan and Arkansas, USA.

TRANSPARENT CRYSTAL OF YELLOW GREEN ELBAITE

Yellow-green elbaite
Although usually thought of as either dark green or red, most elbaite is yellow-green, as in this triangular cushion-cut specimen.

$Na(Li_{0.5}Al_{0.5})_3Al_6(BO_3)_3Si_6O_{18}(OH)_3(F)$

ELBAITE

The name elbaite is given to one of the 11 members of the tourmaline family of minerals. Most tourmaline is dark, opaque, and not particularly attractive. Elbaite provides the most gemstone material, although a small amount comes from another tourmaline, liddicoatite, nearly indistinguishable from elbaite.

Elbaite often occurs as beautifully formed, elongated crystals with a distinctive "rounded triangular" shape in cross section. Several gem varieties of elbaite and liddicoatite are named after their colors: indicolite (blue), achroite (colorless), rubellite (pink or red), and verdelite (green). Pink and green stones are the most popular, although emerald-green ones are rarer and more valuable. In watermelon tourmaline, pink and green colors can be found in the same stone, with different colors occurring at either end of the crystal or forming a core of one color and a rim of another. Yellow-green is the most common of all gem tourmaline colors. Elbaite is strongly pleochroic, exhibiting different colors when viewed from different directions. This means that gem cutters must orient the rough carefully.

The superb red and green elbaite crystals from the Pala district in San Diego, USA, the color-zoned watermelon crystals from Brazil, and the magnificent red prismatic crystals from Madagascar and Mozambique are stunningly beautiful gem-grade materials. Most emerald green stones come from Brazil, Namibia, and Tanzania.

ANCIENT GEM

Elbaite is named for a deposit at Elba, Italy, where it has been mined for at least two millennia. A pink elbaite Roman cameo dates back to the 1st century CE and a pink cabochon is set in a Nordic gold ring that dates back to 1000 CE.

Roman cameo
This cameo in elbaite depicts the head of Alexander the Great.

Rubellite ring
This ring has a 50-plus carat step-cut rubellite (red elbaite) stone set in platinum with diamond accents.

Oval brilliant-cut achroite
Achroite, the colorless gem variety of elbaite, has been faceted into an oval brilliant cut.

Indicolite rough
This gem-quality crystal of the blue variety of elbaite known as indicolite has transparent areas.

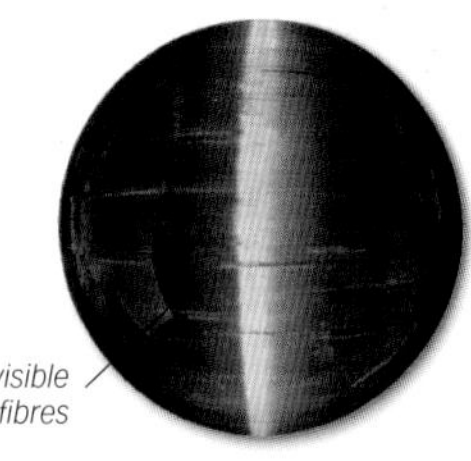

Rubellite cabochon
This rubellite, or red elbaite, cabochon has produced a sharp cat's eye.

Arts and Crafts pin
This 1920s pin has a dark green baguette-cut elbaite mounted in a hand-wrought gold frame.

Watermelon section
Crystal sections of watermelon tourmaline such as this are often mounted and worn as jewelry.

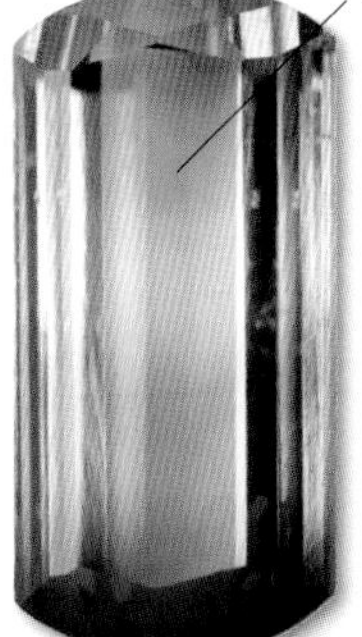

Watermelon tourmaline
This example of watermelon tourmaline has been skillfully faceted to show both of its colors in the same stone.

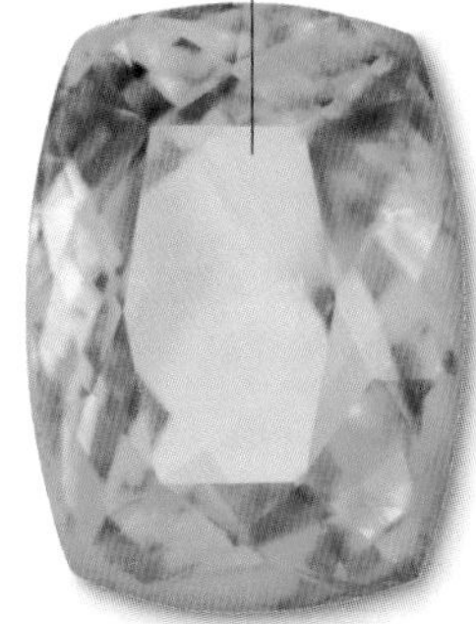

Paraiba tourmaline
This variety of elbaite comes from Brazil, Mozambique, and Nigeria. Its colors are often described as "neon."

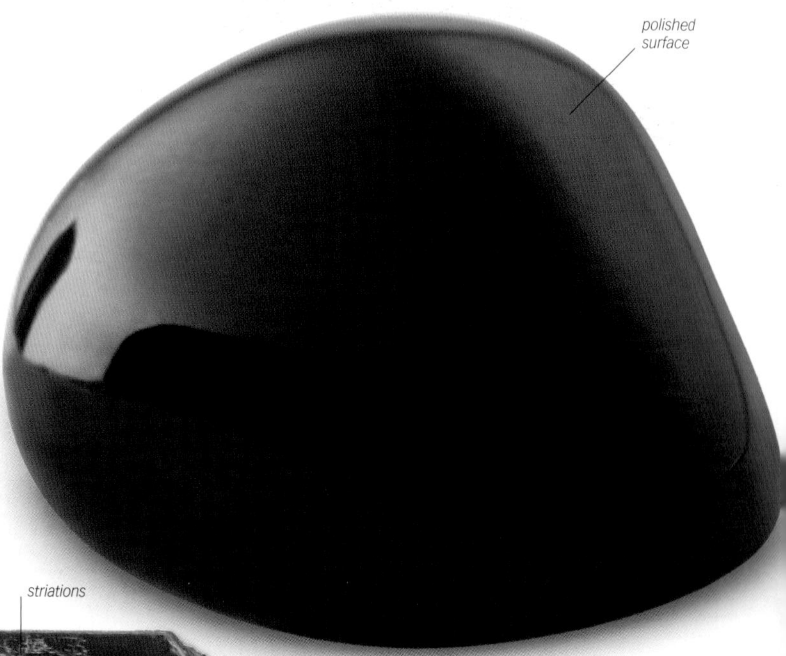

polished surface

striations

SCHORL CRYSTAL

Tumble polished schorl
This piece of schorl has been tumble-polished to show its perfect inky blackness.

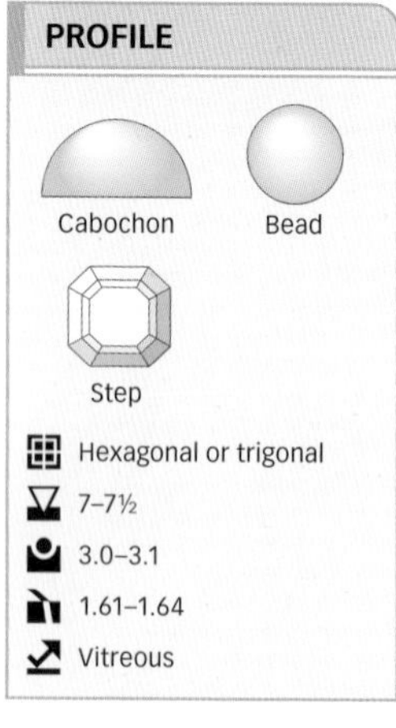

$NaFe_3^{2+}Al_6(BO_3)_3Si_6O_{18}(OH)_3(OH)$

SCHORL

Also called iron tourmaline, schorl is the most abundant species of tourmaline, a borosilicate. A black, opaque, iron-rich mineral, it is highly valued for its superb crystallization and fine mineral specimens. Prismatic crystals may reach 10 feet in length. Schorl was used extensively in black mourning jewelry during the Victorian era in the mid-19th century, cut into rounded and faceted cabochons. Jet (p.204) was also widely used in mourning jewelry. However, jet can be distinguished from schorl by its lighter weight and inferior hardness. Schorl is rarely cut as a gemstone now. When cut, it is almost exclusively fashioned into faceted cabochons. Nevertheless, cut schorl is still abundant in old jewelry.

The name "schorl" developed in the late Middle Ages, from a word relating to worthlessness—a reference to its occurrence with valuable tin minerals. Schorl accounts for a very high percentage of all tourmalines in nature. High-quality schorl comes from Brazil, Germany, Finland, Afghanistan, and the USA.

PROFILE

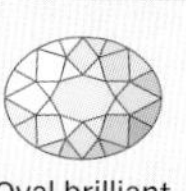
Oval brilliant

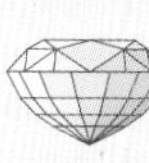
Mixed

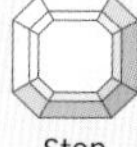
Step

Hexagonal or trigonal

7–7½

3.0–3.1

1.61–1.64

Vitreous

CLASSICALLY SQUAT GEM CRYSTAL OF DRAVITE

Mixed-cut dravite This richly colored specimen of dravite has been faceted into a complex mixed cut to show maximum brilliance.

VARIANT

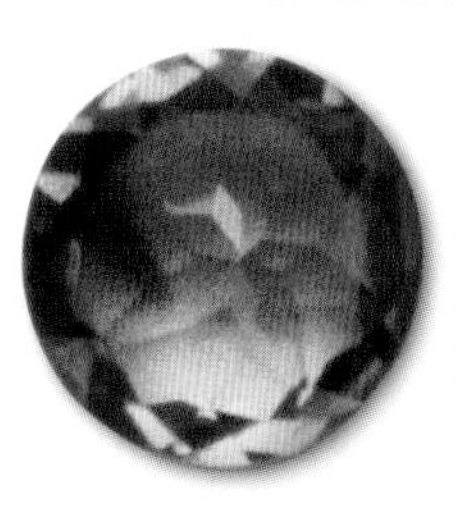
Dravite bead A faceted bead of light-colored dravite

$NaMg_3Al_6(BO_3)_3Si_6O_{18}(OH)_3(OH)$

DRAVITE

One of the distinct mineral species that make up the tourmaline group of minerals, dravite is distinguished by its specific chemical composition and is one of the sodium-rich tourmalines. Like all tourmalines, dravite has a highly complex structure and chemistry. It is black to brown, with the brown material generally being cut for gems. Much brown dravite is treated with heat to lighten its color, often yielding a rich golden brown shade. Dravite is strongly dichroic, exhibiting two different colors when viewed from different angles. The darkest color appears along the length of the crystal. As a result, gemstones are commonly cut through the side of the crystal to prevent the gem from appearing too dark.

Dravite is named after the Drava River in the Republic of Slovenia. Tourmalines are resistant to weathering so they accumulate in gravel deposits, although most dravite is mined from pegmatites. Dravite occurs in Brazil, Canada, Sri Lanka, Mexico, Australia, and the USA.

PROFILE

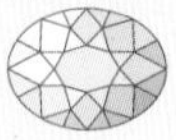

Oval brilliant 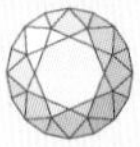 Round brilliant

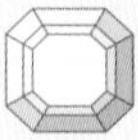

Step  Mixed

Hexagonal

7½

2.7

1.58–1.59

Vitreous

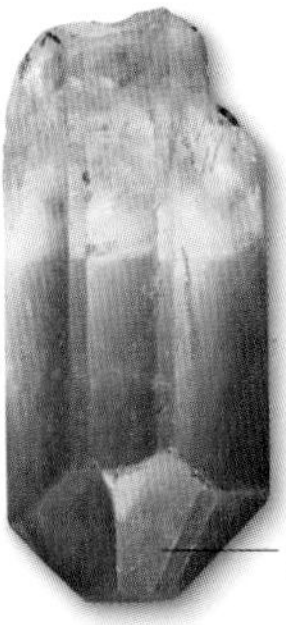

intricate facets

Oval brilliant-cut aquamarine This blue-green specimen of aquamarine has been faceted into a complex oval brilliant cut.

pyramidal termination

BLUE-GREEN, PRISMATIC CRYSTAL OF AQUAMARINE

fine blue-green color

VARIANTS

Cat's eye cabochon A specimen of fibrous aquamarine cut *en cabochon*

Step-cut aquamarine A type of cut popular for aquamarine

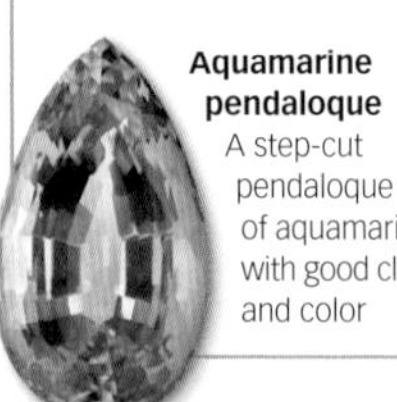

Aquamarine pendaloque A step-cut pendaloque of aquamarine with good clarity and color

$Al_2Be_3Si_6O_{18}$

AQUAMARINE

The most common gemstone variety of beryl, aquamarine is colored greenish blue by traces of iron. In ancient times, aquamarine amulets engraved with images of the Greek god of the sea, Poseidon, were thought to protect sailors against harm. In the 19th century, sea-green aquamarine was highly valued; today, sky-blue specimens are preferred.

Almost all aquamarine, which means "sea water", is found in cavities in pegmatites or concentrated in alluvial deposits. It typically forms larger and clearer crystals than emerald (p.169), which is another variety of beryl. A transparent crystal from Brazil, the most abundant source of aquamarine, weighed 242.5lb (110kg). At 14,000ft (4,250m), the aquamarine locality of Mt. Antero, USA, is the highest gemstone source in North America.

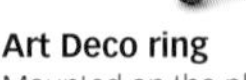

Art Deco ring Mounted on the platinum shank of this ring are a large, rectangular aquamarine and baguette-cut diamonds.

PROFILE

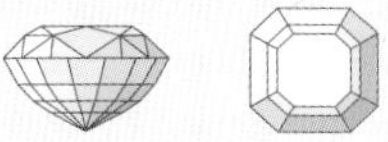

Mixed Step

- Hexagonal
- 7½
- 2.7
- 1.58 –1.59
- Vitreous

Oval mixed-cut morganite This pink specimen of morganite has been cut into an oval mixed cut, with a step-cut pavilion and a brilliant-cut crown.

rectangular faces of step-cut facets

rich color

well-formed crystal

FINE MORGANITE CRYSTAL

VARIANTS

Pendeloque cut A highly transparent specimen of morganite

Brilliant oval A gem cut often used to deepen the color of light stones

$Al_2Be_3Si_6O_{18}$

MORGANITE

A pink gem variety of beryl, morganite has also been called pink beryl, rose beryl, pink emerald, and cesian (or caesian) beryl. It is colored pink, pinkish yellow, peach, rose-lilac, or orange by the presence of manganese impurities. Stones with a yellow or orange tinge may be treated with heat to improve the pink color. Morganite crystals often show color banding, with a sequence from blue near the base to nearly colorless in the center, to peach or pink at the upper end. Morganite is also dichroic, often displaying two shades of color when viewed from different angles. Gems are almost always faceted.

Morganite commonly occurs in pegmatites with lepidolite and tourmaline. It is found in a number of localities in Minas Gerais, Brazil, where crystals can be up to 55lb (25kg) in weight. Other important localities include Pala in California, USA; Muiane in Mozambique; Elba in Italy; and several localities in Madagascar. The New York Academy of Sciences named morganite after the financier and gem enthusiast J.P. Morgan.

Brilliant-cut goshenite
This goshenite gem has been faceted in a complex octagonal brilliant cut to emphasize its brilliance.

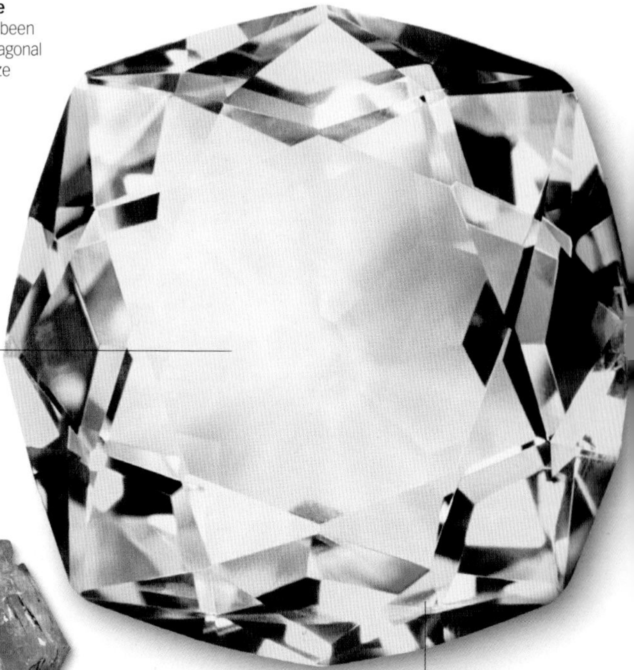

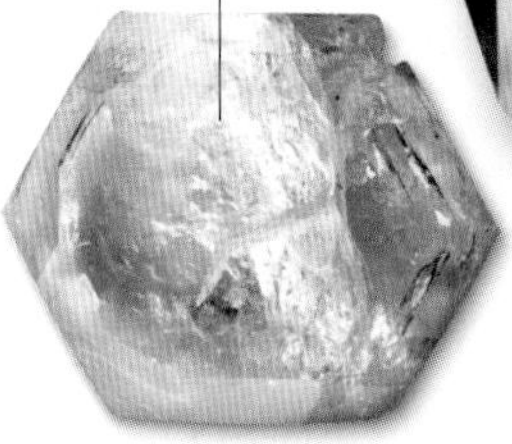

good transparency

vitreous luster

complex faceting

HEXAGONAL CRYSTAL OF ROUGH GOSHENITE

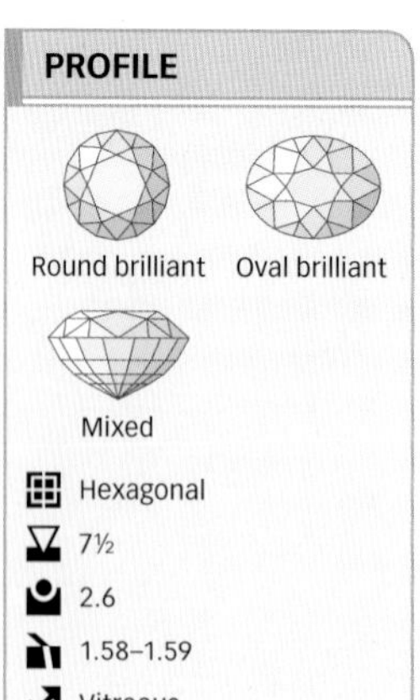

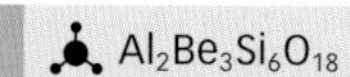

GOSHENITE

A beryllium aluminum silicate, goshenite is the gemstone name given to the colorless variety of the mineral beryl. However, goshenite can also turn yellow, green, pink, or blue when the trace elements held within some specimens are activated by irradiation. The fact that even small amounts of trace elements included in the beryl structure can impart color under the right geological circumstances makes goshenite the least common of the gem beryls. It is nearly always cut in brilliant cuts to emphasize its clarity. Specimens mined in Germany were once used to make eye glasses and lenses because of their transparency.

Goshenite is named after Goshen in Massachusetts, USA, where it was first recognized. The name goshenite is commonly used in gemstone markets, but it is not used as a mineral name. As with most other beryls, goshenite is mainly found in pegmatites. Current sources are Brazil, Russia, Pakistan, and Madagascar.

PROFILE

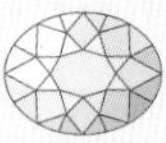

Oval brilliant 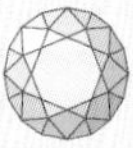 Round brilliant

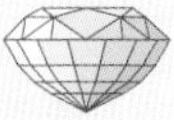

Mixed 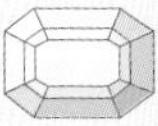 Emerald

Hexagonal

7½

2.7

1.58 –1.59

Vitreous

excellent clarity

main facet

highly transparent crystal

rock matrix

GEM-QUALITY HELIODOR CRYSTAL ON MATRIX

Good clarity and color
This brilliant-cut cushion of heliodor shows excellent color and clarity.

VARIANTS

Rectangular mixed cut
A dark gold specimen of heliodor

Heart-shaped heliodor
A specimen of heliodor fashioned into a heart shape—a difficult shape to achieve

$Al_2Be_3Si_6O_{18}$

HELIODOR

The pale yellow to brilliant gold variety of the mineral beryl, heliodor is a beryllium aluminum silicate. Although pure beryl is colorless, heliodor is colored golden yellow by the presence of iron in its crystal structure. Heliodor crystals are generally columnar, hexagonal prisms. Unlike emerald (p.169), the green variety of beryl, heliodor is commonly found as crystals with very few flaws.

The name heliodor means “gift from the sun”—it is derived from the Greek words *hēlios* and *dōron*, which mean “sun” and “gift,” respectively. Heliodor occurs in granitic pegmatites. The Ural Mountains of Russia produce the best-quality stones. Heliodor is also found in Nigeria, Namibia, Brazil, Ukraine, and the USA. The largest cut heliodor is probably the flawless 2,054 carat stone on display in the Hall of Gems at the Smithsonian Institution in Washington, D.C., USA.

Fine color and quality
Although it contains a few flaws, this brilliant-cut red beryl is of excellent color and quality for the mineral.

natural flaws

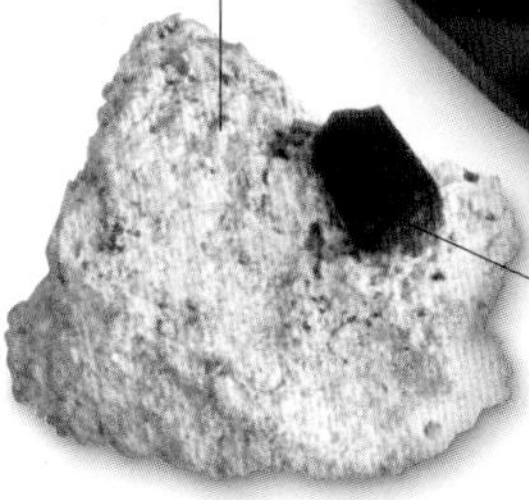

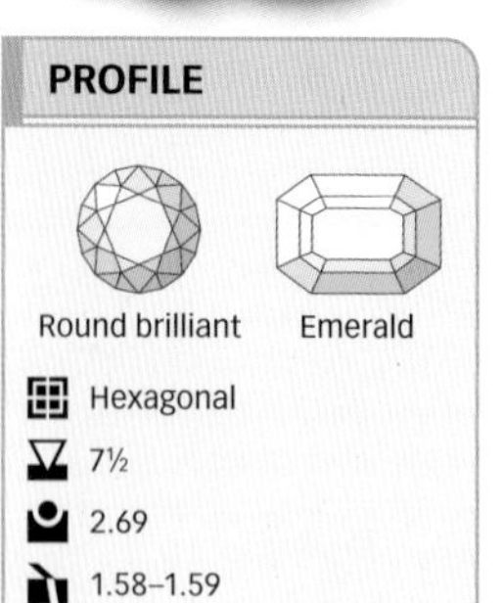

HEXAGONAL CRYSTAL OF RED BERYL

PROFILE

Round brilliant | Emerald

- Hexagonal
- 7½
- 2.69
- 1.58–1.59
- Vitreous

$Al_2Be_3Si_6O_{18}$

RED BERYL

A beryllium aluminum silicate, red beryl is the rarest of the beryls. Its dark red color is induced by natural radiation and is attributed to the presence of manganese atoms in its structure. Faceted red beryls are so rare that they command higher prices than diamond on a carat-for-carat basis.

Red beryl is found almost exclusively in cavities in topaz-bearing rhyolites under conditions of low pressure and high temperature (1,065°F/575°C or above). It was first discovered in 1904 in the Thomas Range of Utah, USA. The largest deposit of gem-quality red beryl has been found in the Wah Wah Mountains of midwestern Utah, but deposits have also been found in New Mexico, USA. Red beryl has also been called "red emerald" and "scarlet emerald"—neither of which are recognized gemstone names. Its former mineral name bixbite is no longer used because of its close similarity to another mineral name: bixbyite.

PROFILE

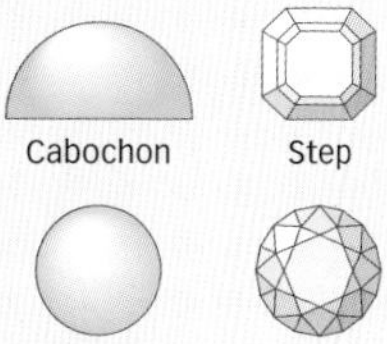

Cabochon Step

Bead Round brilliant

Hexagonal

7½–8

2.7

1.58–1.59

Vitreous

natural inclusions (flaws)

hexagonal face

WALNUT-SIZED EMERALD CRYSTAL

Emerald-cut gem
This emerald-cut stone is valuable despite being internally flawed. The emerald cut was specifically created for emeralds.

VARIANT

Emerald cabochon
An octagonal cabochon of emerald

$Al_2Be_3Si_6O_{18}$

EMERALD

The grass-green variety of beryl, emerald was mined as early as 1300 BCE. The ancient Egyptians believed emeralds were a symbol of fertility and life. In Europe, they were worn to prevent epilepsy. Rich deposits of emeralds were discovered and exploited after the Spanish conquest of Colombia. Around 1830, emeralds were discovered in the Ural Mountains of Russia. They have also been found in Austria, Norway, and Australia. Other sources include Brazil, South Africa, Zambia, Zimbabwe, Pakistan, and the USA.

The "emerald cut" was devised to fit the shape of emerald's normally prismatic crystals and to emphasize its color. Flawless stones are rare, and various treatments are used to hide flaws. Inferior stones may be oiled to fill cracks and enhance color. Beads, intaglios, and cameos are made from flawed specimens.

Maximillian emerald
This 21.04-carat, clear and transparent emerald was set in a ring worn by Emperor Maximillian of Mexico.

ANCIENT GEMS FROM EGYPT

Gold and gemstones were a notable feature of ancient Egypt, and were prized for much more than their ornamental value. Gemstones such as Afghan lapis lazuli were even imported by the Egyptians as far back as 3100 BCE.

Gemstones have played an important role throughout ancient Egyptian culture. Egypt has produced some of the world's most beautiful jewelry using gold from the former Egyptian province of Nubia, and gemstones, such as lapis lazuli from Afghanistan, emeralds from "Cleopatra's Mines," and amber, carnelian, turquoise, and amazonite from elsewhere. Gemstones had both medical and mystical connotations for the ancient Egyptians. The use of colored stones for healing is described in the Ebers medical papyrus, which dates back to about 1500 BCE. Pharaohs were buried with their wealth, especially gold and gems, so that they could intercede with the gods on behalf of Egypt and Egyptians.

Ancient amulets
These amulets from Tutankhamun's tomb represent Egyptian gods: Thoth, god of writing and magic; Horus, god of the Sun, war, and protection; and Anubis, god of the afterlife.

Calcite statue
Like many Egyptian statues routinely described as alabaster, this ancient Egyptian "alabaster" statue with a basalt base is actually made of the mineral calcite.

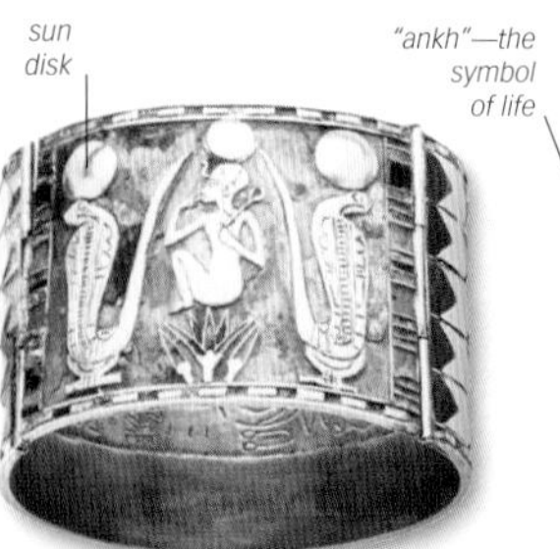

Gold bracelet
The god Horus as a child is the central figure in this ancient Egyptian royal bracelet made for Prince Nemareth. The bracelet is also decorated with lotus flowers and cobras.

Gold plaque
This ancient Egyptian plaque, with gold inlay and hieroglyphics, depicts the Sun god Amun-ra—the creator—and a pharaoh carrying the symbols of his office.

Scarab pectoral
The scarab was the Egyptian symbol of rebirth. This pectoral from the tomb of Tutankhamun depicts a lapis lazuli scarab, and also features turquoise, carnelian, and amazonite.

Sacred scorpion
Selket, the ancient Egyptian goddess who protected her people against poisons and snakebites, was worshipped in the form of a scorpion, represented here in gold.

From the pharaoh's tomb
This calcite stopper in the form of a king's head is from the tomb of Pharaoh Tutankhamun. It is a part of one of the four canopic urns containing the king's embalmed organs.

Complex brilliant cut
In this danburite gem, the cutter has increased the brilliance by splitting the main facets on the crown horizontally.

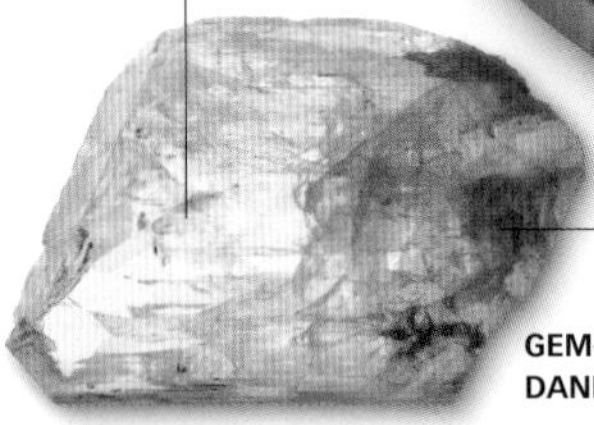

greasy luster

transparent crystal

main facet

GEM-QUALITY DANBURITE ROUGH

PROFILE

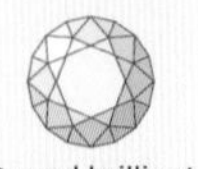

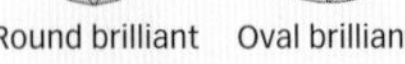

Round brilliant 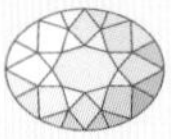 Oval brilliant

Mixed

Orthorhombic

7–7½

3.0

1.63–1.64

Vitreous to greasy

$CaB_2Si_2O_8$

DANBURITE

A calcium borosilicate, danburite is named after its place of discovery—Danbury in Connecticut, USA. Danburite crystals are glassy and prismatic, resembling topaz (pp.198–99), but they can be easily distinguished by their poor cleavage. Generally colorless, danburite can also be amber, yellow, gray, pink, or yellow-brown. The best stones are yellowish or brownish. As a gemstone, danburite is either faceted or cut *en cabochon*.

Danburite is generally a contact metamorphic mineral formed at low to moderate temperatures (up to 1,065°F/575°C) and occasionally in ore deposits formed at higher temperatures and in pegmatites. Yellowish to brownish gem-grade specimens in the form of water-rounded pebbles are found in Mogok, Myanmar. A 138-carat, pale yellow faceted stone is held in a collection at the Natural History Museum in London. Other gem-quality stones come from Switzerland, Italy, Japan, Mexico, and Dalnegorsk, Russia.

PROFILE

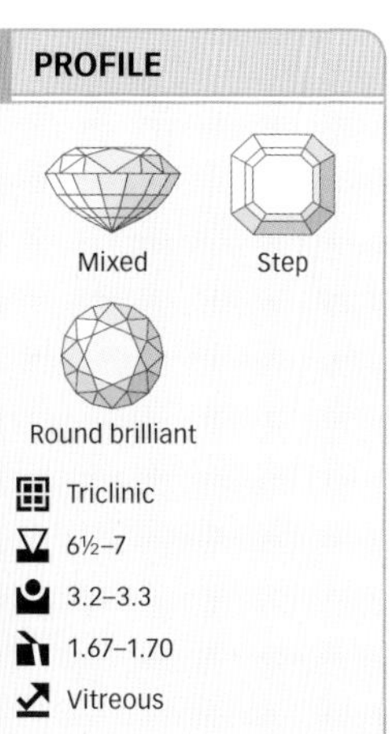

Triclinic

6½–7

3.2–3.3

1.67–1.70

Vitreous

natural inclusions

INTERPENETRATING CRYSTALS OF AXINITE

iron gives brown color

Brown axinite This oval cushion step-cut specimen shows off the rich brown color of axinite.

VARIANT

Purple axinite A brilliant-cut, plum-purple variety of axinite

$Ca_2FeAl_2(BSi_4O_{15})(OH)$

AXINITE

The four minerals in the axinite group—ferroaxinite (the most common), magnesioaxinite, manganaxinite, and tinzenite—are virtually indistinguishable from one another. Axinite takes its name from the axhead shape of its crystals. It also occurs as rosettes and in massive and granular forms. The most familiar color of axinite is clove-brown, but it can also be gray to bluish gray; honey-, gray-, or golden-brown; or pink, purple, yellow, orange, or red. A rare variety from Tanzania is blue. Axinite crystals are hard and brittle, and gems cut from them are easily chipped. This means that axinite is faceted only for collectors.

Axinite is usually found in contact metamorphic rocks and metamorphic rocks formed at low temperatures (up to 400°F/200°C). It also occurs in magnesium- and iron-rich igneous rocks. The mineral is found worldwide but gem-quality axinite comes from Mexico, France, Sri Lanka, Russia, Australia, and the USA.

PROFILE

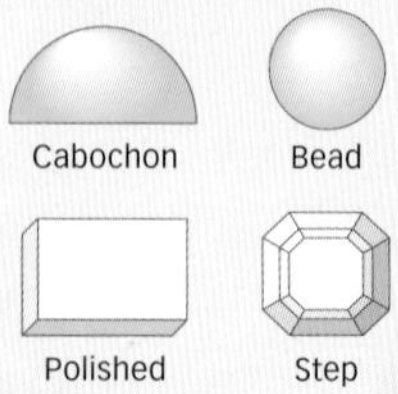

Cabochon | Bead | Polished | Step

Tetragonal or monoclinic

6½

3.4

1.70–1.75

Vitreous to resinous

good brilliance

Brilliant-cut vesuvianite This brilliant-cut cushion of vesuvianite exhibits fine clarity and excellent faceting.

well-formed crystal

GEM-QUALITY, GREENISH VESUVIANITE CRYSTALS

VARIANTS

Vesuvianite cabochon A cabochon cut from translucent vesuvianite

Cushion-cut vesuvianite A cushion-cut vesuvianite gem with internal flaws

Emerald-cut gem A dark brown vesuvianite specimen

$Ca_{10}(Mg,Fe)_2Al_4(SiO_4)_5(Si_2O_7)_2(OH,F)_4$

VESUVIANITE

This mineral is named after Mount Vesuvius in Italy, its place of discovery. Vesuvianite is the new name for the mineral previously called idocrase. The name idocrase is still used for older specimens, and for cabochons and transparent vesuvianite gems. Vesuvianite crystals are pyramidal or prismatic and glassy. They are usually green or chartreuse in color but can also be yellow to brown, yellow-green, purple, red, black, or blue. The largest crystals are more than 3 in (7 cm) long. Numerous elements, including tin, lead, manganese, chromium, zinc, and sulfur, may substitute in the vesuvianite structure. An unusual bismuth-bearing vesuvianite from Langben, Sweden, is bright red. A greenish blue, copper-bearing vesuvianite is called cyprine.

Vesuvianite is formed by the contact metamorphism of impure limestones, and it is also found in marble. The name californite is sometimes used for a massive, jadelike vesuvianite. Gemstone localities include Siberia and the USA.

PROFILE

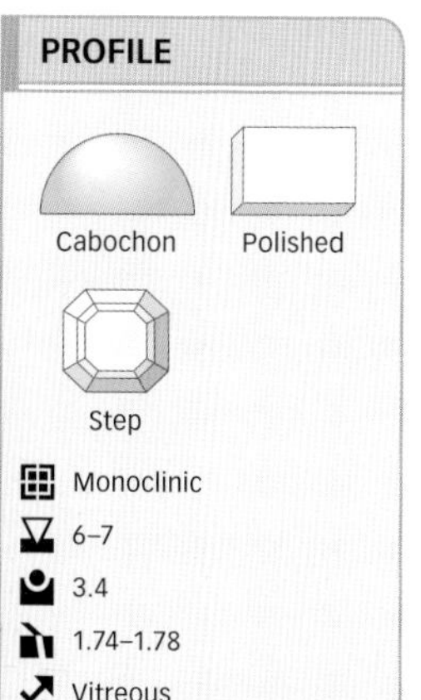

Monoclinic
6–7
3.4
1.74–1.78
Vitreous

CLUSTER OF GEM-QUALITY EPIDOTE CRYSTALS

Step-cut oval This specimen of epidote has a relatively good degree of clarity for this mineral.

VARIANT

Brown epidote A rectangular step-cut gem of brown epidote

$Ca_2Al_2(Fe,Al)(SiO_4)(Si_2O_7)O(OH)$

EPIDOTE

Although abundant as a rock-forming mineral, epidote is less well known as a gemstone. It often forms well-developed crystals and is pleochroic—exhibiting different shades of green when viewed from different angles. This is taken into consideration when faceting. Transparent, dark green crystals of epidote from Austria, Pakistan, and Brazil have been faceted for collectors, as have other colors from time to time. Being a fairly fragile mineral with a distinct cleavage, its faceted stones are not suitable to be worn as jewelry.

Epidote derives its name from the Greek word *epidosis*, which means "increase"—a reference to the fact that one side of the crystal prism is always longer than the others. It occurs widely in low-grade metamorphosed rocks. A bright green, chromium-rich variety of epidote is called tawmawlite. An epidote-rich granitic rock is cut *en cabochon* and sold under the trade name unakite. Unakite is found in various shades of green and pink and is usually mottled in appearance.

PROFILE

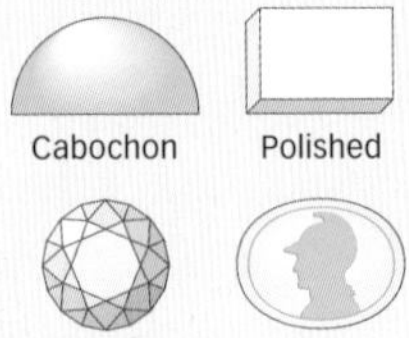

Cabochon Polished

Round brilliant Cameo

Orthorhombic

6–7

3.2–3.4

1.69–1.70

Vitreous

irregular broken surface

THULITE ZOISITE ROUGH

pinkish red color from manganese

Thulite cabochon
This oval cabochon has been cut from the thulite, the pink variety of zoisite.

VARIANTS

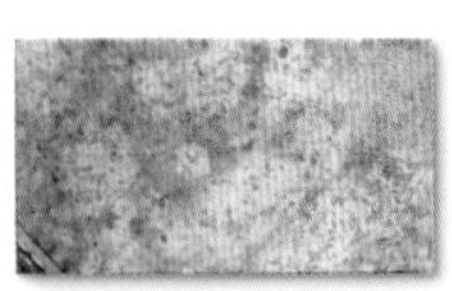

Thulite slab A slab of polished thulite

Anyolite sphere A sphere cut from anyolite, a variety of zoisite with rubies

$Ca_2Al_3(SiO_4)_3(OH)$

ZOISITE

A member of the epidote group of minerals, zoisite is a calcium aluminum silicate hydroxide. It is best known for its transparent, sapphire-blue form called tanzanite (p.177), but there are other gemstone varieties as well. Zoisite can also be green, yellowish green, green-brown, white, colorless, or gray. A pink variety found in Norway is called thulite and is named after Thule, which is an old name for the country. It is usually massive, and is carved or polished for use as a decorative stone, beads, or cabochons.

A brilliant green variety of zoisite known as anyolite is popular as a carving and ornamental stone. It is sprinkled through with red rubies (p.60) that are often distorted and irregularly spread throughout the massive green zoisite. These rubies are not of gem quality, but their color provides a striking contrast to the green zoisite, greatly enhancing the decorative pieces that are carved from the rock. Localities for zoisite include Spain, Japan, Germany, and Scotland. Thulite occurs in Norway, Italy, and the USA.

PROFILE

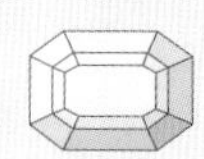
Emerald

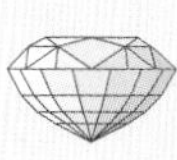
Mixed

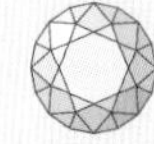
Round brilliant

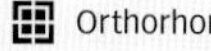
Orthorhombic

6–7

3.2–3.4

1.69–1.79

Vitreous

Mixed-cut tanzanite
This specimen of tanzanite is faceted in a complex mixed cut to bring out its beauty and brilliance.

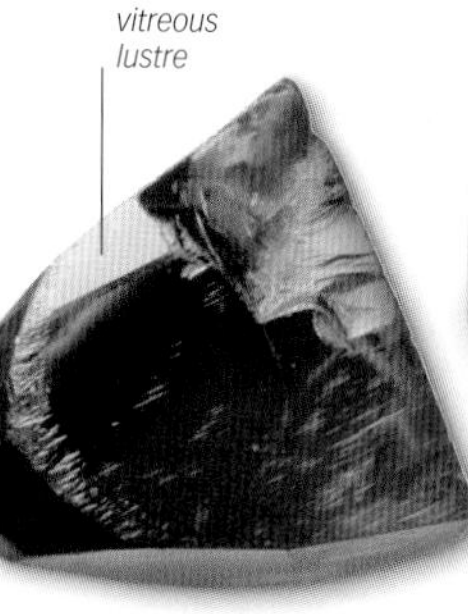

FINE-COLORED TANZANITE ROUGH

VARIANTS

Purple-tinged tanzanite
An oval cushion mixed-cut tanzanite with a purple tinge

Light blue tanzanite
An octagonal step-cut, light blue tanzanite gem

$Ca_2Al_3(SiO_4)_3(OH)$

TANZANITE

Sometimes mistaken for sapphire, tanzanite is the dark blue, purplish blue, or lilac- to sapphire-blue variety of zoisite (p.176). It was named after Tanzania—its place of discovery in 1967. Its crystals are distinctly pleochroic, exhibiting rich blue, magenta, and yellowish gray colors when viewed from different angles. The gem cutter has to carefully orient the rough to obtain the prime color. Tanzanite cleaves easily and can shatter when cleaned with ultrasonic cleaners. For this reason, specimens need careful handling.

The desirable blue color of tanzanite is created by heating the various other colors of zoisite, including yellow, green, and brown. Zoisite typically occurs in medium-grade schists, gneisses, and amphibolites resulting from the metamorphism of calcium-rich rocks. It is also found in quartz veins and pegmatites. Virtually all gem tanzanite is found in Tanzania.

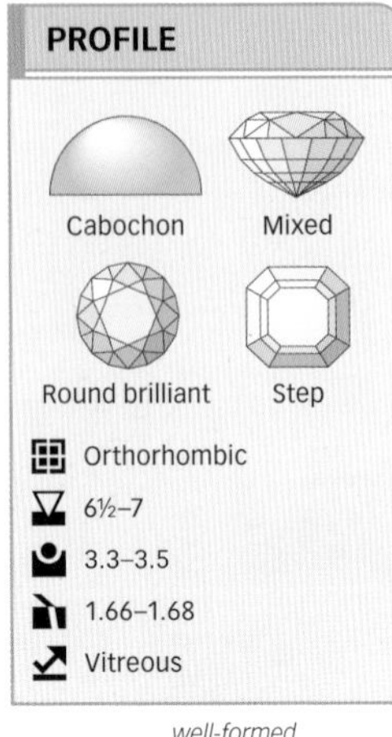

KORNERUPINE CRYSTAL ON ROCK MATRIX

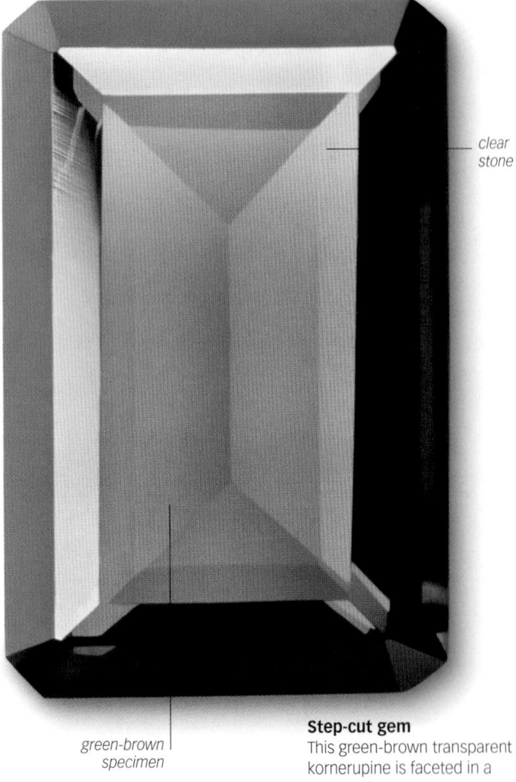

Step-cut gem This green-brown transparent kornerupine is faceted in a rectangular step cut.

VARIANT

Scissors cut A highly transparent specimen faceted in a scissors cut (a type of complex mixed cut)

$(Mg,Fe,Al)_{10}(Si,Al,B)_5(O,OH,F)_{22}$

KORNERUPINE

A rare borosilicate mineral containing magnesium, iron, and aluminum, kornerupine was named in honor of the Danish geologist Andreas Nikolaus Kornerup in 1884. However, the first gem-quality material was discovered nearly 30 years later. Kornerupine crystals can be brown, green, yellow to colorless, and can resemble tourmaline prisms. Emerald-green and blue specimens are most highly valued as gemstones; however, yellowish and yellow-green stones are also cut. Kornerupine is strongly pleochroic and exhibits different colors when viewed from different angles. To bring out the best color, the orientation of the cut stone to the rough should be such that the table facet is parallel to the prism faces of the crystal.

Kornerupine occurs in boron-rich volcanic rocks and in sedimentary rocks that have undergone high-grade metamorphism. Large, sea-green, gem-grade crystals come from Madagascar, while other gem-quality material is extracted from the gem gravels of Sri Lanka.

PROFILE

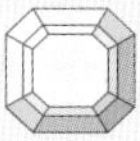

Step 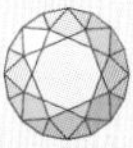 Round brilliant

Cabochon

Cubic

7–7½

4.3

1.76–1.83

Vitreous

star facet

rich color

Brilliant-cut almandine The vibrant red color of this almandine is enhanced by a brilliant cut.

dodecahedral crystal

ALMANDINE CRYSTALS ON SCHIST MATRIX

VARIANT

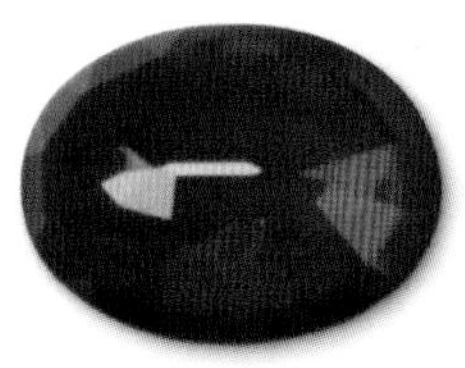

Oval-cut almandine A dark specimen of almandine that has been faceted

$Fe_3Al_2(SiO_4)_3$

ALMANDINE

The most common garnet, almandine is always red, often with a pink or violet tinge, and can sometimes be nearly opaque. Transparent specimens tend to be a pinker red than other garnets. Crystals often have well-developed faces and are dodecahedral or trapezohedral. Almandine is cut extensively for gems, but it is somewhat brittle and cut stones tend to chip on the edges. Some specimens are cut *en cabochon* and may have rutile (p.71) needles as ordered inclusions, which show as four- or six-rayed stars.

Almandine occurs worldwide and in some places is found as well-formed crystals weighing 17 lb (8 kg) or more. Star material is abundant in Idaho, USA, and facet-grade material is found globally in mica schists, gneisses, and igneous rocks.

Unusual gem The almandine specimen set in this silver ring is faceted in a step cut and shows internal inclusions.

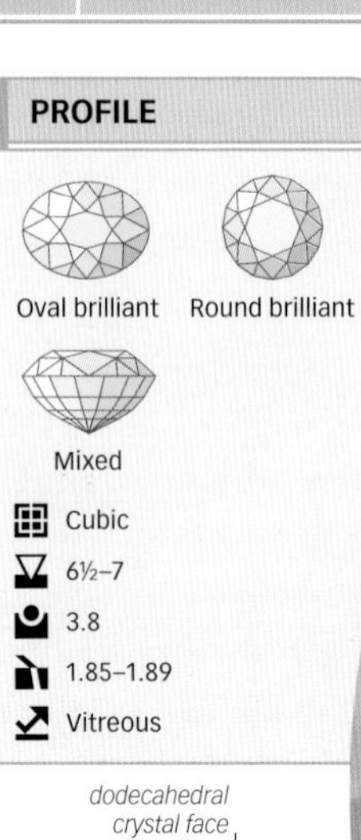

Oval mixed-cut demantoid
This oval mixed-cut specimen of demantoid shows the "horsetails" that are characteristic of this variety of Russian andradite.

DODECAHEDRAL ANDRADITE WITH ADDITIONAL FACES

VARIANTS

Rich-green demantoid
A faceted gemstone exhibiting fine green color and transparency

Brilliant-cut topazolite
A specimen of topazolite—the rare, yellow variety of andradite

$Ca_3Fe_2(SiO_4)_3$

ANDRADITE

A type of garnet, andradite has several named varieties, differing in color. A yellowish variety resembling topaz (pp.198–99) is called topazolite. Demantoid, a yellowish green or emerald-green variety, is the most highly valued form of andradite. Black andradite is called melanite. Andradite can also be brownish red, brownish yellow, grayish green, or green. The green color of andradite is caused by the presence of chromium and the yellow to black color by titanium.

Andradites of all colors except black make spectacular gems, with greater color dispersion than diamond (pp.50–51). Melanite is rarely transparent, but when it is, it can be of facet grade. Andradite commonly occurs with grossular garnet in metamorphosed limestone and some igneous rocks.

Demantoid-studded ring
A transparent faceted gem of demantoid—a variety of andradite—has been mounted on this gold ring.

main facet

star facet

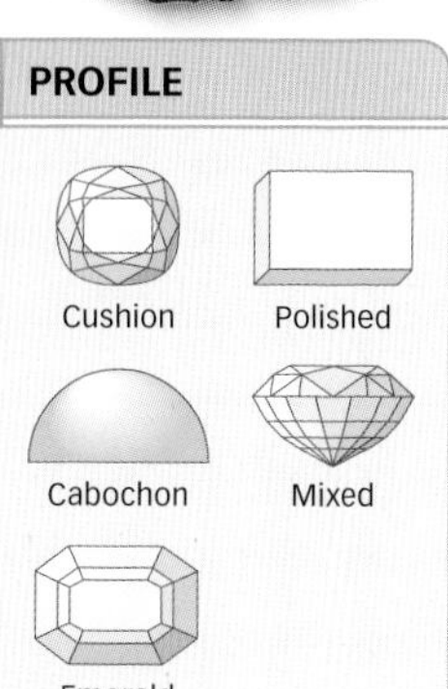

DODECAHEDRONS OF GREEN GROSSULAR

Brilliant-cut grossular
This fine green grossular has been faceted into an oval brilliant cut to emphasize its clarity and brilliance.

PROFILE

Cushion
Polished
Cabochon
Mixed
Emerald

Cubic
6½–7
3.6
1.69–1.73
Vitreous

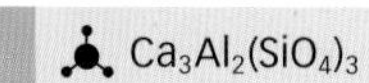
$Ca_3Al_2(SiO_4)_3$

GROSSULAR

A member of the garnet group, grossular is commonly gooseberry-green in color and is named after the Latin word *grossularia*, which means "gooseberry." It can also be white, cream, colorless, pink, orange, red, black, or yellow. A cinnamon-brown variety is called hessonite (p.182). Crystals are usually dodecahedral or trapezohedral. Specimens can also be granular or massive. Most grossular is opaque to translucent and is cut *en cabochon* or polished as a decorative stone. Some transparent, pale to emerald-green material from Kenya and Tanzania called tsavorite is faceted. The name gooseberry garnet is sometimes used for faceted stones.

Grossular is widespread, although relatively little is of gem quality. Massive greenish grossular may be marketed as Transvaal Jade, South African Jade, or African Jade.

Grossular beads
This choker necklace is made from graded and color-matched beads of grossular.

PROFILE

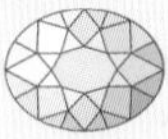

Oval brilliant 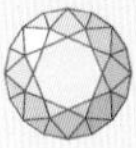 Round brilliant

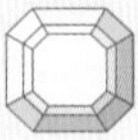

Step

Cubic

6½–7

3.7

1.73–1.75

Vitreous

dark inclusions

Mixed-cut hessonite
This round, mixed-cut specimen of hessonite has an orange color tinged with brown.

star facet

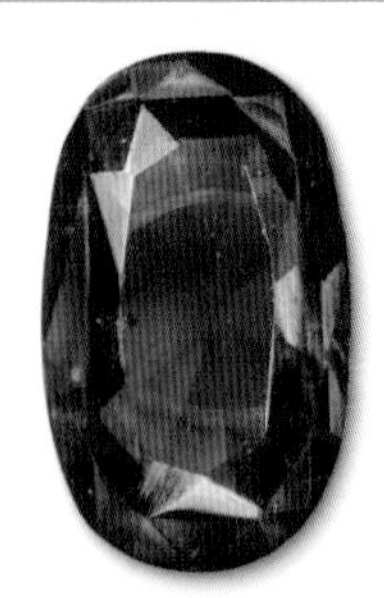

GEMMY HESSONITES ON MATRIX

VARIANT

Oval brilliant-cut hessonite
An elongated oval brilliant-cut hessonite showing good cinnamon color

$Ca_3Al_2(SiO_4)_3$

HESSONITE

Popularly called cinnamon stone, hessonite is the reddish brown variety of grossular garnet (p.181). It is colored by manganese and iron impurities and is mostly found as dodecahedral crystals. Deep-colored hessonite is cut using broad facets to display its color more effectively. The color of lighter hessonite is deepened by cutting many small facets. Hessonite is very similar in color to a variety of zircon (pp.190–91), and gems cut from hessonite have been mistaken for it for centuries. Hessonite is readily distinguished from zircon by its significantly lower specific gravity.

Hessonite is named after the Greek word *hesson*, which means "inferior"—a reference to its low hardness and density compared with most other garnet species. The ancient Greeks and Romans favored hessonite, which they used for cameos, intaglios, and cabochons. The gem gravels and metamorphic rocks of Sri Lanka are a key source of gem-quality hessonite. Excellent material is also found in Mexico, Italy, Canada, and the USA.

excellent color

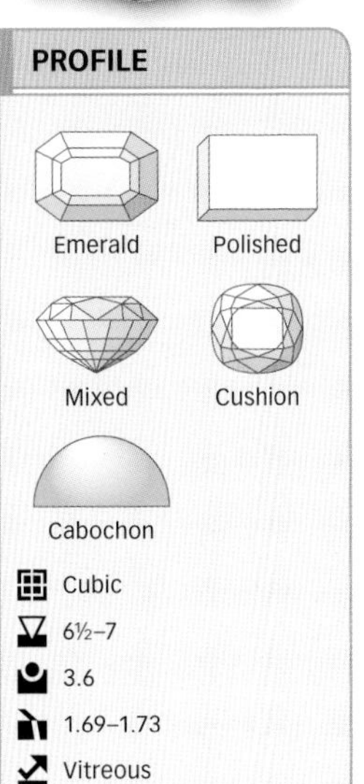

PINK GROSSULAR CRYSTAL IN MATRIX

Fine color
This oval cushion brilliant-cut specimen of pink grossular from Tanzania weighs about 5 carats and exhibits excellent color.

PROFILE

Emerald
Polished
Mixed
Cushion
Cabochon

Cubic
6½–7
3.6
1.69–1.73
Vitreous

$Ca_3Al_2(SiO_4)_3$

PINK GROSSULAR

A member of the garnet group, grossular is a calcium aluminum silicate. Pink is one of the most popular colors of grossular to be used as a gemstone. Other colors, such as the cinnamon-brown hessonite (p.182) and the emerald-green tsavorite, are also used as gemstones. The color of pink grossular ranges from pale pink to dark pink, almost grading into raspberry. Curiously enough, in spite of the vibrancy of its color, pink grossular has never acquired a specific gemstone name. Its crystals are generally dodecahedral or trapezohedral, but it can also be granular or massive. Crystals up to 5 in (13 cm) across have been found, although gem-quality crystals tend to be smaller. Transparent material is faceted, and translucent or massive material is cut into cabochons or polished as a decorative stone.

Pink grossular typically forms in impure calcium-rich rocks that have undergone metamorphism. Like other grossular, pink grossular is fairly widespread, although relatively little is of gem quality.

PROFILE

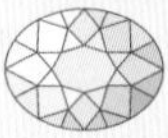

Oval brilliant

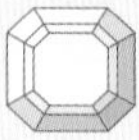

Step

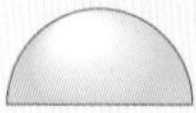

Cabochon

Cubic

7–7½

3.6

1.73–1.76

Vitreous

Rich color This pendaloque-cut specimen exhibits the rich purple-red color for which pyrope is well known.

typical deep color

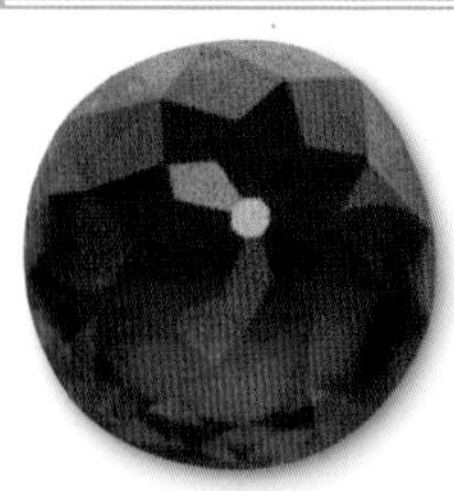

STREAM-ROUNDED PYROPE ROUGHS

VARIANT

Pavilion facets A pyrope gem resting on its table facet and displaying the intricacies of its pavilion facets

$Mg_3Al_2(SiO_4)_3$

PYROPE

A member of the garnet family, pyrope is a magnesium aluminum silicate. It takes its name from *pyr* and *õps,* the Greek words for “fire” and “to appear” respectively—a reference to the fact that, unlike other garnets, natural samples of pyrope always display red coloration. Iron, chromium, titanium, and manganese all substitute in the pyrope structure. They act as coloring agents by changing the composition, producing variation from the rich red of pure pyrope to violet-red, rose-red, or reddish orange. Pyrope with high chromium content can change color according to the type of light source.

With increasing substitution of other elements in its structure, pyrope gradually grades into other garnet minerals. Rhodolite for example, often cut as a gemstone, is a garnet of about 70 percent pyrope by composition. Although it is most often found in rounded grains or pebbles, pyrope can occur as crystals. These are dodecahedrons and trapezohedrons and have been found up to 5 in (12 cm) in diameter.

PROFILE

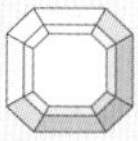

Step 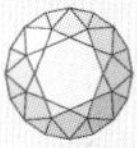 Round brilliant

Cubic

7–7½

4.2

1.79–1.81

Vitreous

internal inclusions (flaws)

dodecahedron face

Triangular cushion
This spessartine is faceted in a triangular brilliant-cut cushion and has a number of interesting internal inclusions.

GEM-QUALITY CRYSTAL OF SPESSARTINE

VARIANT

Emerald-cut spessartine
A specimen faceted in an emerald cut to highlight its color

$Mn_3Al_2(SiO_4)_3$

SPESSARTINE

A manganese aluminum silicate and a member of the garnet family, spessartine is named after Spessart, Germany. Pure spessartine garnet is rare—it is almost always compositionally between spessartine and almandine (p.179), which gives a common orange to red color. It can also be pale yellow, deep red, black, or brown. Well-formed dodecahedral or trapezohedral crystals up to 5 in (13 cm) across are known. Spessartine can also be granular or massive. Gem-quality material is relatively rare, and is cut more for collectors than for use in jewelry.

The Rutherford Mine in Virginia, USA, produces some of the largest spessartines, one of which weighed 6,720 carats. Gemstone material is found in Madagascar, Nigeria, Brazil, Namibia, Sri Lanka, and the USA. A garnet with a composition intermediate between that of spessartine and pyrope is called Malaya garnet. Some of these garnets, containing small amounts of vanadium and chromium, change color according to the type of light source.

Free-form uvarovite
This cabochon has a surface of fine uvarovite crystals that are too small to facet.

small uvarovite crystals

free-form shape

crust of uvarovite crystals

UVAROVITE CRYSTALS ON MATRIX

PROFILE

Oval brilliant

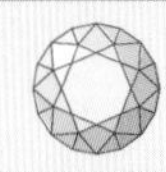
Round brilliant

- Cubic
- 6½–7
- 3.8
- 1.86–1.87
- Vitreous

$Ca_3Cr_2(SiO_4)_3$

UVAROVITE

A calcium chromium silicate, uvarovite is the rarest of all gem garnets and a rarity among gemstones. Its crystals are mostly dodecahedral and are almost always too small to be cut. Uvarovite is usually brilliant green in color—the only consistently green garnet species. Its color comes from chromium—a coloring agent that is also present in emerald (p.169) and ruby (p.60). Gems faceted from the relatively rare crystals of sufficient size are in great demand by collectors.

Uvarovite was named in 1832 after the Russian nobleman Count Uvarov, a noted amateur mineral collector. It is found in igneous and metamorphic rocks associated with chromium-bearing ores. Some of the largest crystals come from Outokumpu, Finland. It is also found in the Ural Mountains of Russia, where transparent crystals are found lining cavities and fissures in rock. Other localities include Silesia, Poland; Québec, Canada; and California, USA. The name uvarovite is sometimes incorrectly applied to other dark green garnets.

PROFILE

Cabochon 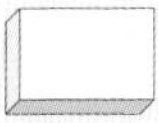 Polished

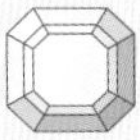

Step

Orthorhombic

6½–7½

3.2

1.63–1.64

Vitreous

elongated andalusite crystal

rock matrix

ANDALUSITE CRYSTALS ON ROCK MATRIX

main facet

Pleochroic andalusite The strong pleochroism of andalusite causes flashes of various colors throughout this emerald-cut stone.

color flashes

VARIANT

Chiastolite A cross section of the andalusite variety known as chiastolite

Al_2OSiO_5

ANDALUSITE

This mineral is named after Andalusia, Spain, where it was discovered. A transparent variety that was first found there can be cut into attractive gemstones. Andalusite can be green, white, gray, violet, yellow, blue, or pink to reddish brown. Faceted stones exhibit a play of colors that resembles iridescence. This is a result of strong pleochroism, which causes the same stone to appear yellow, green, or red depending on the original color and the direction of viewing. When faceting, pleochroism must be taken into account to get the desired gem color.

Gem-quality andalusite is found in Minas Gerais, Brazil, and in the gem gravels of Sri Lanka, mainly as water-worn pebbles. Sri Lanka also produces a grayish white material that shows a cat's eye effect when cut *en cabochon*. Attractive blue stones have been found in Myanmar. A yellowish gray variety called chiastolite occurs as long prisms enclosing symmetrical wedges of carbonaceous material, which form a cross in cross section. Slices of chiastolite are worn as talismans.

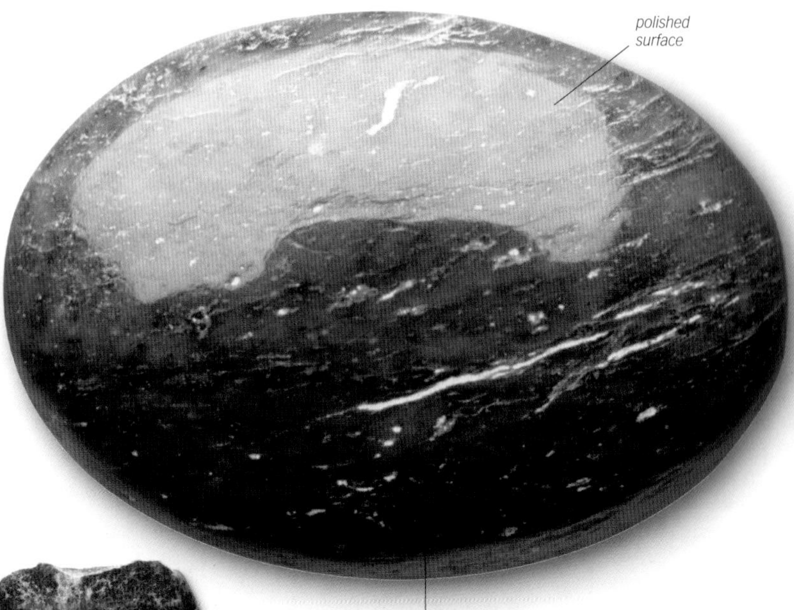

polished surface

blue shade from titanium substitution for iron

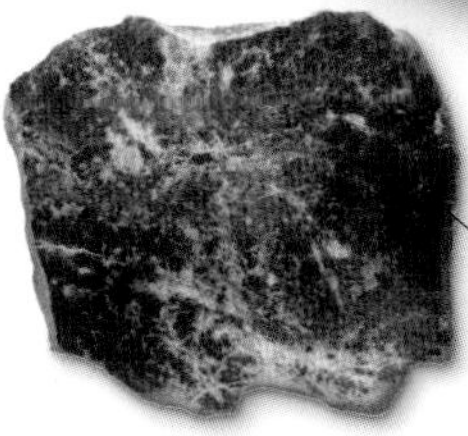

deep blue color

FINE BLUE DUMORTIERITE ROUGH

Dumortierite cabochon
This oval cabochon of dumortierite exhibits an intense blue—the stone's most prized color.

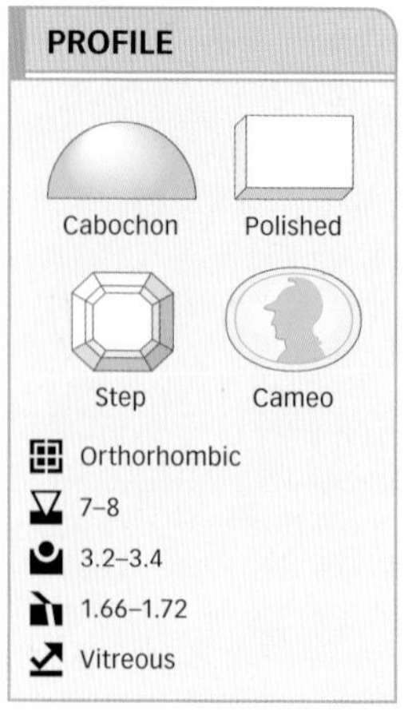

$(Al,Fe)_7(BO_3)(SiO_4)_3O_3$

DUMORTIERITE

A fibrous aluminum-iron borosilicate, dumortierite is usually pinkish red or violet to blue, but it can also be brown or greenish in color. Intense deep blue to violet specimens are particularly prized. Dumortierite is best known in its massive form, which is used for gemstones cut *en cabochon* and in carvings. The mineral is sometimes found as small crystals that are pleochroic and appear red to blue to violet when seen from different directions. On rare occasions, these crystals are faceted for collectors. Dumortierite can resemble sodalite (p.134) or lapis lazuli (pp.130–31), but its colors are more vivid.

Dumortierite occurs in pegmatites, aluminum-rich metamorphic rocks, and rocks metamorphosed by boron-bearing fluids from intruding bodies of granite. Deep blue, titanium-rich gem material comes from Cape Province in South Africa. Other gem material is found in Madagascar, Japan, Canada, Sri Lanka, Italy, and Nevada and Colorado, USA.

PROFILE

Mixed 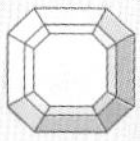 Step

Monoclinic

7½

3.0

1.65–1.67

Vitreous

fragile stone

pyramidal termination

COLORLESS, PRISMATIC EUCLASE CRYSTAL

Emerald-cut euclase
This deep blue specimen of euclase is faceted in a step cut to accentuate its color.

VARIANT

Colorless euclase
A colorless step-cut specimen of euclase

$BeAlSiO_4(OH)$

EUCLASE

A beryllium aluminum hydroxide silicate, euclase is generally white or colorless, but it can also be pale green or pale to deep blue. The most desirable gems are pale aquamarine blue, although other colors are also faceted. Transparent euclase is mostly faceted for collectors. Darker blue material is distinctly pleochroic, requiring careful orientation of cut stones. Euclase takes its name from the Greek words *eu* and *klasis*, which mean "good" and "fracture" respectively – a reference to its perfect cleavage. The ready cleavage of euclase makes it a fragile stone with a tendency to chip; hence care must be taken while setting and mounting. To prevent fragments from popping off in the cutting process, faceters must avoid orienting a major face of the gem along a cleavage plane.

Euclase forms striated prisms, often with complex terminations. It occurs mainly in veins formed at low temperatures (up to 400°F/ 200°C) and in pegmatites. Gem-quality euclase comes from Brazil, India, Russia, Tanzania, Austria, and the USA.

Natural color The color of this cushion brilliant-cut zircon has not been altered by heat treatment.

ZIRCON ROUGH (WITHOUT HEAT TREATMENT)

$ZrSiO_4$

ZIRCON

Known since antiquity, zircon is named after the Arabic word *zargun*, derived in turn from the Persian words *zar* and *gun*, which mean "gold" and "color" respectively. In addition to the gold color referred to in its name, zircon can also be colorless, yellow, gray, green, red, blue, or brown. Many of the colored zircons on the market today have been obtained by heating brown zircons. Heating in an oxygen-free atmosphere yields blue zircon, which itself may be heated in air to yield a golden color. Both of these processes produce some colorless material, provided trace elements are absent from the brown zircon.

Zircon has a high refractive index and superb color dispersion. It is one of the few stones to approach diamond (pp.50–51) in fire and brilliance. As a result, colorless zircons have been both mistakenly identified as diamonds and purposely used as diamond simulants. Zircon occurs as tetragonal crystals that can reach a considerable size: single crystals weighing up to 4²⁄₄ lb (2 kg) have been found in Australia and examples up to 8¾ lb (4 kg) in Russia.

A zirconium silicate, zircon is widespread in silica-rich igneous rocks and in some metamorphic rocks. Because it is resistant to weathering and has a relatively high specific gravity, it concentrates in stream and river gravels and in beach deposits. Gem material comes from France, Thailand, Cambodia, Vietnam, Myanmar, Australia, Tanzania, Nigeria, and Brazil.

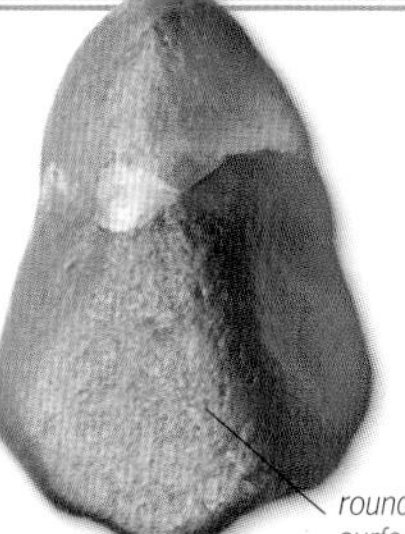

Water-rounded pebble
This water-worn pebble of zircon is typical of much gem material recovered from placer deposits.

Heat-treated zircon
The blue color of this round brilliant-cut gem has been achieved by subjecting brown zircon to heat.

Brown zircon
This pale brown zircon has been faceted into a step cut to emphasize its color.

Green zircon
This oval brilliant-cut green zircon is in its natural color.

Zircon bracelet
This gold-plated bracelet is set with colorless zircons and other orange gemstones.

diamond border

Edwardian zircon ring
This gold and platinum ring has a large, brilliant-cut blue zircon in the center, surrounded by small diamonds.

EASTERN GEM

Zircon has been mined and used for jewelry in India and Sri Lanka for many centuries. Some of its obsolete Eastern names are hyacinth or jacinth for the red, orange, or yellow varieties and jargon or jargun for all other gem colors. The *Kalpataru*, a symbolic offering to Hindu gods, was described as a mass of jewels that included zircon.

The Kalpataru
This 10th-century CE temple has two Kinnari (mythical creatures) guarding *Kalpataru*—the tree of life.

Floral brooch
The zircons in this silver floral brooch are naturally colorless.

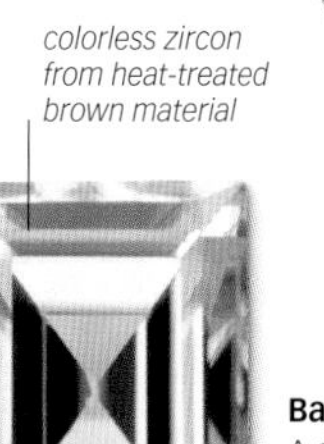

Baguette-cut zircon
A specimen of colorless zircon has been cut into a baguette to emphasize its brilliance.

Oval brilliant-cut kyanite
This kyanite gem showing fine blue color and clarity has been faceted into an oval brilliant cut.

unpolished girdle

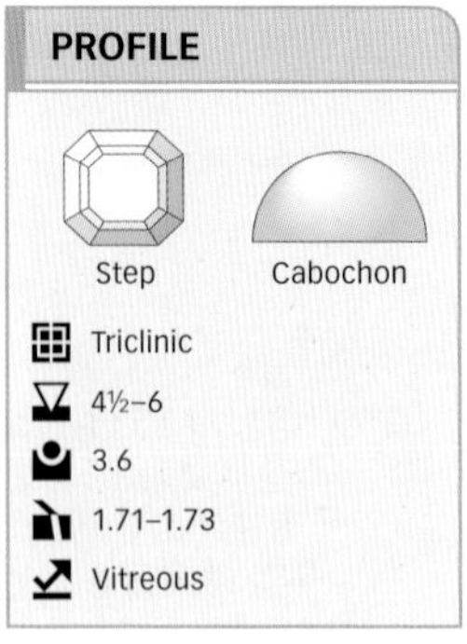

BLUE KYANITE BLADES IN MATRIX

PROFILE

Step | Cabochon

Triclinic

4½–6

3.6

1.71–1.73

Vitreous

Al_2SiO_5

KYANITE

A mineral that occurs principally as elongated, flattened blades, kyanite is usually blue in color. This explains the fact that it derives its name from the Greek word *kyanos*, which means "dark blue." Within a single crystal, the blue is generally mixed or zoned with blue-gray. In color-zoned crystals, the darker colors appear toward the centre. Specimens can also be green, orange, or colorless. Blue kyanite is distinctly pleochroic, appearing blue, violet-blue, and colorless when viewed from different directions. Kyanite can be difficult to facet due to its variable hardness—about 4½ parallel to the long axis, but 6 along the perpendicular direction. Kyanite's former name, disthene, which means "two strengths," derives from this.

The fibrous nature and cleavage of kyanite make it liable to break along its length, adding to the cutter's difficulties. Kyanite may be cut *en cabochon* to show a cat's eye effect. Cut stones tend to be collectors' gems. Kyanite is found in mica schists, gneisses, and associated quartz veins and pegmatites.

PROFILE

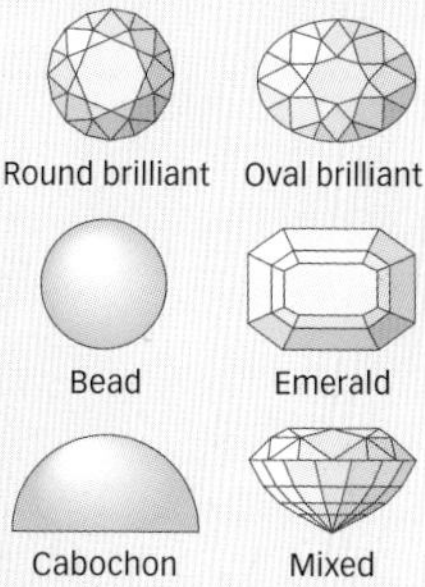

Round brilliant
Oval brilliant
Bead
Emerald
Cabochon
Mixed

Orthorhombic
6½–7
3.3–4.3
1.64–1.69
Vitreous to greasy

highly transparent

Pendaloque-cut peridot The light green color of this peridot indicates a relatively low concentration of iron in its structure.

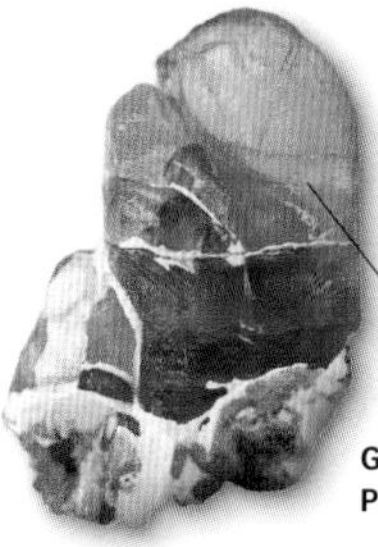

distinctive color

GEM-QUALITY PERIDOT CRYSTAL

VARIANTS

Oval cut A light green specimen of peridot faceted in a mixed oval cut

Octagonal cut An octagonal scissors-cut, dark green, iron-rich peridot

$(Mg,Fe)_2SiO_4$

PERIDOT

The name peridot is French and may have been derived from the Arabic word *faridat*, which means "gem." It is a transparent gem variety of the mineral group olivine. The most valued color of peridot is a rich green, but it can range from pale golden green to brownish red. The proportion of iron present determines the shade and depth of color. In general, stones with small amounts of iron exhibit better color.

As a gemstone, peridot is relatively soft. It is doubly refractive, so facets on the underside of the stone appear doubled. Peridot has been mined for over 3,500 years. St. John's Island in the Red Sea was the ancient source of peridot. It is currently found in Pakistan and China, and also in South Africa, Norway, Canary Islands, Australia, Myanmar, and the USA.

Peridot earrings These antique earrings have matched peridots and pearls in a gold setting.

"steely" appearance

vitreous luster

blocky crystals

PARALLEL-GROWTH, GEM-GRADE PHENAKITE CRYSTALS

Brilliant oval gem
This superbly transparent oval phenakite shows a quality of brilliance sometimes described as "steely."

PROFILE

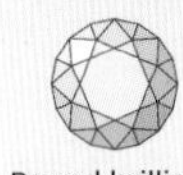
Round brilliant

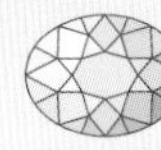
Oval brilliant

Mixed

 Hexagonal or trigonal

 7½–8

 2.9

1.65–1.67

Vitreous

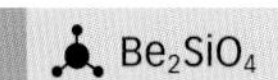 Be_2SiO_4

PHENAKITE

A rare beryllium mineral, phenakite is named after the Greek word for "deceiver"—a reference to the fact that it can be mistaken for quartz, which it can resemble. Phenakite crystals can be colorless and transparent, but they are more often grayish or yellowish, and occasionally pale rose-red. Colorless, transparent crystals are faceted for collectors. Because of their high refractive index—higher than topaz (pp.198–99)—faceted stones are usually brilliant-cut. Phenakite's brilliance approaches that of diamond (pp.50–51), with which faceted phenakite is sometimes confused.

Phenakite usually occurs as isolated crystals, which are mostly rhombohedral and, less commonly, short and prismatic. It occurs in pegmatites that form at high temperatures (1,065°F/575°C or above) and in granites and mica schists. Large crystals are found in the Ural Mountains of Russia and in the Pikes Peak region of Colorado, USA. Phenakite is also found in Zimbabwe, Namibia, and Sri Lanka.

PROFILE

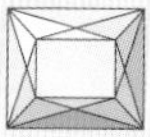

Scissors

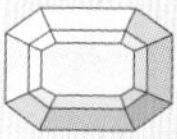

Emerald

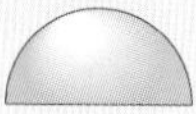

Cabochon

Orthorhombic

7

3.2–3.3

1.66–1.68

Silky or vitreous

elongated prismatic crystals

SILLIMANITE CRYSTALS ON ROCK MATRIX

crisscross facets

Scissors-cut sillimanite
The scissors cut is used to enhance the brilliance of colorless or light-colored stones, like this otherwise pale violet sillimanite.

VARIANT

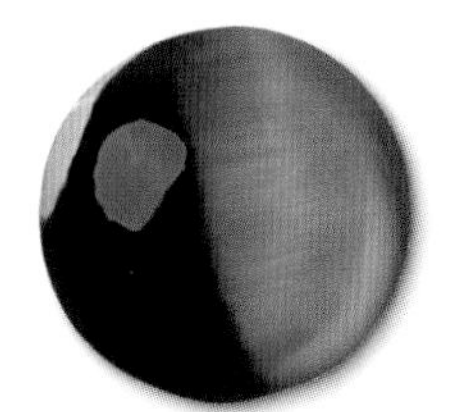

Fibrolite cabochon
A specimen of the fibrolite variety of sillimanite cut *en cabochon*

Al_2OSiO_5

SILLIMANITE

Named after the American chemist Benjamin Silliman, sillimanite is commonly colorless to white, but it can also be pale yellow to brown, pale blue, green, or violet. Although sillimanite is often thought of as an industrial mineral, attractive faceted gems can be cut from transparent material. Blue and violet gemstones are the most prized. Sillimanite is distinctly pleochroic, appearing yellowish green, dark green, or blue when seen from different angles; consequently, the gem rough needs to be carefully oriented while cutting to achieve the best color. Crystals of sillimanite are long, slender, and glassy, or occur as blocky prisms. Cabochons are cut from a variety of sillimanite called fibrolite, so named because the mineral appears like a bunch of fibers twisted together.

An aluminum silicate, sillimanite is a common mineral in some metamorphic rocks. Most gem-quality material is recovered from placer deposits. Localities include India, Myanmar, the Czech Republic, Sri Lanka, Italy, Germany, Brazil, and the USA.

PROFILE

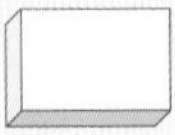

Polished

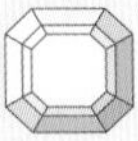

Step

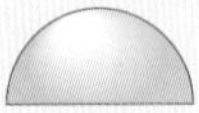

Cabochon

Monoclinic

7–7½

3.7

1.74–1.75

Vitreous to resinous

Fairy cross
A twinned staurolite crystal like this is sometimes called a "fairy cross" and worn uncut as jewelry.

staurolite crystal

STAUROLITE CRYSTALS IN MICA SCHIST MATRIX

twinned crystal

VARIANT

Faceted staurolite
An oblique step-cut specimen of transparent staurolite

$(Fe,Mg)_4Al_{17}(Si,Al)_8O_{45}(OH)_3$

STAUROLITE

An aluminum iron hydroxysilicate, staurolite is one of the few minerals that are worn as a gem straight out of the ground. A special property of staurolite is that it often occurs twinned in a characteristic cross shape. It is this crosslike form that gives the mineral its name. The word "staurolite" is derived from the Greek words *stauros* and *lithos*, which mean "cross" and "stone" respectively. Staurolite is locally known as "Fairy Stones" or "Fairy Crosses" in the USA, based on a legend about the origin of the stone's curious shape. Staurolite is reddish brown, yellowish brown, or nearly black. It is frequently worn as ornaments and talismans. Charms made from staurolite are in great demand, and President Theodore Roosevelt was said to wear a watch charm made from staurolite.

Staurolite is occasionally found as translucent to transparent crystals. These can be cut *en cabochon* or faceted for collectors. It is found in Georgia, USA, and is the state gem of Georgia. It is also found in Brazil, France, and New Mexico, USA.

PROFILE

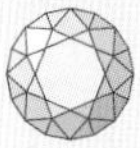

Round brilliant 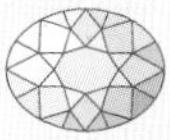 Oval brilliant

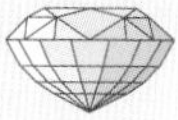

Mixed

Monoclinic

5–5½

3.5–3.6

1.84–2.03

Vitreous to greasy

Cushion-cut sphene This cushion mixed-cut gem shows the doubling of facets on the stone due to its strong dispersion.

doubling of facets

wedge-shaped crystal

SPHENE CRYSTAL ON ROCK MATRIX

VARIANTS

Triangular cut A triangular cushion-cut specimen showing good yellow color

Step cut An oval yellow sphene with modified step-cut

$CaTiSiO_5$

SPHENE

A calcium titanium silicate, sphene is the former name for titanite gemstones. Titanite derives its name from the titanium content of the mineral, while sphene persists as the informal name. Sphene is one of the few stones with color dispersion higher than that of diamond (pp.50–51). It is strongly pleochroic as well, appearing nearly colorless, greenish yellow, and reddish or brownish yellow when seen from different directions. Gem-quality sphene is yellow, green, or brown, but specimens can also be red, pink, black, blue, or colorless.

Faceted stones cut from transparent crystals are fiery and brilliant. Sphene is relatively soft so faceted stones must be set in deep mountings to protect them when worn as jewelry. This means that despite their brilliance, most stones are cut only for collectors.

Gold ring This round, multifaceted yellow titanite is set in a gold ring and shows its superb fire and intense color.

Fine topaz
This oval mixed-cut topaz has a fine intense golden color.

$Al_2SiO_4(F,OH)_2$

TOPAZ

It was once believed that all yellow gems were topaz and that all topaz was yellow. Yellow sapphire (pp.62–63), for example, was once called oriental topaz. Topaz is, in fact, found in a wide range of colors, and sherry-yellow stones from Brazil are considered particularly valuable.

The name topaz is thought to have been derived from the Sanskrit word *tapaz*—which means "fire." Because it is very refractive, brilliant-cut stones faceted from colorless topaz have been mistaken for diamond (pp.50–51). Some blue topaz is almost indistinguishable from aquamarine (p.164) with the naked eye. Topaz is found as well-formed, prismatic crystals, with a characteristic lozenge-shaped cross section and striations parallel to the length. Natural pink stones are rare; therefore, pink is the most highly valued color. Much of the colored topaz on today's market is "enhanced"—treated by heat or radiation to change its color. Even in Victorian times, the popular pink color was produced by treating golden brown topaz from Guro Freto, Brazil. Current sources of topaz include Russia, Brazil, and Nigeria.

An aluminum silicate, topaz contains up to 20 percent fluorine or water. It is formed by fluorine-bearing vapors given off during the last stages of the crystallization of various igneous rocks. It is typically found in cavities in rhyolites, granites, pegmatites, and hydrothermal veins. It is resistant to weathering and relatively heavy, so it concentrates in stream deposits.

TOPAZ MEGAGEMS

A number of large crystals of topaz have been found to date. The world's largest preserved topaz crystal weighs 596 lb (271 kg). In the 1980s, a gem weighing 22,892.5 carats—4.6 kg (10 lb)—was faceted from a Brazilian cobble for the American Smithsonian Institution's National Gem Collection.

Megatopaz
The two gigantic crystals flanking the girl and the huge faceted stone at her feet show how large topaz can be.

Brazilian topaz
This 8.87-carat, pear-shaped imperial topaz was one of the first to be recovered from San Luis Potosi, Mexico.

cleavage plane

Gem-quality crystal
This gem-quality, pyramidal topaz crystal has a fine blue color above its cleavage plane.

Topaz necklace
Designed by Elsa Schiaparelli, this necklace has a matched set of emerald-cut topaz stones.

amber-colored stone

multiple reflections

Step-cut topaz
The clarity and depth that can be achieved in topaz are illustrated in this step-cut stone.

prong mounting

Topaz ring
This gold ring has been set with an eight-sided, step-cut topaz in a fine pink color.

prism face

mixed cut stone

rare color

Imperial crystal
The red-brown color of this Brazilian crystal makes it prime gemstone material.

Topaz brooch
This gold and platinum brooch has been set with a natural pink topaz that is surrounded by diamonds.

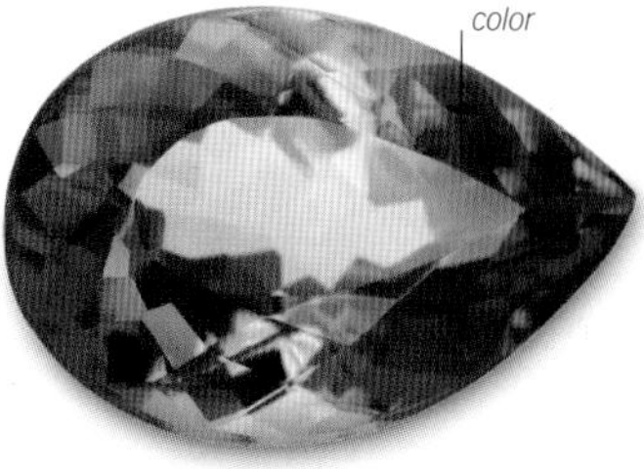

Pink topaz
The pink color of this pendaloque-cut stone is the rarest in topaz.

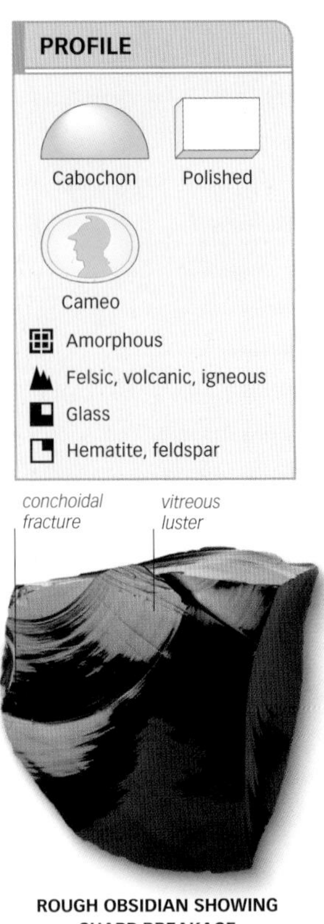

ROUGH OBSIDIAN SHOWING SHARP BREAKAGE

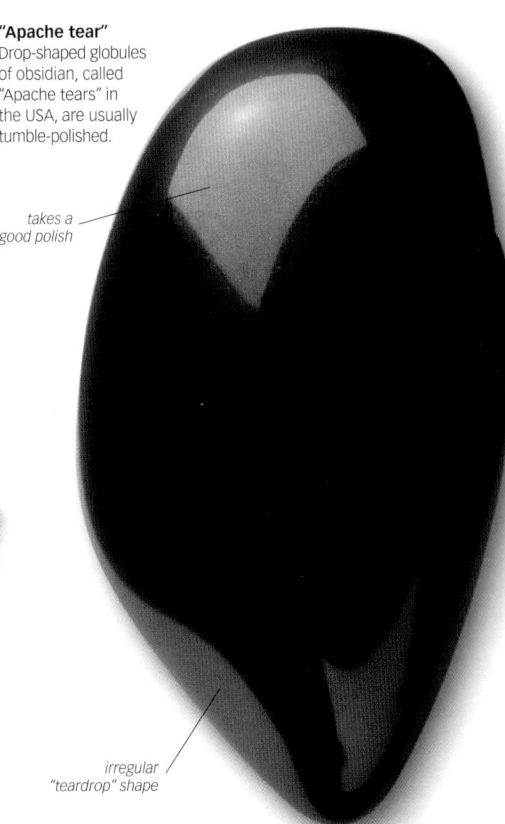

"Apache tear" Drop-shaped globules of obsidian, called "Apache tears" in the USA, are usually tumble-polished.

Variable, mainly silicates

OBSIDIAN

This rock is a natural volcanic glass that forms when lava solidifies so quickly that mineral crystals do not have time to grow. Obsidian is typically jet-black, but the presence of the iron oxide hematite (p.57) produces red and brown varieties, and the inclusion of tiny gas bubbles can create a golden sheen. Another variety, called snowflake obsidian, has spherical clusters of light-colored, needlelike crystals, which are usually around 3⁄16 in (5 mm) in diameter, scattered throughout the black mass.

Although obsidian can have a range of chemical compositions, it is usually the product of silica-rich magmas. It is harder than glass and can be chipped to razor-sharp edges. The Native Americans and other ancient peoples used this rock to make weapons, tools, and ornaments. It is now carved and cut *en cabochon*. Well-known occurrences of obsidian are on the Eolie Islands off the coast of Italy, Mount Hekla in Iceland, and the Obsidian Cliff in Yellowstone National Park, Wyoming, USA.

VARIANTS

Thunder egg A sliced ball of thunder egg, a variety of obsidian

Snowflake obsidian A tumble-polished piece of snowflake obsidian

airflow ripples

aerodynamic shaping

visible internal flow structures

internal color variations

UNCUT MOLDAVITE

Faceted gem
This transparent specimen of moldavite has been faceted into an oval brilliant gem.

PROFILE

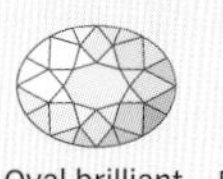

Oval brilliant

Round brilliant

Amorphous

5

2.4

1.48–1.51

Vitreous

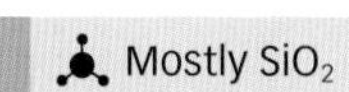

Mostly SiO_2

MOLDAVITE

Pieces of glass that are typically olive green to dull greenish yellow, moldavites are one of several types of tektite that sometimes form when large meteorites hit Earth. Moldavite is found in sizes ranging from 1⁄16 in (1 mm) or less to several inches across. Uncut specimens are worn as pendants. Moldavite is also faceted, although it is a relatively brittle stone.

Moldavites are now recognized to have been formed 15 million years ago when a giant meteorite fell in present-day Nördlinger Ries, Bavaria, Germany. The local sandstone melted from the heat of the impact, was flung up several hundred miles toward the east, and cooled in flight to form glass. Much of it fell in the Bohemia region in the Czech Republic. Moldavite gets its name from Moldauthein, a town in the region where it fell. It is also found occasionally in Germany and Austria. Other types of tektites have been found on every continent except Antarctica and South America.

ORGANICS

Many organic substances, such as feathers, leaves, shell, and bone, have been carved or otherwise used for personal adornment over centuries. The usual definition of an organic gem is a gem that is created by or made from living organisms.

REAL GEMS

Within the broad definition of organic gems there are many subgroups. The largest group consists of organic gems that contain crystalline matter, such as calcite and aragonite—the same mineral matter as that generated through geological processes. Gems in this group include shell, pearl, mother-of-pearl, and red coral.

EASILY WORKED

Like gemstones of purely mineral origin, organic gems are valued for their beauty and durability. Organic gems were popular in ancient times because they are softer than minerals and were easily worked by primitive methods.

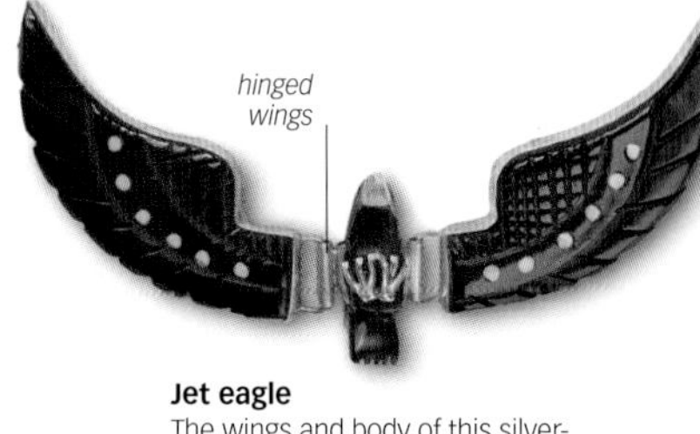

Jet eagle
The wings and body of this silver-mounted Native American eagle are carved from jet. Turquoise has been used for the beak and as an inlay in the wings.

graduated sizes

Maya shell pendant
This pre-Columbian Maya shell pendant is carved with a Maya god in profile and Mayan hieroglyphics around the periphery.

Coral necklace and brooch
This 1950s necklace is made of tumble-polished red coral branches. The brooch is made of red coral beads and polished coral disks.

Pearls in oyster
Pearls of assorted sizes and colors can be seen in this oyster shell. A black pearl sits on top.

PROFILE

Cabochon  Polished

Bead  Cameo

None

2–2½

1.1

1.54–1.55

Resinous

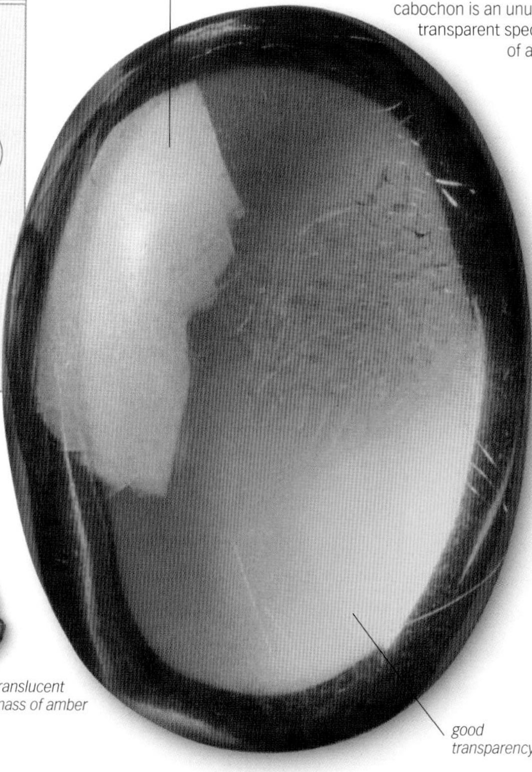

resinous appearance

Transparent cabochon This high-domed, double-sided cabochon is an unusually transparent specimen of amber.

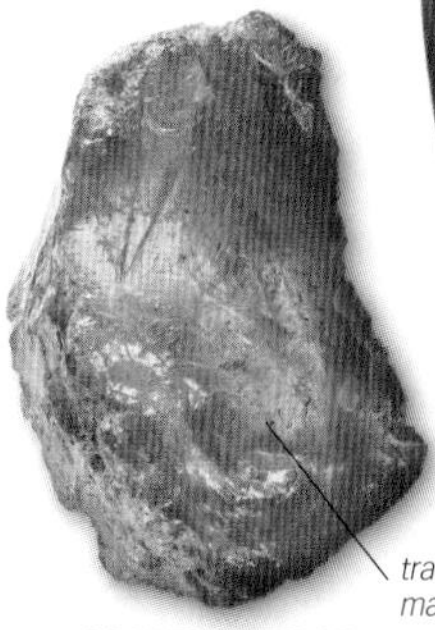

translucent mass of amber

BROKEN PIECE OF FINE-QUALITY AMBER

good transparency

VARIANT

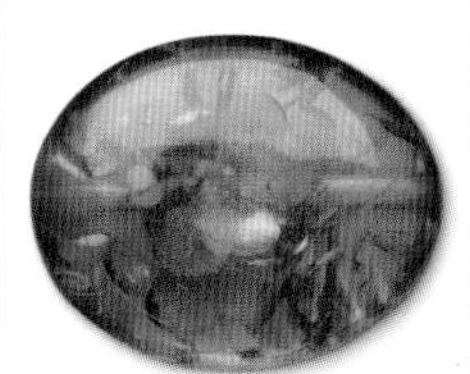

Polished bead A bead of amber, possibly cracked during drilling

(C,H,O)

AMBER

This gem is fossilized resin from extinct coniferous trees. Amberlike substances from even earlier trees are also known. Amber is most often yellow to golden in color, although red, green, violet, and black specimens are sometimes found. It can be transparent or opaque and can have inclusions of plant and animal debris. Amber can acquire a static charge when rubbed; this helps distinguish it from plastic and modern resin lookalikes.

Amber has been widely used and traded since ancient times. Beads of amber that date back to the 3rd millennium BCE have been found. A cup carved from amber was discovered in a British Bronze Age burial site. For several thousand years, Europe's Baltic coast has been the largest source of the gem.

Amber earrings This pair of earrings has cut and polished, teardrop shaped stones of amber set on silver mountings.

PROFILE

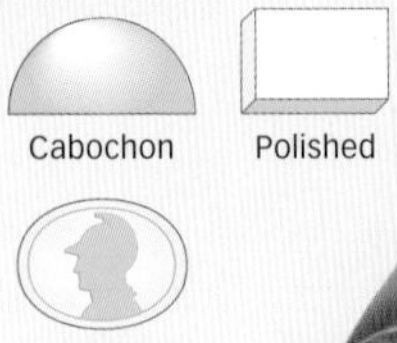

Cabochon Polished

Cameo

Amorphous

2½

About 1.3

1.64–1.68

Velvety to waxy

best-quality jet takes a high polish

rose carving

Victorian carving This late 19th-century carving of a rose set in a swirl of foliage illustrates the intricate detail possible when carving fine jet.

bedded structure

other organic material

PIECE OF RAW WHITBY JET

VARIANT

Jet egg An ornamental egg made from jet

Various

JET

Jet carvings found in caves dating back to prehistoric times show that humans have had a long association with this material. The ancient Romans carved jet into bangles and beads. In medieval times, powdered jet drunk in water or wine was believed to have medicinal properties. The mineral also has a long history of religious association. During the Middle Ages, jet carvings were sold to pilgrims in Spain. Jet has also traditionally been used for rosaries for monks.

Generally classified as a lignite coal, jet has a high carbon content and a layered structure. Unlike ordinary lignite, which usually forms from peaty deposits on land, jet occurs in rocks of marine origin, perhaps derived from waterlogged driftwood or other plant material. Jet sometimes contains tiny inclusions of pyrite (p.55), which have a metallic luster.

Jet pendant This carved and polished pendant of jet shows a dove carrying a heart in its beak.

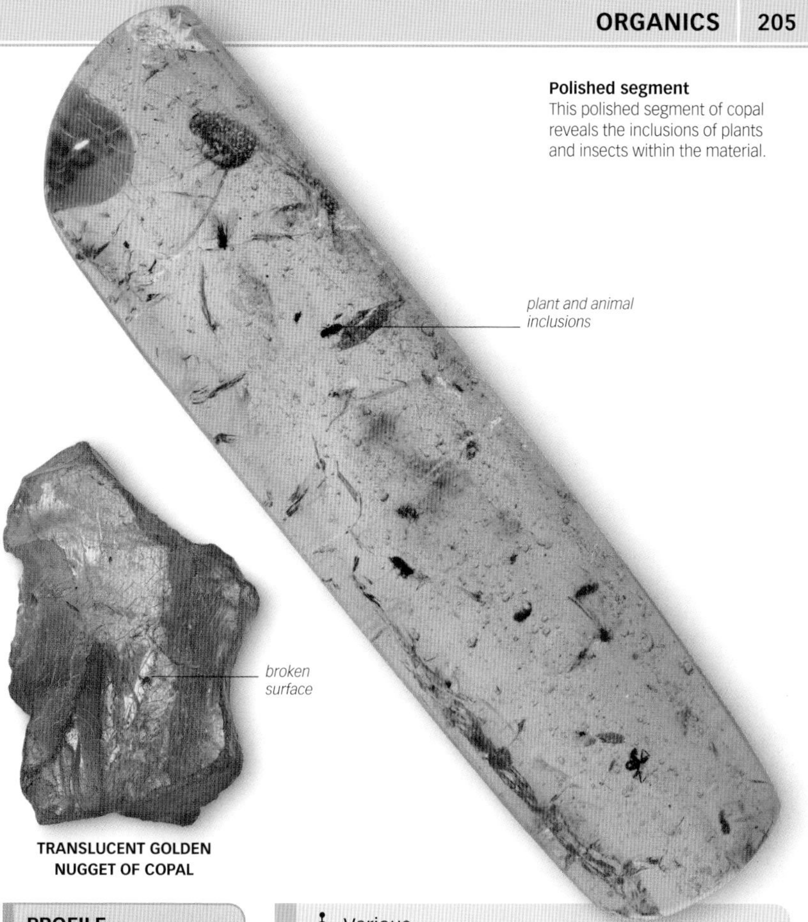

Polished segment
This polished segment of copal reveals the inclusions of plants and insects within the material.

plant and animal inclusions

broken surface

TRANSLUCENT GOLDEN NUGGET OF COPAL

PROFILE

Polished

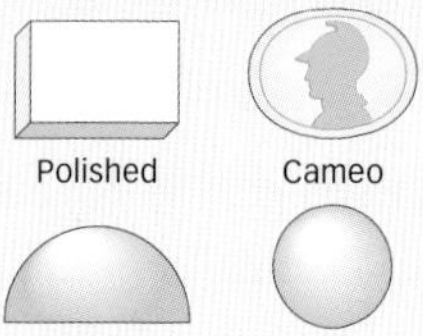

Cameo

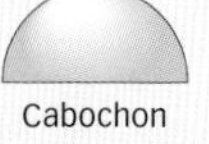
Cabochon

Bead

None

2–2½

About 1.1

Variable

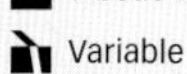
Resinous

Various

COPAL

The name copal probably originates from the Mesoamerican word *nahuatl copalli*, which means "resin." Copal refers to resins obtained from tropical trees and more generally to resinous substances in a stage of hardening between "gummier" resins and amber (p.203). Copal has the look of hardened tree resin, and tends to have the same yellow to yellow-orange color. Copal resins have the same approximate hardness as amber and can easily be mistaken for it; like amber, they often contain plants and insects. Buried copal mined from the soil under living trees is the nearest to amber in durability and is often virtually indistinguishable from it.

As a gem, copal is used in the same applications as amber. Buried copal comes from Zanzibar, South America, and China.

Copal necklace
This necklace is made of amberlike beads of copal alternating with beads carved from seeds or nuts.

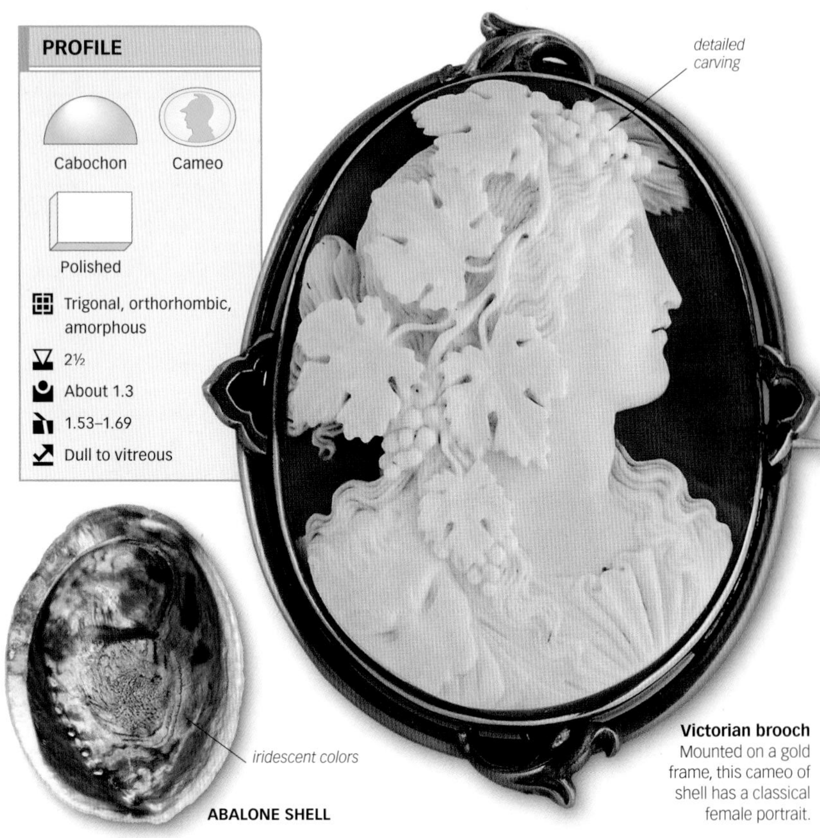

ABALONE SHELL

Victorian brooch Mounted on a gold frame, this cameo of shell has a classical female portrait.

Mostly $CaCO_3$

SHELL

Both marine and freshwater shells have been used as ornamentation and a carving medium for millennia. In the late 18th century and throughout the 19th century, the use of pearly shells in button making increased with the mechanization of production. The demand for seashells became so great that mother-of-pearl (p.209) shells were more popular than the pearls themselves. Shells have also been used in inlays, beads, and other decorative items. Those shells with differently colored layers have been carved into cameos since antiquity. Shells have also been used as money (see panel, opposite).

Shell comes in a huge variety of sizes, shapes, and colors. Like coral (p.212), it is mineral matter generated by biological processes. Shell forms as the hard outer covering of many mollusks. The mineral component of shell occurs as calcite or aragonite—two different crystal forms of calcium carbonate. Shell is secreted in layers by cells in the mantle, which is a skinlike tissue in the body wall of the mollusk. However, not all mollusks secrete shell in the same way. This results in distinct microstructures that have different mechanical properties and, in some shells, different colors. Groups of mollusks can be characterized by the number of calcareous layers, the composition of the layers (aragonite or aragonite and calcite), and their arrangement.

turquoise overlay

Native American pendant
This *Spondylus* shell pendant is partially encrusted with turquoise, jet, and mother-of-pearl.

Perfume bottle
This Victorian mussel-shell perfume bottle has a pinchbeck (brass) stopper, chain, and ring.

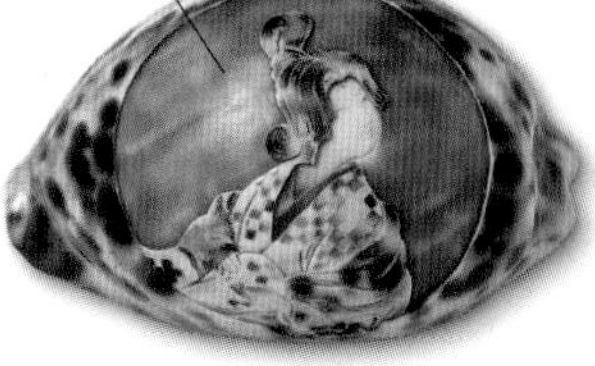

polished mussel shell

rich purple color

Tiger cowrie cameo
This cameo is carved on a Tiger Cowrie and features a portrait of a Japanese female figure.

pink lining

imitation pearl

Tortoiseshell comb
This Gui comb is made of exquisitely carved tortoiseshell.

delicate shell petals

Flower pin
This flower pin by Ian St. Gielar has iridescent shell petals and a central gem encircled by rhinestones.

Spider conch
The layering of colors in spider conch makes it a good choice for cameos.

SHELL MONEY

Cowrie barter
In this lithograph dated *c.*1845, cowrie shells are being bartered between Arab traders.

Shells were a medium of exchange on every continent from antiquity until the 19th century. They were either used whole or as pieces worked into beads or other shapes. The most famous shell variety to be used as money was the cowry species, *Cyprae moneta*. It was popular in the trade networks of Africa, south Asia, and east Asia.

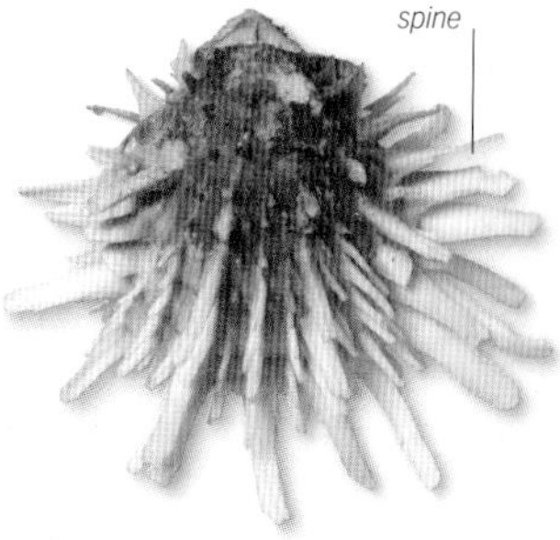

spine

Thorny oyster
The thorny oyster is one of the shells with a mother-of-pearl lining that is useful for inlays.

Ammolite cabochon
This free-form cabochon of ammolite shows the color play that makes this material desirable.

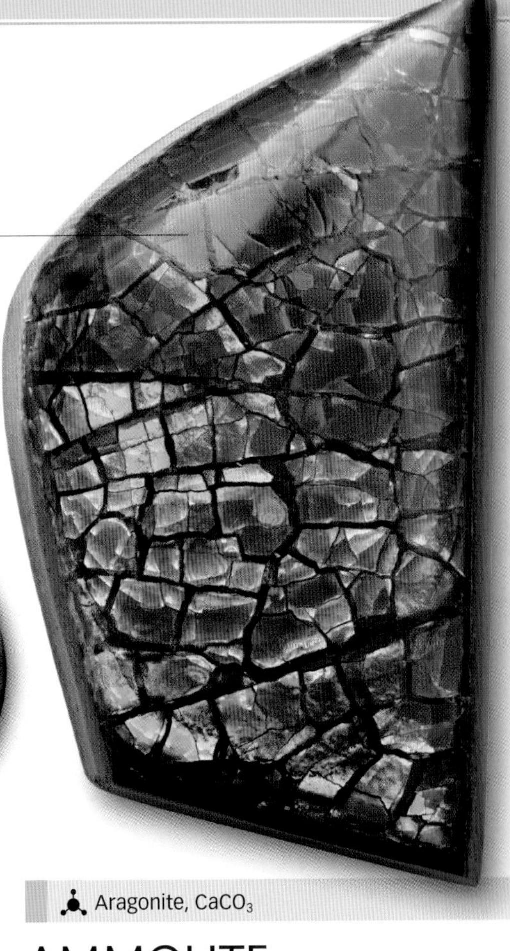

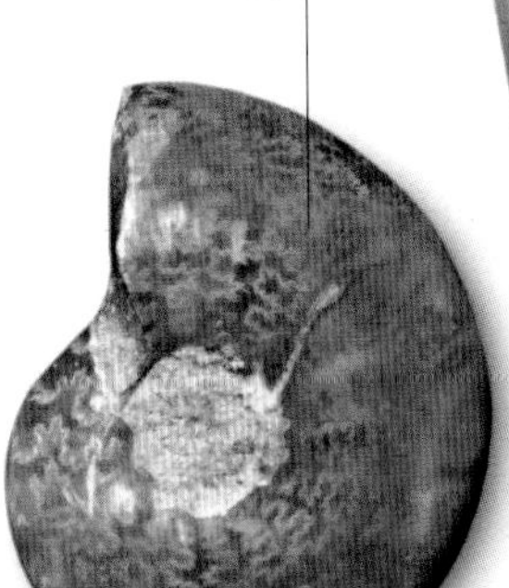

AMMONITE SHELL

PROFILE

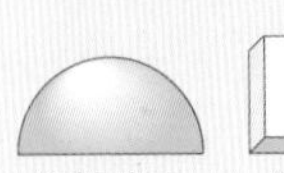

Cabochon Polished

Orthorhombic

4½–5

2.6–2.8

1.52–1.57

Resinous

Aragonite, $CaCO_3$

AMMOLITE

An organic gemstone made up of the fossil shells of ammonites—extinct coiled cephalopods related to the nautilus—ammolite is a relatively new gemstone in the market. Like pearl (p.209), ammonite shells are principally composed of the mineral aragonite (p.79). Gem ammolite may also include calcite (p.76), silica, pyrite (p.55), or other minerals.

The best specimens show an iridescent, opal-like play of color, mostly in shades of green and red, although other colors appear in varying amounts. The iridescence is due to the microstructure of aragonite, which is made up of stacked layers of thin platelets. Ammolite itself is very thin—up to 0.02–0.03 in (0.5–0.8 mm) in thickness—and is usually backed by its matrix—normally shale, chalky clay, or limestone. Because it is so thin, it is often cut as doublets or triplets. Gem-quality ammolite is found from Alberta to Saskatchewan in Canada and from Montana to southern USA. Small deposits have been found as far south as central Utah, USA.

PROFILE

Cameo 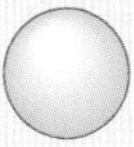 Bead

Orthorhombic

3

2.7

1.55–1.68

Pearly

Pearl necklace
This multistranded necklace from the Italian jewelry design company Coppola e Toppo has alternating pearls and clear, faceted beads.

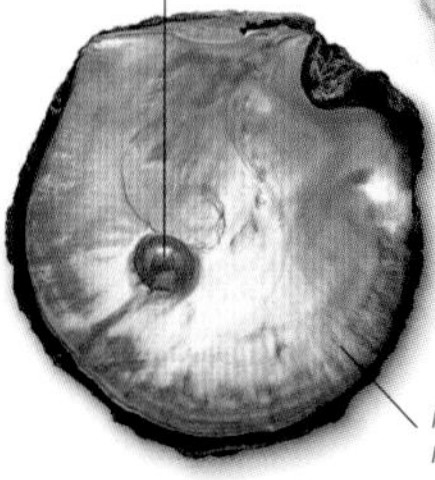

clear bead

multiple interwoven strands

black pearl

iridescent mother-of-pearl

BLACK PEARL ON MOTHER-OF-PEARL

VARIANTS

Baroque pearl An irregularly shaped pearl

Cultured pearls Four marine cultured pearls showing color variation

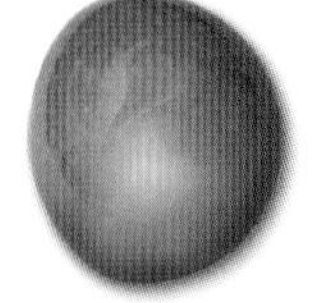

Conch pearl A rare specimen of Queen Conch pearl

Mostly $CaCO_3$

PEARL

A mollusk creates a pearl when a foreign particle enters its mantle—a layer of body tissue where its shell-secreting cells are located. These cells build up concentric layers of pearl around the particle to protect the mantle. The layers consist of the same material as the shell—mainly aragonite (p.79). Some shells also contain small amounts of conchiolin, a hornlike organic substance. Together, the aragonite and conchiolin are called nacre, or mother-of-pearl. The finest pearls come from mollusks whose shells are lined with mother-of-pearl.

Pearls can be yellow, white, cream, green, black, blue, or pink. The most valuable are spherical or droplike, with deep luster and good color play. Saltwater pearls are commonly referred to as Oriental pearls and those from freshwater mollusks are called freshwater pearls.

Art Deco pin
Black and white pearls and diamante accents are set in this Art Deco pin from the 1930s.

CULTIVATING AND HARVESTING PEARLS

Recovered by diving, natural pearls have always been scarce and highly variable in shape, color, and quality. Modern culturing of pearls has brought greater supply to the market, and has allowed for consistent size, color, and quality.

HISTORY OF PEARL CULTURING

The cultivation of pearls is thought to have begun in 13th-century China, initially in freshwater mussels. The first cultured pearls were "blister" pearls—hemispherical pearls that form between the mussel and its shell and are attached to the shell. The production of fully round cultured pearls, and subsequently an associated industry, was started in the 1890s in Japan by Mikimoto Kokichi. After much experimentation, he discovered that a tiny mother-of-pearl bead introduced into the tissue of a mollusk—a process known as "seeding"—would stimulate it to produce a perfectly round pearl.

Pearl fishing in Kublai Khan's era
This illustration is from a 15th-century book based on the travels of the Venetian merchant-traveler Marco Polo. It shows the Mongolian emperor Kublai Khan, who monopolized pearl-fishing and turquoise-digging at the time.

PEARL FARMING

Modern pearl farms can be found both in seawater and freshwater. Immature pearl oysters are raised in containers until they are two to three years old and then implanted with a tiny sphere of mother-of-pearl. Next, the oysters are taken to coastal waters or deeper freshwater, where they are suspended in wire nets, or are otherwise contained so that growth takes place in natural conditions. Divers tend to the growing oysters, ensuring that they have enough plankton to feed on and are not overcrowded. The oysters are ready for harvesting 13 months to 2 years later, when the pearls are extracted.

Harvesting pearls
These pearl oysters are suspended from cords to allow maximum growth. The diver in the background is preparing to harvest them.

PEARL COLORS

The value of a pearl depends on its color, which in turn depends on the waters from which the pearl comes. Japanese pearls are cream or white with greenish tones; those from the Persian Gulf are cream; Mexico, black or reddish brown; Sri Lanka, pink; and Australia, white with greenish or bluish shades.

Ornate cream pearls
This 1960s necklace is strung with baroque cultured pearl beads and drops. It is set with rose montees (rhinestones premounted on a pronged setting).

String of pink pearls
Pink is one of the most desirable colors for pearls. The ones shown here are closely matched in size and color.

Pink pearl comb
This elaborate gold comb is made up of a number of baroque pearls of varying shapes and sizes, highlighted with faceted gems.

Cultured pearl brooch
A part of the Smithsonian collection, this brooch features a diamond-set owl with an oblong pearl body, perched on a spherical pearl.

White pearl brooch
The two halves of this oval brooch are set with graduated cultured pearls. Diamonds are mounted on white metal in the center.

Black pearl necklace
Black pearls are a considerable rarity in nature, and the culturing process for them is more complex than for other colors. As a result, they are considered more valuable.

PROFILE

Cabochon  Polished

Bead

Trigonal, amorphous, or orthorhombic

3½

2.6–2.7

1.49–1.66

Opaque

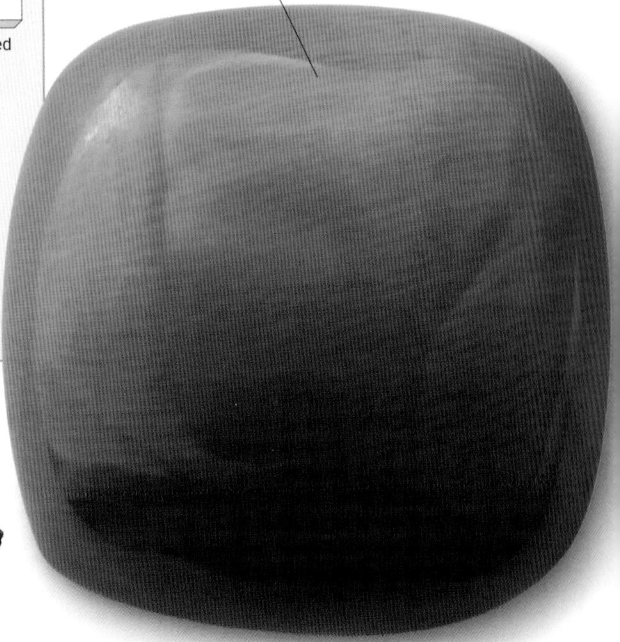

highly polished surface

Coral cabochon
This high-domed cabochon is cut from solid coral with a good color.

branch

BRANCHES OF RED CORAL

VARIANTS

Black coral cabochon
An elongated oval cabochon cut from rare black coral

Red coral cabochon
A thickly cut, high-domed oval cabochon of coral

$CaCO_3$/conchiolin

CORAL

Coral is skeletal material generated by sea-dwelling coral polyps. In most corals, the material is calcium carbonate, but in black and golden corals, it is a hornlike substance called conchiolin. Coral has a dull luster when harvested, but gem corals take a bright polish. This polish can become dull with extensive wear and can be etched by even mild acids. Coral is used in carvings, beads, and inlays; cut as cabochons for use in jewelry; and used as polished, branchlike strands.

Red coral was used as an ornament in Western European shields, helmets, and jewellery in pre-Roman times. Red and pink precious coral comes from the warm seas around Japan and Malaysia, the Mediterranean, and African coastal waters. Black and golden coral are found around the West Indies, Australia, and the Pacific Islands.

Coral pin
This gold-plated maple leaf pin is set with oval and teardrop coral cabochons.

PROFILE

Cameo Bead

Amorphous

2

1.9

1.53–1.54

Dull to greasy

deep cut

Carved ivory Made of African elephant ivory, this Roman head was carved in the 4th or 5th century BCE style.

natural striation

WALRUS TUSK IVORY

VARIANT

Fossil ivory A fossilized tooth of a mastodon—an extinct elephant-like mammal

Calcium hydroxophosphate and organic

IVORY

A variety of dentine, the tissue that makes up the bulk of the teeth and tusks of animals, ivory is used to make many items. It was carved in ancient Greece and Rome to create works of art, religious objects, and decorative boxes. It has a long history of use in China, from where it was traded along the Silk Road—a trade route linking Asia, Europe, and Africa—as early as the 1st century BCE. Elephants have been the prime source of ivory. It also comes from animals such as hippopotamus, walrus, pig, sperm whale, and narwhal.

Before the introduction of plastic and other synthetics, ivory was used to make billiard balls, buttons, and other ornamental items. The import and sale of ivory is now banned or severely restricted in many countries.

Ivory necklace This early 20th-century necklace includes finely carved beads of ivory.

GLOSSARY

ACCESSORY MINERAL
A mineral that occurs in a rock in such small amounts that it is disregarded in the definition of the rock.

ACICULAR HABIT
A needlelike crystal habit of some minerals. See also *habit*.

ADAMANTINE LUSTER
A type of bright mineral luster similar to that of diamond. See also *luster*.

AGGREGATE
An accumulation of mineral crystals or rock fragments.

ALEXANDRITE EFFECT
The effect noted when a gem appears one color in artificial light and a different color in natural light.

ALKALINE ROCK
A class of igneous rocks abundant in potassium- and sodium-rich minerals.

ALTERATION
The chemical, thermal, or pressure process or processes by which one rock or mineral is changed into another.

ALTERATION PRODUCT
A new rock or mineral formed by the alteration of a previous one. See also *alteration*.

ASSOCIATED MINERALS
Minerals found growing together but not necessarily intergrown. See also *intergrowth*.

BOTRYOIDAL HABIT
A mineral habit in which crystals form globular aggregates similar to bunches of grapes. See also *aggregate*, *habit*.

CABOCHON
A gemstone cut with a domed upper surface and a flat or domed under surface; gemstones cut in this way are said to be cut *en cabochon*. See also *cut*, *gem*, *gemstone*.

CAMEO
A design in low relief cut into layered stone or shell, with the background material cut away. See also *cut*, *gem cutting*.

CARAT
A unit of gemstone weight, equivalent to 0.007 oz (0.2 g). Carat (also spelled "karat") is also a measure of gold purity, the number of parts of gold in 24 parts of a gold alloy: 24 kt is pure gold; 18 kt is three quarters gold. See also *gem*, *gemstone*.

CHATOYANCY
The cat's-eye effect shown by some stones cut *en cabochon*. See also *cabochon*.

CLAY
Mineral particles smaller than about 0.00008 in (0.002 mm).

CLEAVAGE
The way certain minerals break along planes dictated by their atomic structure.

COLOR DISPERSION
The separation of white light into its constituent colors.

CONCHOIDAL FRACTURE
A curved or shell-like fracture in many minerals and some rocks. See also *fracture*.

CONCRETION
A rounded, nodular mass of rock formed from its enclosing rock and commonly found in beds of sandstone, shale, or clay.

CONTACT TWINNING
The phenomenon of two or more crystals growing in precisely oriented contact relationships with each other and sharing a common face. See also *twinned crystals*.

CRYPTOCRYSTALLINE HABIT
A mineral habit that is crystalline but very fine-grained. Individual crystallized components can be seen only under a microscope. See also *habit*.

CUT
The final shape of a ground and polished gem, as in emerald cut. See also *gem*, *gemstone*, *gem cutting*.

DENDRITIC HABIT
A type of habit in which crystals form branching, treelike shapes. See also *habit*.

DICHROIC, DICHROISM
The phenomenon of a mineral or gem presenting two different colors to the eye when viewed from different directions.

DIFFRACTION
The splitting of light into its component colors. See also *x-ray diffraction*.

DISCOVERY LOCALITY
Also known as type locality, the site where a mineral was first recognized as a new mineral.

DODECAHEDRAL
A crystal showing the faces of a dodecahedron—a 12-sided geometric figure.

DOUBLE REFRACTION
The splitting of light into two separate rays as it enters a stone.

DULL LUSTER
A type of luster in which little or no light is reflected. See also *luster*.

EARTHY LUSTER
A nonreflective mineral luster. See also *luster*.

EXTRUSIVE ROCK
A rock formed from lava that either flowed onto Earth's surface or was ejected as pyroclastic material. See also *intrusive rock*, *lava*.

FACES
The external flat surfaces that make up a crystal's shape.

FACETING
The process of cutting flat faces onto a gemstone in a three-dimensional, geometric pattern. See also *cut*, *gem*, *gemstone*, *gem cutting*.

FELSIC ROCK
An igneous rock with more than 65 percent silica and more than 20 percent quartz. It is also known as acidic rock.

FIRE
The splitting of white light into its constituent colors as it passes through a gemstone.

FOSSIL
Any record of past life preserved in the crustal rocks. Apart from bones and shells, fossils can include footprints, excrement, and borings.

FRACTURE
Mineral breakage that occurs at locations other than along cleavage planes. See also *cleavage*.

GARNET
A member of a group of silicates with the general formula $A_3B_2(SiO_4)_3$ in which A can be Ca, Fe^{2+}, Mg, or Mn^{2+}; and B can be Al, Cr, Fe^{3+}, Mn^{3+}, Si, Ti, V, or Zr.

GEODE
A hollow, generally rounded nodule lined with crystals. See also *nodule*.

GEM, GEMSTONE
A cut stone worn in jewelry, valued for its color, rarity, texture, beauty, or clarity. It may even be an unset stone cut for use as jewelry. See also *cut*, *rough gemstone*.

GEM CUTTING
The process of shaping a gemstone by grinding and polishing. See also *cut*, *gem*, *gemstone*.

GLASS
A solid substance showing no crystalline structure—in effect, a very thick liquid. See also *glassy texture*.

GLASSY TEXTURE
The smooth consistency of an igneous rock in which glass formed due to rapid solidification. See also *glass*, *texture*.

GRANITIC ROCKS
Rocks composed principally of the minerals feldspar, quartz, and mica.

GRANULAR TEXTURE
A rock or mineral texture that either includes grains or is in the form of grains. See also *texture*.

HABIT
The mode of growth and appearance of a mineral. The habit of a mineral results from its molecular structure.

HACKLY FRACTURE
A mineral fracture that has a rough surface with small protuberances, as on a gold nugget. See also *fracture*.

HYDROTHERMAL DEPOSIT
A mineral deposit formed by hot water ejected from deep within Earth's crust.

HYDROTHERMAL VEIN
A rock fracture in which minerals have been deposited by fluids from deep within Earth's crust. See also *hydrothermal deposit*, *pegmatite*, *vein*.

IGNEOUS ROCK
A rock that is formed through the solidification of molten rock.

INCLUSION
A crystal or fragment of another substance within a crystal or rock.

INTERFERENCE
The reflection of light from thin layers within a gemstone, which causes light waves to either cancel or reinforce each other.

INTERGROWTH
Two or more minerals growing together and interpenetrating each other. See also *associated minerals*.

INTRUSIVE ROCK
A body of igneous rock that invades older rock. See also *extrusive rock*.

IRIDESCENCE
The reflection of light from the internal elements of a stone, yielding a rainbowlike play of colors.

LAVA
Molten rock extruded onto Earth's surface. See also *magma*.

LITHIFICATION
The process by which unconsolidated sediment turns to stone. See also *recrystallization*.

LUSTER
The shine of a mineral caused by reflected light.

MAGMA
Molten rock that may crystallize beneath Earth's surface or be erupted as lava. See also *lava*.

MASSIVE
A mineral form having no definite shape.

MATRIX
A fine-grained rock into or on top of which larger crystals appear to be set. It is also known as a groundmass.

METAL
A substance characterized by high electrical and thermal conductivity as well as by malleability, ductility, and high reflectivity of light.

METALLIC LUSTER
A shine similar to the typical shine of polished metal. See also *luster*.

METAMORPHIC ROCK
A rock that has been transformed by heat or pressure (or both) into another rock.

METEORITE
A rock from space that reaches Earth's surface.

MICA
Any of a group of hydrous potassium or aluminum silicate minerals. These minerals exhibit a two-dimensional sheetlike or layerlike structure.

MICROCRYSTALLINE HABIT
A mineral habit in which crystals are so minuscule that they can be detected only with the aid of a microscope. See also *habit*.

MINERAL GROUP
Two or more minerals that share common structural and/or chemical properties.

MOONSTONE
A gem-quality feldspar mineral that exhibits a silvery or bluish iridescence. Several feldspars, especially some plagioclases, are called moonstone.

NATIVE ELEMENT
A chemical element that is found in nature uncombined with other elements.

NODULE
A generally rounded accretion of sedimentary material that differs from its enclosing sedimentary rock.

OCTAHEDRAL CRYSTAL
A crystal composed of two base-to-base square pyramids.

OPTICAL GRADE
The highest grade of transparency—that is, internally flawless.

ORE
A rock or mineral from which a metal can be profitably extracted.

OXIDATION
The process of combining with oxygen. In minerals, the oxygen can come from the air or water.

PEGMATITE
A hydrothermal vein composed of large crystals. See also *hydrothermal vein*.

PENETRATION TWINNING
The phenomenon of two or more crystals forming from a common center and appearing to penetrate each other. See also *twinned crystals*.

PLACER, PLACER DEPOSIT
A deposit of minerals derived by weathering and concentrated in streams or beaches because of the mineral's high specific gravity.

PLATY HABIT
The growth habit shown by flat, thin crystals. See also *habit*.

PLEOCHROIC, PLEOCHROISM
The phenomenon of a mineral or gem presenting different colors to the eye when it is viewed from different directions.

POTCH OPAL
Opaque or translucent opal with no color-play, considered waste opal.

PREFERENTIAL ABSORPTION
The tendency of certain crystal faces to absorb trace elements during crystallization in preference to other faces.

PRISMATIC HABIT
A mineral habit in which parallel rectangular crystal faces form prisms. See also *habit*.

PYRAMIDAL HABIT
A crystal habit in which the principal faces join at a point. When two such pyramids are placed base to base, the crystal is said to be di- or bi-pyramidal. See also *habit*.

PYROXENE
A member of a group of 21 rock-forming silicate minerals that typically form elongate crystals.

RARE-EARTH MINERAL
A mineral containing a significant portion of one or more of the 17 rare-earth elements, principally ytterbium, gadolinium, neodymium, praseodymium, cerium, lanthanum, yttrium, and scandium.

RECRYSTALLIZATION
The redistribution of components to form new minerals or mineral crystals; in some cases new rocks form. It occurs during lithification and metamorphism. See also *lithification*.

REFRACTIVE INDEX
A measure of the slowing down and bending of light as it enters a stone. It is used to identify cut gemstones and some minerals. See also *cut*, *gem*, *gemstone*.

REPLACEMENT DEPOSIT
A deposit formed from minerals that have been altered. See also *alteration product*.

RESINOUS LUSTER
A shine having the reflectivity of resin. See also *luster*.

RETICULATED
Having a network or a netlike mode of crystallization.

RHOMBOHEDRAL CRYSTAL
A crystal shaped like a skewed cube.

ROUGH GEMSTONE
An uncut gemstone. See also *cut*, *gem*, *gemstone*.

SCALENOHEDRAL CRYSTAL
A crystal composed of two base-to-base hexagonal pyramids.

SCHILLER EFFECT
The brilliant play of bright colors in a crystal, often due to minute, rodlike inclusions.

SEDIMENTARY ROCK
A rock that either originates on Earth's surface as an accumulation of sediments or precipitates from water.

SEMIMETAL
A metal, such as arsenic or bismuth, that is not malleable. See also *metal*.

SILICA-POOR ROCKS
Rocks containing less than 50 percent silica. See also *silica-rich rocks*.

SILICA-RICH ROCKS
Rocks containing more than 50 percent silica. See also *silica-poor rocks*.

SOLID-SOLUTION SERIES
A series of minerals in which certain chemical components are variable between two end members with fixed composition.

SPECIFIC GRAVITY
The ratio of the mass of a mineral to the mass of an equal volume of water. Specific gravity is numerically equivalent to density (mass divided by volume) in grams per cubic centimeter.

STALACTITIC HABIT
A mineral habit in which the crystalline components are arranged in radiating groups of diminishing size, giving the appearance of icicles. See also *habit*.

STREAM ROUNDING
The process by which rocks and minerals are rounded by being tumbled through moving water.

STRIATION
Parallel grooves or lines appearing on a crystal.

SUNSTONE
A gemstone variety of feldspar with minute, platelike inclusions of iron oxide oriented parallel to one another throughout. See also *gem*, *gemstone*.

TABULAR HABIT
A crystal habit in which crystals take the shape of a cereal box. See also *habit*.

TERMINATION
Faces that make up the ends of a crystal.

TETRAHEDRAL CRYSTAL
A crystal composed of four triangular faces in pairs, rotated 90 degrees from each other.

TEXTURE
The size, shape, and relationships between rock grains or crystals.

TRAPEZOHEDRAL CRYSTAL
A crystal showing the faces of a trapezohedron, a 24-sided geometric figure.

TRISOCTAHEDRAL CRYSTAL
A crystal showing the faces of a trisoctahedron, a 24-sided geometric figure.

TUMBLE POLISHING
The process by which gemstones are rounded and polished by being rotated in a barrel with abrasives.

TWINNED CRYSTALS
Crystals that grow together in precise crystallographic orientations as mirror images with a common face (contact twins) or grow at angles up to 90 degrees to each other and appear to penetrate each other (penetration twins).

TYPE LOCALITY
See *discovery locality*.

VEIN
A thin, sheetlike mass of rock that fills fractures in other rocks.

VITREOUS LUSTER
A shine resembling that of glass. See also *luster*.

X-RAY DIFFRACTION
The passing of x-rays through a crystal to determine its internal structure by the way in which the x-rays are scattered. See also *diffraction*.

ZEOLITE
A group of hydrous aluminum silicates characterized by their easy and reversible loss of water.

INDEX

Page numbers in **bold** indicate main entries.

ACKNOWLEDGMENTS

Smithsonian Enterprises
Carol LeBlanc, Vice President; Brigid Ferraro, Director of Licensing; Ellen Nanney, Licensing Manager; Kealy Wilson, Product Development Coordinator.

The publisher would like to thank Steve Setford for proofreading.

The publisher would also like to thank the following people: Greg Dennis, Mark Cook, and Steve and Karen Ottewill at Ottewill Silversmiths (http://www.ottewill.co.uk); Jason Holt, Susi Smither, and Laure Berdoz at Holts Lapidary (www.holtslapidary.com) for their help with images; and Richard Leeney for the photography.

DK India would like to thank Rohini Deb for editorial assistance; and Amit Malhotra and Suhita Dharamjit for design assistance.

The publisher would like to thank the following for their kind permission to reproduce their photographs:

(Key: a-above; b-below/bottom; c-center; f-far; l-left; r-right; t-top)

2–3 Alamy Images: blickwinkel. **6–7 Getty Images:** John W Banagan. **8 Smithsonian Institution, Washington, DC, USA:** (cl, cr, b). **9 Smithsonian Institution, Washington, DC, USA:** (c, cr). **11 Getty Images:** Siegfried Layda (b). **13 Dorling Kindersley:** Courtesy of the Natural History Museum, London / Colin Keates (tr). **Smithsonian Institution, Washington, DC, USA:** (bc, br). **16 Smithsonian Institution, Washington, DC, USA:** (cr). **17 Corbis:** Atlantide Phototravel (b); Hulton-Deutsch Collection (tr). **Smithsonian Institution, Washington, DC, USA:** (ca). **18 Corbis:** Scientifica / Visuals Unlimited (t). **19 Smithsonian Institution, Washington, DC, USA:** (tr). **21 Smithsonian Institution, Washington, DC, USA:** (t). **24–25 Corbis:** Frederic Soltan / Sygma (b). **25 Getty Images:** LatinContent (t). **26 Getty Images:** DEA (tr); Brendan Ryan (cr). **26–27 Corbis:** John Carnemolla (b). **27 Getty Images:** Lihee Avidan (tl); Per-Anders Pettersson (cr). **28 Corbis:** Charles O'Rear (bl). **31 Corbis:** Dean Conger (br). **Dorling Kindersley:** Bonhams / Judith Miller (tc). **32 Alamy Images:** The Natural History Museum (b). **33 Alamy Images:** Greg C. Grace (crb); PhotoStock-Israel (c). **34 Corbis:** Peter Ginter (b). **Dorling Kindersley:** Courtesy of the Natural History Museum, London / Colin Keates (cr). **35 Alamy Images:** Zoonar GmbH (tr). **Dorling Kindersley:** Courtesy of the Natural History Museum, London / Colin Keates (tc). **Robert Fosbury:** (br). **36 Alamy Images:** The Art Archive (clb). **Corbis:** Bettmann (c). **Dorling Kindersley:** Courtesy of the Natural History Museum, London / Colin Keates (cb); Sloan's / Judith Miller (br). **Getty Images:** A. DAGLI ORTI / DEA (bc). **37 The Bridgeman Art Library:** (br). **38 Corbis:** Charles O'Rear (b). **39 Corbis:** Alain Denize / Kipa (tr); Bob Krist (br). **42 Corbis:** Steve Vidler (b); Werner Forman Archive / Werner Forman (tr). **Dorling Kindersley:** Courtesy of the Natural History Museum, London / Colin Keates (clb). **Science Photo Library:** Jim Amos (crb). **43 Trustees of the National Museums of Scotland:** Geoff Dann (t). **44 Corbis:** David Lees (t). **Dorling Kindersley:** Courtesy of the Natural History Museum, London (tl). **45 Corbis:** Araldo de Luca (c). **Dorling Kindersley:** The Trustees of the British Museum (br); N. Bloom & Son Ltd. / Judith Miller (clb); Courtesy of the Natural History Museum, London / Colin Keates (crb); Christi Graham and Nick Nicholls / The Trustees of the British Museum (bl). **Science Photo Library:** Chris Gunn (tl). **46 Corbis:** Bettmann (cl). Getty Images: MPI / Stringer (tr). **46–47 Getty Images:** Don Grall (b). **47 Corbis:** (t). **Smithsonian Institution, Washington, DC, USA:** (clb). **48 Dorling Kindersley:** Macklowe / Judith Miller (br). **The Goldsmiths' Company:** Leo De Vroomen (t). **49 Getty Images:** Orien Harvey (b). **Smithsonian Institution, Washington, DC, USA:** (t, cl, c, clb). **51 Dorling Kindersley:** Courtesy of the Natural History Museum, London / Colin Keates (tr); Wallis and Wallis / Judith Miller (br). **Getty Images:** Time & Life Pictures (tl). **Science Photo Library:** Vaughan Fleming (ca). **Smithsonian Institution, Washington, DC, USA:** (bc, cl, cr, clb, crb). **52 Corbis:** Michael Freeman (bl). **Smithsonian Institution, Washington, DC, USA:** (tl). **52–53 Smithsonian Institution, Washington, DC, USA:** (c). **53 Getty Images:** Tim Graham (cr). **Smithsonian Institution, Washington, DC, USA:** (tl, tr, br). **61 Alamy Images:** Rhea Eason (cl). **63 Alamy Images:** Greg C. Grace (tr). **Ron Bonewitz:** (br). **Dorling Kindersley:** Sloan's / Judith Miller (cra); HY Duke and Son / Judith Miller (cr). **Smithsonian Institution, Washington, DC, USA:** (cl). **64 Getty Images:** Hector Mata / AFP (cl). **Smithsonian Institution, Washington, DC, USA:** (c, bl). **65 Smithsonian Institution, Washington, DC, USA:** (t, tr, bl). **68 Dorling Kindersley:** Courtesy of the Natural History Museum, London / Colin Keates (cl). **Smithsonian Institution, Washington, DC, USA:** (t). **69 Smithsonian Institution, Washington, DC, USA:** (cl). **71 Corbis:** José Manuel Sanchis Calvete (t). **73 Alamy Images:** The Natural History Museum (t). **74 Smithsonian Institution, Washington, DC, USA:** (t). **75 Alamy Images:** Greg C. Grace (br). **Science Photo Library:** Paul Biddle (tr). **Smithsonian Institution, Washington, DC, USA:** (clb). **76 Corbis:** Sandro Vannini (t). **78 Dorling Kindersley:** Courtesy of the Natural History Museum, London / Harry Taylor (cl). **79 Gem Testing Laboratory, Jaipur, India:** Gagan Choudhary (t). **82 Dorling Kindersley:** Courtesy of the Natural History Museum / Colin Keates (tr). **86 Smithsonian Institution, Washington, DC, USA:** (br). **87 Alamy Images:** Caroline Eastwood (tl). **Dorling Kindersley:** Ark Antiques / Judith Miller (tr); Van Den Bosch / Judith Miller (bc). **93 Dorling Kindersley:** Clevedon Salerooms / Judith Miller (t). **94 Alamy Images:** Fabrizius Troy (t). **97 Alamy Images:** Guillem Lopez (bl). **Dorling Kindersley:** Courtesy of the Statens Historiska Museum, Stockholm / Peter Anderson (c); Courtesy of the Natural History Museum, London / Colin Keates (tl, tr); Courtesy of the Natural History Museum, London / Harry Taylor (cl); John Jesse / Judith Miller (cb); Gorringes / Judith Miller (br). **Smithsonian Institution, Washington, DC, USA:** (clb). **98 Dorling Kindersley:** Jewellery design by Maya Brenner Designs / Ruth Jenkinson (bl). **101 Dorling**

Kindersley: Courtesy of the Natural History Museum, London / Colin Keates (cl). **103 Dorling Kindersley:** ARF/TAP (tl); Circa 1900 / Judith Miller (cl). **Smithsonian Institution, Washington, DC, USA:** (tr). **106 Dorling Kindersley:** Jewellery design by Maya Brenner Designs / Ruth Jenkinson (br); Courtesy of the Natural History Museum, London / Colin Keates (t, clb). **109 Corbis:** Francis G. Mayer (t). **Dorling Kindersley:** Fellows & Sons / Judith Miller (br). **110 Dorling Kindersley:** N. Bloom & Son Ltd. / Judith Miller (br). **112 Dorling Kindersley:** Courtesy of the Natural History Museum, London / Colin Keates (tr). **115 akg-images:** historic-map (tl). **Dorling Kindersley:** Courtesy of the Natural History Museum, London / Colin Keates (bl); Lynn & Brian Holmes / Judith Miller (cl); Wallis and Wallis / Judith Miller (br); N. Bloom & Son Ltd. / Judith Miller (crb). **116 Alamy Images:** Natural History Museum, London (cl). **Smithsonian Institution, Washington, DC, USA:** (clb). **118 Dorling Kindersley:** Joseph H. Bonnar / Judith Miller (br). **119 Dorling Kindersley:** Courtesy of the Natural History Museum, London / Colin Keates (cl). **120 Alamy Images:** Zoonar GmbH (t). **Corbis:** Visuals Unlimited (cla). **121 Corbis:** Stéphane Lemaire / Hemis (tc). **Dorling Kindersley:** Fellows & Sons / Judith Miller (clb). **Smithsonian Institution, Washington, DC, USA:** (cla, ca, tr, c, cb). **123 Dorling Kindersley:** Courtesy of the Natural History Museum, London / Harry Taylor (cl). **Smithsonian Institution, Washington, DC, USA:** (bl). **126 iRocks.com/Rob Lavinsky Photos:** (t). **128 Dorling Kindersley:** Courtesy of the Natural History Museum, London / Colin Keates (cl, br). **129 Dorling Kindersley:** Courtesy of the Natural History Museum, London / Colin Keates (bl); Van Den Bosch / Judith Miller (br). **130 Smithsonian Institution, Washington, DC, USA:** (tc). **131 Getty Images:** De Agostini (tr); A. DAGLI ORTI / DEA (cr). **Science Photo Library:** Joel Arem (cl). **132 Corbis:** Sheldan Collins (b). **Getty Images:** Danita Delimont (tl). **133 Alamy Images:** Charles Stirling (Travel) (br). **Corbis:** Mark Moffett (ca). **Getty Images:** G. DAGLI ORTI / DEA (c, bl); Robert Nickelsberg (tl). **135 iRocks.com/Rob Lavinsky Photos:** (t). **137 iRocks.com/Rob Lavinsky Photos:** (t). **138 Dorling Kindersley:** Courtesy of the Natural History Museum, London / Colin Keates (cl). **139 Dorling Kindersley:** Courtesy of the Natural History Museum, London / Colin Keates (clb). **142 Dorling Kindersley:** T W Conroy / Judith Miller (br). **147 Smithsonian Institution, Washington, DC, USA:** (tr). **148 Smithsonian Institution, Washington, DC, USA:** (clb, br). **150 Dorling Kindersley:** Sloan's / Judith Miller (br). **151 Dorling Kindersley:** Courtesy of the Natural History Museum, London / Colin Keates (cb). **Getty Images:** Universal Images Group (br). **152 Dorling Kindersley:** Courtesy of the Natural History Museum, London / Colin Keates (cl). **153 Dorling Kindersley:** Courtesy of the Natural History Museum, London / Colin Keates (cr); Blanchet et Associes / Judith Miller (br). **156 iRocks.com/Rob Lavinsky Photos:** (t). **158 Dorling Kindersley:** Courtesy of the Natural History Museum, London / Colin Keates (cl, bl). **159 Alamy Images:** The Natural History Museum (t). **161 The Bridgeman Art Library:** Ashmolean Museum, University of Oxford, UK (tl). **Dorling Kindersley:** Ark Antiques / Judith Miller (c). **Smithsonian Institution, Washington, DC, USA:** (tr). **162 Alamy Images:** Arco Images GmbH (t). **163 Dorling Kindersley:** Courtesy of the Natural History Museum, London / Colin Keates (clb). **164 Dorling Kindersley:** HY Duke and Son / Judith Miller (br). **167 Dorling Kindersley:** Courtesy of the Natural History Museum, London / Colin Keates (bl). **168 iRocks.com/Rob Lavinsky Photos:** (t). **169 Smithsonian Institution, Washington, DC, USA:** (br). **170 Dorling Kindersley:** Peter Hayman / The Trustees of the British Museum (bc, br). **Getty Images:** De Agostini (cl); S. Vannini / DEA (c). **171 Corbis:** Sandro Vannini (t). **Dorling Kindersley:** Peter Hayman / The Trustees of the British Museum (br). **Getty Images:** Robert Harding (b). **176 Alamy Images:** Greg C. Grace (bl). **179 Dorling Kindersley:** Courtesy of the Natural History Museum, London / Colin Keates (cl, br). **180 Smithsonian Institution, Washington, DC, USA:** (cl). **183 Dorling Kindersley:** Courtesy of Oxford University Museum of Natural History / Gary Ombler (cl). **Science Photo Library:** Joel Arem (t). **184 Dorling Kindersley:** Courtesy of the Natural History Museum, London / Colin Keates (cl). **191 akg-images:** Gerard Degeorge (bl). **Dorling Kindersley:** Joseph H. Bonnar / Judith Miller (c). **193 Alamy Images:** Antiques & Collectables (br). **197 Dorling Kindersley:** Courtesy of the Natural History Museum, London / Colin Keates (bl). **198 Dorling Kindersley:** Courtesy of the Natural History Museum, London / Colin Keates (tr); Courtesy of the Natural History Museum, London / Harry Taylor (t). **199 Dorling Kindersley:** Courtesy of the Natural History Museum, London / Colin Keates (cla, bl); Cristobal / Judith Miller (cr); Courtesy of the Natural History Museum, London / Colin Keates (cla, bl). **Getty Images:** L. Douglas / DEA (bc). **Smithsonian Institution, Washington, DC, USA:** (tl, tr). **200 Dorling Kindersley:** Courtesy of the Natural History Museum, London / Colin Keates (bl); Courtesy of the Natural History Museum, London / Harry Taylor (cl). **202 Corbis:** Werner Forman (cr); Tetra Images (b). **Dorling Kindersley:** Take-A-Boo Emporium / Judith Miller (cl). **206 Dorling Kindersley:** N. Bloom & Son Ltd. / Judith Miller (tc). **207 Dorling Kindersley:** Wallis and Wallis / Judith Miller (tc); Cristobal / Judith Miller (clb). **Getty Images:** De Agostini Picture Library (cl); SSPL (bl). **208 Gem Testing Laboratory, Jaipur, India:** Gagan Choudhary (cl). **209 Dorling Kindersley:** Roxanne Stuart / Judith Miller (t); Terry & Melody Rodgers / Judith Miller (br). **210 Getty Images:** Tobias Bernhard (b); DEA (cl). **211 Corbis:** Elio Ciol (br). **Dorling Kindersley:** William Wain at Antiquarius / Judith Miller (tl); Fellows & Sons / Judith Miller (bc). **Smithsonian Institution, Washington, DC, USA:** (c, clb). **212 Dorling Kindersley:** Cristobal / Judith Miller (br). **213 Dorling Kindersley:** Courtesy of the University Museum of Zoology, Cambridge / Frank Greenaway (cl).

All other images © Dorling Kindersley
For further information see: www.dkimages.com